Praise for
75 Green Businesses You Can Start to Make Money and to Make a Difference

"*75 Green Businesses* is a compendium of opportunity for the next generation of entrepreneurs. Deeper in scope than its 'green' title belies, Croston has developed a virtual barrel full of ducks to shoot when looking for new mission-driven business opportunities."

—JOHN ROOK
FOUNDER AND PRESIDENT OF DWELL CREATIVE

"*75 Green Businesses* is a comprehensive overview of the green-business revolution. This timely book highlights numerous ways in which people around the world, who are concerned about the environment, are making a difference. Croston needs to be commended for researching and presenting examples of innovative and credible business opportunities which contribute toward an environmentally sustainable Planet Earth!"

—ELIZABETH ISRAEL
FOUNDER AND PRESIDENT OF GREEN MICROFINANCE

"Anyone wanting to be part of the swelling green wave is in luck with this book. Since I think the green wave is really a green tsunami, now is the time for anyone interested in being part of the rebuilding of the economy to buy this book. This can be your first step in building a greener America."

—KIT CASSINGHAM
FOUNDER OF SAGE BLOSSOM CONSULTING

"We are at a critical time as a species, a time of knowing the right path to take yet uncertain how to get there. The world our generation has inherited cannot simply be passed on to our heirs without the issues of sustainability addressed. In the near future, every career, every business and every job will address green concerns in some way. This must be the case if we are to survive.

"In his new book, *75 Green Businesses*, Glenn Croston provides us with this ever important direction of how to reach this important path. The book is divided into some telling and intriguing chapters, including: Energy, Waste, Food, Water, among others. Browsing through these pages will inspire some directly toward a new career and prompt others to invent new business models. Expect to see a dog-eared copy sitting on every shelf of the next generation of entrepreneurs."

—ERIC COREY FREED
PRINCIPAL, organicARCHITECT
AUTHOR OF *GREEN BUILDING & REMODELING FOR DUMMIES*

"As you read this book, looking through the eyes of a man who sees not problems, but opportunities for new ways to inhabit our world, you can't help but get excited. Often I am asked by eager fans of sustainability, "What can I do to make a difference? I have all this passion and energy, but I don't know where to start!" Well, now there's a much better answer than I've been able to give before. Quite simply, it's this: Read this book, then take the first step. Reinvent the work you do and watch what happens. The inspiration you'll find herein is worth its weight in gold (and sunshine!)."

—SARAH SUSANKA, ARCHITECT AND AUTHOR OF
THE NOT SO BIG HOUSE SERIES, AND *THE NOT SO BIG LIFE*

Innovative Startups for Eco Entrepreneurs  Key Issues and Solutions
Tap into this $200 Billion Industry Insights from Green Revolution Leaders

75

GREEN
BUSINESSES

YOU CAN START
to MAKE MONEY and
MAKE A DIFFERENCE

GLENN CROSTON, PH.D.

EP
Entrepreneur
Press

Editorial Director: Jere L. Calmes
Cover Design: Desktop Miracles
Production and Composition: Eliot House Productions

This publication is designed to provide accurate and authoritative information in regard to
the subject matter covered. It is sold with the understanding that the publisher is not
engaged in rendering legal, accounting or other professional services. If legal advice or other
expert assistance is required, the services of a competent professional person should be
sought.

Plant image ©pakhnyushcha/Shutterstock

Library of Congress Cataloging-in-Publication Data
Croston, Glenn E., 1964–
  75 green businesses you can start to make money and make a difference/by Glenn
Croston.
   p.   cm.
   ISBN-13: 978-1-59918-180-6 (alk. paper)
   ISBN-10: 1-59918-180-0
   1. Green products. 2. Green movement—Economic aspects. 3. New business enterprises. I. Title. II. Title: Seventy five businesses you can start to make money and make a
difference.
HD9999.G742C76 2008
333.72—dc22   2008015787

Printed in Canada
12 11 10 09 08   10 9 8 7 6 5 4 3 2

Contents

Acknowledgments

This book would not have been possible without incredible help from friends and family. I thank my wife Guadalupe for always being there, my daughter Gaia for her wisdom beyond her years, Thomas Howell for tireless critical insight, Konsuelo Howell for constant support in innumerable ways, and Rafael Petrone, Mike Dunn, and Rob Meadows for their insight and guidance. For helping me get started I owe thanks to Taylor Wilshire, Sharon Wampler, and Ray Smilor. I would also like to thank Karen Billipp of Eliot House Productions, and Jere Calmes and Courtney Thurman of Entrepreneur

Press for seeing the book's potential and keeping it on track. Finally, I thank the many green entrepreneurs who have been so generous with their time and thoughts. They are too numerous to mention, but by living the change they are creating a greener future for us all.

Preface

The biggest business opportunities of the 21st century are for green businesses solving environmental challenges such as climate change. The opportunities are as large as the challenges, and innovative entrepreneurs taking on these challenges are moving green from the fringes to Wall Street, Main Street, and everywhere in between. With the green economy estimated to be over $200 billion in the United States in 2005 (Natural Marketing Institute, 2006) and growing globally, going green is both good for the environment and a smart business move.

Going green means different things to different people, but it generally means reducing pollution; conserving resources and ecosystems; being energy efficient; and reducing climate change. For many people, being green also means being aware of social issues such as fair trade and labor practices. Green businesses ensure that the natural systems on which our lives and economies rely will be around for the long term, and provide an environmentally sustainable world with profitable and rewarding ventures.

The rapid growth of green business is seen in many fields. In response to the concern about the impact of food and agriculture on our planet and our bodies, sales of organic food have been growing 15 to 21 percent a year for more than a decade (Organic Trade Association's 2006 Manufacturer Survey). To fight climate change, reduce pollution, and lower our dependence on oil, businesses increased U.S. wind power capacity 45 percent in 2007 (American Wind Energy Association, *AWEA 2007 Market Report*, awea.org). Entrepreneurs are transforming the buildings where we live and work to be safer and more efficient as part of the booming green-building movement. The pattern is repeated over and over with startup businesses providing clean water, green clothing and services, efficient transportation; and many other solutions. Never before has there been such a broad range of opportunities for entrepreneurs with almost any background to do well in business and help the environment at the same time.

People around the globe are rolling up their sleeves and getting to work on solutions for habitat loss, air pollution, declining oil supplies, water pollution, and climate change. An estimated 30 percent of the U.S. adult population are considered Lohas (lifestyles of health and sustainability) and are spending money in ways consistent with the belief in the need for a greener world. Every day, more people are changing to more efficient light bulbs, buying more fuel-efficient cars, and doing whatever else they can in their daily lives to make a difference. Going green is not just a fad or a trend but a lasting change in how we live and do business.

In a major shift, the old war between business and environmental concerns is fading. Major corporations such as Wal-Mart, General Electric, and

DuPont are "greening" their businesses to help the environment and their bottom line. British Petroleum (BP) is investing $500 million in a biofuels center as part of its transition from British Petroleum to Beyond Petroleum. Venture-capital investment in fledgling green companies grew 78 percent in 2006 with the expectation that green companies are a good investment and will continue to boom as key to business growth in the 21st century.

Going green also may be the best way to protect against the loss of business that may result from a globalized economy and other economic challenges. Former bastions of industrial strength are giving way to new industrialized powers, such as China and India, and this shift has eliminated or moved millions of jobs from the United States to other parts of the world. Developing green technologies and companies helps developed economies offset their diminishing role in old industries, and going green makes companies more efficient and more competitive when the economy slows.

Eco-entrepreneurs have many advantages in the rapidly growing green economy. Entrepreneurs with small, innovative firms don't have to worry about changing their mind-set or about losing investments in old technologies; instead new business owners start with a clean slate to build profitable and environmentally sound companies from the ground up. Eco-entrepreneurs are seeding change in almost every business field with innovative approaches. They are proving to be potent catalysts for greening the rest of the economy.

75 Green Businesses You Can Start helps you get your own business started by looking at opportunities to join the green-business revolution. As part of the burgeoning green economy, there are unprecedented opportunities to build profitable and rewarding businesses while providing solutions for the challenging environmental problems we face. These 75 opportunities identify markets, products, resources, challenges, and strategies for success. Explore these possibilities to find the green business that best fits your personal interests, skills, and resources, but don't feel constrained by these ideas.—get inspired; blend and combine ideas to create something entirely new.

The opportunities are grouped into the following chapters:

* *Chapter 1: Fueling Green Energy*—building innovative businesses to provide renewable energy.
* *Chapter 2: Seeding Entrepreneurial Green Careers*—joining the green wave wherever you are.
* *Chapter 3: Building Green Homes and Businesses*—renovating homes and other buildings in a green way.
* *Chapter 4: Investing Green Money*—bridging the green path and Wall Street.
* *Chapter 5: Finding Business Solutions in the Living World*—learning from nature to build strong, clean businesses.
* *Chapter 6: Wasting Less*—turning waste into a resource, increasing efficiency, and decreasing pollution.
* *Chapter 7: Providing Green Food*—helping people eat well, for themselves and the planet.
* *Chapter 8: Using Water Wisely*—ensuring clean water for all of us.
* *Chapter 9: Delivering Green Services*—bringing services to people who have a shared desire to do the right thing.
* *Chapter 10: Green Transportation and Cities*—shaping the urban and suburban landscapes of the green future.
* *Chapter 11: Green Farms*—helping farms produce clean, healthy food for today and tomorrow.

Who is joining the green-business revolution? A 2006 Gallop poll revealed that 77 percent of Americans are concerned about the environment and feel it is urgent to get involved and make a difference. Plus the millions of Americans who start their own businesses are seeking the right opportunity (Global Entrepreneurship Monitor, 2005 Executive Report). Combined, these statistics show the potential of green business opportunities. Whatever your background or motivation, this book provides the seeds for a wide range of businesses you can tailor to your own personal goals and interests. For each idea, the book also identifies:

- *The Market Need.* The opportunity in a nutshell that a business can address

- *The Mission.* What the business will set out to do, how it will meet the needs of customers and the environment in order to succeed

- *Special Challenges.* Identifying unique challenges a business will face in moving from an idea to a successful enterprise.

- *Knowledge to Start.* From businesses that require minimal specialized knowledge to fields benefiting from experience in areas such as food, farming, or finance

- *Capital Required.* From minimal upfront investment costs to businesses requiring research and product development to get going ($ = thousands of dollars, $$ = tens of thousands, $$$ = hundreds of thousands, and $$$$ = millions).

- *Timing to Start.* The time it takes for a business to get the essentials in place, establish a product (or service), and open doors for business, from weeks to months or years.

As important as climate change is, going green is not just about slowing the melting of ice caps and protecting polar bears. We have the opportunity to develop our economies while maintaining an environment with clean energy, clean air, clean water, and meaningful work. Eco-entrepreneurs are helping to create a healthy, rewarding, and enriching world for future generations. The place to start is with a vision. I hope this book presents the visions eco-entrepreneurs can use to build this future. Each of the 75 opportunities described is one way to get there, and each path has limitless variations. There's no telling exactly where each idea will lead, but with a vision of a brighter future in place, you already have taken the most important step forward.

If you have changed your light bulbs and are ready to do more, this book is for you.

If you are looking for the biggest business opportunity of your lifetime and are ready to get started, this book is for you.

If you are worried about climate change and want to make a difference, this book is for you.

If you are bored with your work and looking for a business with a purpose you can commit to, this book is for you.

If you lie awake at night worried about how your business is going to compete in challenging economic times, this book is for you.

If you want to do well by doing right, this book may reveal your path to a greener future.

If one of the following ideas is a good match for you, pursue it by doing more research, fleshing out the plan, and making it your own. The website for this book (75GreenBusinesses.com) provides many resources, and the associated site for *Starting Up Green* (StartingUpGreen.com) provides further support for eco-entrepreneurs as they move their businesses forward. There are many additional resources that can help any business get started. There are also many books on environmental topics, a few of which are mentioned throughout this book to provide useful background information. You are not alone in your path toward a successful green business, and with a little help, you will make it.

While working on this book, I met and talked to many amazing eco-entrepreneurs who are making a difference with the businesses they are building. I know there are many more who want to get involved but are not sure what to do, what route to take, or what business to start. Maybe you are one of these people. The hardest part is getting started, but now is the time. A Chinese proverb says that the longest journey begins with a single step. Let this be the first step on your journey to a bright, green future.

Fueling Green Energy

We need energy and lots of it. According to the 2003 book by Vijay Vaitheeswaran (*Power to the People*), the global energy business totals more than $2 trillion a year (yes, that's trillion), and as the economy of the developing world grows rapidly, the global appetite for energy could increase another 50 percent by 2030 (International Energy Agency, World Energy Outlook, 2006). Mitigation of climate change is an important

factor shaping public policy and the energy market, and is creating vast opportunities for fledgling energy companies to provide renewable, clean energy. With oil soaring to more than $120 per barrel and rising prices at the fuel pump, everybody is paying attention. This, in turn, drives the development of alternative fuels and the supporting, innovative businesses that supply those alternative fuels.

Worldwide, energy production from renewable resources is growing rapidly. As concern about climate change and energy security grows, the market for renewable energy is booming. Government-mandated contributions from green power are giving the sector a big boost and the confidence that the drive for green power will last. In California, utilities are required to supply 20 percent of electrical generation from renewable energy by 2010 and 33 percent by 2020. The U.S. Department of Energy has targeted 30 percent of our transportation fuel to come from biofuels by 2030. Achieving these aggressive goals for renewable energy production is not easy. It is a huge change, creating equally huge opportunities for entrepreneurs.

Venture capitalists know an opportunity when they see one and are pouring money into green energy, investing more than $900 million in cleantech in 2005, according to the Clean Edge report "Clean-Energy Trends 2006." This investment is primarily in solar, wind, and biofuels. While such actions may be motivated in part by the desire to do the right thing, these are not philanthropic donations. Rather experienced and tough-minded venture capitalists think renewable energy is a good investment. That is the bottom line.

Clean, quiet, and increasingly versatile, solar power is growing 40 percent a year (*The Economist*, March 10, 2007). The growth in solar power and continued technology innovation will drive down prices, further expanding the market and making rooftop solar panels increasingly competitive. In fact, the growth in solar-panel installation is so rapid, it can be difficult to train workers fast enough. This creates an opportunity for "green collar" workers in the energy sector and those who train them (Opportunity 1). Solar power also is increasingly diverse as it becomes integrated into purses and camping gear to power our plugged-in way of living (Opportunity 10). Solar ovens help people in the developing world reduce dependence on dangerous, polluting cooking stoves that burn charcoal, wood, and dung, and solar bar-beques may remove pollutants from U.S. backyards (Opportunity 6). All of these are signs of the brighter solar future that eco-entrepreneurs are creating.

Other forms of green energy also are growing rapidly, particularly wind. Utilities are installing large wind turbines at a breakneck pace, but smaller wind turbines are bringing power to homes and businesses, and architectural turbines on buildings may bring wind power downtown (Opportunity 2). Fuel cells remain costly for applications such as the long-awaited fuel-cell car, but eco-entrepreneurs are making rapid inroads in markets for clean, emergency-backup power (Opportunity 8). Like modern alchemists, researchers are even finding ways to use microbes to turn wastewater into electricity (Opportunity 7)—killing two birds with one stone.

Our cars still rely almost entirely on oil, putting our economy in an increasingly precarious position. Since the oil shocks of the 1970s, our dependence on imported oil has only grown and the remaining oil reserves increasingly are concentrated in the hands of the Organization of Petroleum Exporting Countries (OPEC). Biofuels are being aggressively developed worldwide to provide alternatives, such as ethanol (Opportunities 4 and 5) and biodiesel (Opportunity 3). Biofuel production has increased dramatically but still accounts for only a small percentage of what we consume, ensuring a strong opportunity for many years to come.

One energy resource that is often overlooked is simply using less energy. By living more efficiently, we get more out of the energy we already have. This is not only a good solution, hands down it's the best solution. Power plants are a lot more expensive than compact fluorescent bulbs, insulation, and weather stripping. Conserving a megawatt by using it more efficiently is a better use of capital and natural resources than sinking money into new power plants. Energy saved from efficiency is sometimes measured in units called "negawatts," and generating energy in this way is another opportunity to divert waste into profit (Opportunity 9).

The opportunities could not be bigger for innovative businesses bringing greener energy to consumers. If you are an entrepreneur looking for the next big thing, this could be the field for you; the future is always open for innovators with visions of a bright future and the drive to make it happen.

OPPORTUNITY 1

Training for Solar Workers

The Market Need	Installation of solar systems is growing rapidly, but training of workers is not keeping pace.
The Mission	Create schools and programs for training of solar workers.
Knowledge to Start	Education, renewable energy, electrical
Capital Required	$$
Timing to Start	Months
Special Challenges	Gaining certification

Solar power is booming, with production of solar photovoltaic panels increasing a whopping 40 percent a year from 2000 to 2005 (*The Economist*, March 10, 2007), and reaching $15 billion globally in 2006 (*The Clean Tech Revolution*, Pernick and Wilder, 2007). This growth is stimulated by rebates, tax incentives, and consumers' desire to do what is right. Germany and Japan are leading the way in solar-panel installation, and California has pledged to install solar panels on 1 million roofs in the next ten years. Although solar power produced only 0.04 percent of the world's electricity in 2004 (International Energy Agency), this percentage is growing rapidly.

RELATED TREND

Photovoltaics (PVs) are not the only form of solar power. Other solar panel systems that heat oil or generate steam to produce power are resulting in large-scale production of power by utilities, but for the residential market or commercial rooftops, PVs are still the only way to go.

Solar power has a lot going for it. Once installed, photovoltaic panels sit silently on the roof generating electricity for up to 30 years without any moving parts and with little maintenance. Panels can be installed almost anywhere, and new materials, such as solar roofing tiles are less conspicuous in building designs. Producing solar electricity doesn't have a fuel cost, as sunlight is still pretty much free and doesn't produce carbon dioxide, noise, or pollution. With power like that, what's not to love?

Things are looking sunny for solar power, but it's not out of the woods yet. Even with incentives and rebates, its cost is still a major factor for many. The $25,000 or $30,000 price tag for the average photovoltaic system remains a fair chunk of change for most, and a shortage of silicon held back production and increased prices of panels in 2006. But these limitations are passing. Panel producers are ramping up production, financing is improving, and costs will fall as production continues to increase. According to the Solar Energy Industries Association, the cost of electricity produced by solar panels is expected to drop to about $.08 to $.09 per kilowatt-hour in the next ten years, low enough to compete with natural gas or coal.

As production of solar power continues to grow rapidly and becomes increasingly competitive with electricity from other sources, who is going to install all of these systems? Today, most

IN THE LONG RUN

As new solar-power technologies get better and cheaper, solar panels increasingly will be integrated on building surfaces. As this happens, builders will incorporate renewable-energy production in home design.

RELATED TREND

Many eco-entrepreneurs are working on new thin-film technology and solar concentrators to drive down the cost of solar power and increase efficiency. Novel financing models to reduce the cost barrier are another area of innovation.

OPPORTUNITY TO IMPROVE

It's a fact: Photovoltaic panels work best when they are cool. Unfortunately, some of the places with the best sun for solar—like the Southwest—are hot, thereby decreasing the efficiency of solar panels. Improving the efficiency of panels by cooling them might be a simple way to increase their power output. For example, one hot day, I sprayed the panels on my home with water and power generation went up 36 percent, if only for half an hour until the panels heated up again. ❦

INDUSTRY INFO

See the Solar Energy Industries Association (SEIA) for the solar industry's perspective and support for solar companies. Check their website at seia.org. The American Solar Energy Society is another resource (ASES.org).

photovoltaic systems in the United States are installed in those states that boast the biggest rebates and tax incentives to consumers. If more states join those programs, or nationwide incentives become more attractive, expect the solar wave to spread, creating opportunities for eco-entrepreneurs to install the panels as fast as the industry can produce them.

To install solar panels, the ideal worker needs a strong background in construction and electrical skills, with certified training specific to solar panels. The solar industry is growing so quickly, though, that businesses are having difficulty finding trained installers. Gerald Zepeda at Sun Light and Power of Berkeley, California, says, "We often hire people with construction, plumbing, electrical, or similar experience and train them ourselves," helping employees achieve certification by the North American Board of Certified Energy Practitioners (NABCEP). Zepeda also says he looks for individuals who are committed to a green lifestyle, walking the walk that matches what they do for a living. Once workers get started, the company is motivated to keep them trained to stay abreast of this rapidly evolving field.

Van Jones, founder of Green For All, may have one answer for deploying renewable energy in America's cities and keeping the green wave growing. Millions of people in cities continue to be left behind by economic and environmental progress while manufacturing jobs move overseas. Training these people for new "green collar jobs"—installing solar power and other forms of renewable energy—can help the renewable energy industry keep up its rapid growth, get these people on track to rewarding careers and lives, and help the country and planet in the process. Too often, job training provided by schools and the government has been focused on old industries that are shrinking rather than growing. Green collar jobs, on the other hand, cannot be outsourced, provide viable skills, and craft a

GREEN LEADER

Lyndon Rive, CEO of SolarCity in Foster City, California, told *The New York Times*, "It is hard to find installers. We're at the stage where if we continue to grow at this pace, we won't be able to sustain the growth" (February 1, 2008).

career path for the future. As Jones says, this situation is not just creating jobs, but building "green paths out of poverty."

Although solar installers are doing their best to train the workers they need, in-house programs cannot keep pace with the continuing growth of the industry. Training programs are already springing up at universities, community colleges, and even high schools. Vocational schools and programs like the one incorporated in electrical training at the Electrical Training Institute of Southern California also provide models for training.

One accessible opportunity for eco-entrepreneurs is to establish new training programs for renewable energy workers. Starting a new school for this is not a one-person operation and requires people from a variety of backgrounds. Those with experience in renewable energy would do best collaborating with others who have experience in education and business, making the most of everyone's skills. New schools can specialize in renewable-energy training by partnering with solar companies; taking over existing in-house training; and ensuring a continued stream of workers. To attract students and gain an edge, schools should emphasize practical training with the latest technology and offer job placement.

To get started creating a solar training program, you need to have a strong grasp of the technical and business aspects of the industry. Becoming certified by a group such as the NABCEP is one way to accomplish this, and getting the necessary background by working in the industry, taking courses, talking to industry veterans, going to conferences, and even taking someone else's training program to see how it works. Online courses are offered by some programs, providing a convenient way to learn, and a possible opportunity to develop.

One source of funding for training programs is government grants. The 2007 energy bill provides up to $125 million per year for green-job training, and other government and private investments in training are expected to follow. This funding can provide training for tens of thousands of workers who can be part of the green wave and ride it to success. From the solar industry perspective, Zepeda says, "It's a step in the right direction."

> **INFORMATION RESOURCE**
> The U.S. Department of Energy lists training programs on its Solar Energy Technologies Program website at www1.eere.energy.gov/solar.

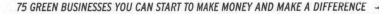

Types of solar opportunities include:

- Building a solar worker-training program
- Developing new solar technologies
- Creating alternative funding for solar power
- Launching a job board for renewable-energy workers
- Creating online courses and programs for renewable training

Although solar power is growing rapidly, solar panels still are found on only a few scattered homes. Those who see the glass as half empty might be discouraged, but others see an opportunity waiting to be realized. Success is when every home generates its own electricity. In addition to solar, wind power and biofuels are growing rapidly, and trained workers are needed in these areas as well. By one estimate, renewable energy already employs 8.5 million people in the United States and might employ as many as 40 million people by 2030 (American Solar Energy Society, "Renewable Energy and Energy Efficiency: Economic Drivers for the 21st Century," 2007). The green wave is growing rapidly, but continuing its growth will take far more trained workers. Now is the time to start training them.

OPPORTUNITY 2
Small Wind-Turbine Installer

The Market Need	Renewable energy other than solar power in cities and suburbia
The Mission	Provide small wind turbines for customers to produce their own clean power
Knowledge to Start	Electrical, mechanical
Capital Required	$
Timing to Start	Weeks to months
Special Challenges	Small market today, but has large potential

When it comes to renewable energy, wind power is cheap, clean, and effective. With strong and steady wind, the cost of electricity from utility-scale wind power can be as low as $.03 or $.04 per kilowatt hour—competitive with natural gas and even coal. Factoring in the additional costs of burning coal—air pollution, destruction of land, and climate change—makes wind power look like a real bargain. This is helping to drive rapid installation of large wind turbines and an emerging market in installing small wind turbines at homes and businesses.

Globally, the wind business grew an incredible 50 percent in 2006 (*The Clean Tech Revolution*, 2007), and wind power will continue to benefit from commitments to increase the use of renewable energy. There are already many winners in wind power: Producers of large wind turbines are doing very well, with manufacturers of towers, blades, and turbines in Europe, Asia, and North America jockeying for a lead position. The turbines being installed increasingly are enormous towers for megawatt-scale wind farms run by utilities—larger towers can produce power more efficiently. Some utility-size wind towers have blades more than 100 meters across, a football field in size. Companies building improved turbines, blades, or other components are expected to continue to find opportunities to grow with utility-scale wind power.

Large wind towers can produce a lot of energy, but they also can raise objections from the local community. To one person, a wind farm may be a thing of beauty, replacing coal with clean, renewable energy. Others feel towers mar the scenery, leading communities to block prominent wind projects in places like Cape Cod, Massachusetts. Some residents have objected to noise or potential harm to birds. Wind power developed in wind-rich rural areas like North Dakota also is a long way away from major urban centers where most of the power is used, leading to transmission

INDUSTRY INFO

The American Wind Energy Association provides support for wind entrepreneurs in many ways. For more info about the opportunities in small-wind-turbine installation see the association's 2007 Small Wind Turbine Global Market Study (awea.org).

RELATED TREND

The cost of importing wind turbines produced outside the United States increased somewhat in 2007, in part due to the declining dollar and increasing cost of imported components. This should increase the competitiveness of turbines and components produced inside the United States.

RELATED TREND

One form of wind investment is community wind projects, described in Greg Pahl's book *The Citizen-Powered Energy Handbook*. With technical, financing, and regulatory issues properly addressed, locally owned wind projects stimulate the local economy and could grow rapidly.

difficulties. A way for wind to contribute to our power needs avoiding some of these problems is with small wind turbines located at homes and businesses, bringing wind power directly to the consumer.

Large wind towers work best for utility-scale energy in open remote areas, and are not generally welcome in urban or suburban environments. Small wind turbines with blades that are, at most, a few meters across are starting to pop up in locations where large turbines would not work. Local regulations permitting, small turbines can generate enough power for the average home's needs. There were about 6,800 small wind systems sold in the United States in 2006 (AWEA Small Wind Turbine Global Market Study, 2007), with U.S. companies dominating this part of the wind business. A variety of state or local tax credits or rebates may apply to wind systems, although there isn't a federal tax credit for small wind systems at this time. The U.S. market for small wind systems in 2006 was $56 million, a figure that is small compared with large wind turbines but growing between 14 and 25 percent a year (AWEA Global Market Study, 2007). If given a federal tax credit similar to that given to solar, the market for small wind systems likely would see much faster growth.

Wind systems like the Turby or Skystream are installed on small towers in rural and suburban markets for homes and small businesses. The Skystream from Southwest Windpower costs between $12,000 and $15,000 installed, and a typical home with a properly sited wind generator and 12 mile-per-hour wind speeds can generate 400 kilowatt hours a month, a large proportion of what most homes use. This cost compares favorably with solar power.

GREEN MARKET

Small wind may really take off in cities such as San Francisco and Chicago that have wind to spare. Wind power might be a harder sell in less windy locations.

According to Miriam Robbins at Southwest Windpower, "Small wind systems, especially our new Skystream design, cost less to install than the same amount of PV." It has been estimated that electricity produced from small wind comes to about $.11 per kilowatt hour, compared with about $.18 for solar power. While small wind has been more common in rural areas, installation in suburban regions is expected to increase as people get used to seeing turbines. "We anticipate that installs will get more and more residential as more and more are installed and accepted within communities," Robbins says. As small wind grows, so do opportunities for small-wind-turbine installers and dealers.

To become a small-wind-turbine installer, turning to the experience of others is helpful. The paper "How to Build a Small Wind Energy Business: Lessons from California" presented at the ASES Solar 2007 Conference (available online at nrel.gov) describes the ins and outs of starting a wind business. The paper describes many factors that come together in a region to help wind entrepreneurs, including permitting requirements, state incentives, the cost of power, and wind in the region.

Another form of small wind power is being designed and installed in architecture on buildings in the suburban and urban landscape. Rather than towers, wind turbines can be fixtures on buildings, capturing the wind gusting through the urban landscape. Ongoing experimentation in this new side of wind is expected to continue to improve output and lower costs. Aerovironment in Monrovia, California, and Aerotecture in Chicago, Illinois, are developing turbines to be installed on commercial buildings and other urban structures.

Types of small-wind-power opportunities include:

- Distributing small wind towers
- Installing small wind towers
- Designing small wind systems
- Developing community wind
- Incorporating architectural wind turbines in urban and suburban building design

Given the early stage of the small wind sector and the small scale of the systems involved, this field is suited to smaller entrepreneurs looking for a way into wind power. Becoming a small-wind distributor or installer is an accessible option, especially for individuals experienced in working with mechanical or electrical systems. As more wind installations start popping up, people's reluctance likely will diminish and the market should grow, similar to photovoltaics. There is plenty of room to grow and plenty of wind to go around.

OPPORTUNITY 3

Biodiesel Production

The Market Need	Renewable fuels
The Mission	Join in the biofuel revolution with small-scale biodiesel production
Knowledge to Start	Autos, fuels
Capital Required	$$
Timing to Start	Months (for small-scale production)
Special Challenges	Source and cost of feedstocks as well as regulations for sales

When it comes to transportation fuels, oil is king. In 2005, the world consumed about 30 billion barrels of oil (Energy Information Administration, eia.doe.gov), most of it for transportation, with millions of new cars coming on the road in the developing world. The consumption of oil accelerates climate change, pollutes the air, and generates geopolitical headaches spanning the globe, creating a massive opportunity for entrepreneurs working to change this with the production of biofuels such as biodiesel derived from plant or animal products.

The number of diesel cars introduced in the United States is increasing as awareness grows of the advantages of diesel. Petroleum diesel produces more power per gallon than gasoline, is more energy efficient, and uses simpler engines (without spark plugs or a distributor) that require

INDUSTRY INFO

For more biodiesel industry information and statistics, see the National Biodiesel Board's website at www.biodiesel.org.

less maintenance. However, petroleum diesel produces significant pollution and is nonrenewable. Biodiesel is superior to petroleum diesel in many ways. Produced from vegetable oils or animal fats, biodiesel burns more cleanly and is a renewable fuel that can fight climate change. Biodiesel can be produced from used cooking oils; grease; palm, canola (called rapeseed in many countries), soybean oil; or just about any other plant that makes oil. Unlike straight vegetable oil, biodiesel is chemically modified to suit engines right out of the factory, and diesel engines have run for hundreds of thousands of miles on the fuel. It is also nontoxic (unlike petroleum diesel or gasoline), and can be blended with petroleum diesel to increase engine lubrication. By improving engine lubrication, biodiesel fuel reduces engine wear and keeps them cleaner, reducing maintenance costs and breakdowns.

The United States consumes about 58 billion gallons of diesel fuel and related petroleum products each year, and the National Biodiesel Board estimates that U.S. demand for biodiesel was about 225 million gallons in 2006. Production of biodiesel is increasing rapidly but remains only 0.4 percent of overall consumption. It has been estimated that even if the United States converted all its cooking oil and animal grease to biodiesel, this would cover only a small fraction of our needs. Planting all spare farmland with biodiesel crops such as canola or rapeseed could increase biodiesel's share of our total diesel use to only between 10 and 20 percent. Entrepreneurs do not need to provide our entire diesel supply from biodiesel to build a business, however. Displacing even a small part of the oil we use can still be a successful business.

Large biodiesel producers include agribusiness giants

ECO-TIP

Straight vegetable oil can fuel a car for a short time, and it looks neat to pour vegetable oil in your car and drive around, but this non-standard fuel quickly burns out engines that are not specifically modified to handle it.

ECO-ISSUE

Although biodiesel has a lot of advantages, it does have a down side or two. Compared to petroleum diesel, biodiesel becomes a gel more easily at low temperatures, requiring specialized engine modification in colder areas.

IN THE LONG RUN

Competition for soy between biodiesel, food, and other uses is driving up its price, causing inflation and controversy about the cost of food. If the rising cost of soy keeps the price of biodiesel high, it will limit the market in the long run, driving production toward alternatives (see Opportunity 74).

BEYOND SOY

Soy beans are the mainstay of U.S. biodiesel production, but the soy plant is neither the only oil-producing plant nor the best one. In Europe, canola is the main source of biodiesel, and a variety of other crops produce oil. There are ongoing opportunities in each region to grow a variety of crops for fuel. Having fuel-specific crops can help avoid the food-fuel controversy.

GREEN MARKETS

Companies trying to improve their environmental impact are fueling their fleets with biofuels. This creates a great market for biodiesel fleet sales, guaranteeing a steady income with a good relationship.

like Archer Daniels Midland (ADM), which is positioning itself as a potent global force in biodiesel and ethanol production. Regional production also is beginning to produce biodiesel locally using the feedstocks available where the fuel will be used. To address this market, regional producers—such as Pacific Biodiesel in Hawaii and Imperium Renewables in the Northwest—are developing production capacity around the country.

Big players like ADM are hard to beat on price alone, with market power and economies of scale on their side, but innovative small businesses can compete by identifying local or regional niches. Establishing a unique brand is one way to carve out a market niche, as is the case with BioWillie biodiesel, endorsed and promoted by country music legend Willie Nelson. Biodiesel enthusiasts may prove loyal to a local brand with which they identify. Another way to differentiate your company is to use sustainable methods, such as avoiding pesticide use, competition with food, or clearing new land for fuel crops.

A growing cadre of dedicated enthusiasts is so committed to biodiesel that they are producing their own. One of the attractive aspects of biodiesel is that it can be done on a small scale, even in your backyard (check your local regulations). On their own and in co-ops, more and more people are using the resources they have available locally—including restaurant grease, used vegetable oil, and virgin vegetable oil—to make themselves self-sufficient for fuel. The higher the price of gas goes, the more the wave of home-brewed biodiesel will grow. Greg Pahl (author of *Biodiesel: Growing a New Energy Economy*) confirms that, although statistics are hard to come by, a growing number of local producers and cooperatives—such as Piedmont Biofuels in North Carolina (biofuels.coop)—are springing up to provide energy security, stimulate economic growth, and fight climate change.

Small producers can find the biodiesel business rewarding but also frustrating due to challenging regulations. Selling fuel to the public requires ASTM compliance, which can be expensive (ASTM International develops technical standards for a wide variety of products and materials). Small producers, such as co-ops, can fly under the radar and deal with minimal regulation as long as they only use the fuel themselves. Experienced veterans, such as Piedmont, provide an invaluable resource for education, consultation, and finding supplies. Piedmont also provides classes and information on their website about ASTM testing of biodiesel.

The growth of biodiesel presents opportunities for distribution and installation of alternative-fueling stations (Opportunity 67). The special properties of biodiesel mean it cannot be handled in the same way as petroleum diesel, creating opportunities for those who specialize in ensuring the delivery of the highest quality biodiesel from production to pump.

Entrepreneurs getting into the fuel market need to find a niche where biodiesel can compete with petroleum products. The more expensive oil becomes, the easier it will be for biodiesel to compete if the cost of feedstocks does not increase to the same extent. As a good lubricant, biodiesel can be blended with petroleum diesel to reduce

GREEN LEADER

Author Greg Pahl's website is gregpahl.com.

RELATED TREND

One business idea is selling materials to enthusiasts, helping them to get started with biodiesel production. For more information, visit homebiodieselkits.com. Piedmont Biofuels also sells systems for production.

ECO-ISSUE

The chemical process that makes biodiesel is also producing tons of glycerol, flooding the market and driving down its price. The oversupply of glycerol is an opportunity to find new ways to use this biodiesel byproduct.

IN THE LONG RUN

Algae can produce high levels of oil that can be converted into biodiesel. From 1978 to 1996, the U.S. Department of Energy spent millions of dollars testing algae oil production in large, outdoor ponds. In the current biofuels boom, several companies—such as Greenfuels and Aurora Biofuels—have created new strategies to use algae as a source of climate-friendly fuel. ❧

engine wear and increase performance. The market for an additive for petroleum diesel would create a demand for hundreds of millions of gallons of biodiesel.

The clean-burning nature of biodiesel should help it to compete in urban markets. For example, hospitals need a backup power system, but having a big, polluting diesel generator running next to the building may not be the best option. Clean-burning biodiesel for electrical generators produces far fewer pollutants and health problems. Plus, in parts of the world where power is unreliable, diesel generators are common, and biodiesel from used cooking oil could provide a clean alternative.

Types of biodiesel opportunities include:

- ◉ Creating biodiesel cooperatives
- ◉ Supplying parts and materials for biodiesel enthusiasts
- ◉ Developing plant oil-based lubricants and solvents
- ◉ Establishing branded biodiesel sales
- ◉ Working in biodiesel distribution and quality control

It's not likely that biodiesel will replace petroleum diesel completely, but entrepreneurs still can build a business. There are many biodiesel niches from which entrepreneurs can profit while reducing reliance on petroleum diesel, at least in small part. Every step forward is a step in the right direction.

OPPORTUNITY 4

Sugarcane Ethanol Production

The Market Need	Clean, green biofuels in addition to corn ethanol
The Mission	Sustainably and cleanly grown sugarcane for ethanol production
Knowledge to Start	Fermentation, sugar market
Capital Required	$$$ to $$$$
Timing to Start	Months (for small-scale production)
Special Challenges	Government policy in sugar program and biofuel incentives

Ethanol production in the United States today comes almost exclusively from the fermentation of corn. Why corn? The United States grows a lot of corn and knows how to make it into ethanol. However, we only have so much corn, which is why billions of dollars are being spent to figure out how to produce cheap cellulosic ethanol from agricultural waste and plants such as switchgrass. Meanwhile, entrepreneurs worldwide are already producing billions of gallons of ethanol from another resource: sugarcane.

Sugarcane has many advantages over corn for ethanol production. In the right climate, sugarcane grows quickly and converts a large percentage of its energy into making sugar. Sugar is the key ingredient needed to make

BALANCING ACT

If increased production of Brazilian ethanol destroys the Amazonian forest, the cost may be too high to overlook. However, Brazilian officials have stated that sugarcane production requires only 6 million hectares, with more than 100 million hectares of land available for expansion without intrusion into the rain forest. Raising cattle is probably a greater threat to Amazonia, using land to provide feed and grazing. Going vegetarian is a more effective way to fight deforestation than fighting cane ethanol. ❦

ethanol, as with the yeasts that produce wine from grapes. While the sugar in corn is locked in starch that must be broken down before it can be fermented by microbes into ethanol, the sugar in cane forms a large part of the liquid content of the plant; fermentation starts almost as soon as the plant is cut. Ethanol from sugarcane yields eight times more energy than is used to produce it—a ratio that is five or six times better than corn—and sugarcane ethanol reduces greenhouse gas emission by between 80 and 90 percent when compared with gasoline—much better than the 10 to 20 percent reduction estimated with corn ethanol (David Tilman and Jason Hill, *Washington Post*, March 25, 2007). Per acre, sugarcane produces about twice as much ethanol as corn. Increasing the production of ethanol from sugarcane may provide a viable route for biofuel businesses.

Sugarcane-ethanol production in Brazil has set the standard, producing the cheapest ethanol in the world. Brazilian ethanol costs about $0.81 per gallon (*Science*, March 16, 2007), compared with a cost of $1 to $1.06 for a gallon of American corn ethanol with subsidies (Energy Information Administration, 2005). Brazil gets about 40 percent of its auto fuel (not including diesel cars) from sugarcane ethanol, producing 282,000 barrels of ethanol a day in 2005 (*Nature*, December 7, 2006). Although the United States currently imposes a $0.54-per-gallon import duty on Brazilian ethanol, it is attracting worldwide attention and money from investors such as George Soros, who is investing $900 million.

Objections often have been raised to the environmental impact of growing sugarcane and producing ethanol from it. The ideal biofuel does not just displace petroleum but can be produced without damaging the environment, providing a sustainable-fuel alternative. The 2006 report "Sustainability of Brazilian Bioethanol" from Utrecht University in the Netherlands, gave it a score of "average" to "very positive," confirming its overall climate benefit. While cane fields in the past were burned, new practices encourage cane to be farmed more sustainably, leaving residue in fields to compost rather than burning it. Many new distilleries in Brazil burn cane waste as fuel instead of burning fossil fuels, and many of

Brazil's sugarcane growers are signing agreements to use sustainable production methods. Increasing awareness of the need for sustainably produced fuel will drive some buyers on the international ethanol market toward fuel that is certified as being produced in an environmentally sustainable manner.

The sugarcane approach is being developed in other regions with tropical and subtropical climates, trying to replicate Brazil's success. The Brazilian story took decades of work farming, harvesting, distilling, distributing, designing fueling stations, and developing cars that could handle the fuel. This process takes time and effort, but if Brazil has done it, others can too, particularly if the price of oil continues its upward climb. Barring policy changes in the United States, it may be more productive to invest in sugarcane production elsewhere. The U.S. market is big for biofuels but it is not the only one. There is room around the world for greater cane production without cutting into food production, and if the cane is grown responsibly and sustainably, it will have the same impact on climate and oil use whether the crop is grown in India or in Florida.

What about importing Brazilian ethanol to the United States? The current tariff makes this expensive, pricing Brazilian ethanol above U.S. corn ethanol. The US corn lobby will put up a stiff fight before the ethanol tariff changes, and it would take a brave politician to support this move. It may not be likely, but if the tariff is lifted, it would create an instant opportunity for importing, distributing, and supplying ethanol from Brazil.

What about U.S. production of ethanol from sugarcane? Sugarcane in the United States is produced mainly in parts of Florida, Louisiana, and Texas along the Gulf Coast. Climate is one factor restricting sugarcane production and use for ethanol, but it's not the only factor. The US Department of Agriculture published a report in 2006 on "The Economic Feasibility of Ethanol Production from Sugar in the United States," finding that production of ethanol from molasses was cost-effective in the United States but production from cane sugar was less so.

INFORMATION RESOURCE
You can find the 2006 report at the USDA website, usda.gov, by searching for "sugarcane ethanol."

Why does ethanol production from cane work so much better in Brazil? One important reason is government policy. The U.S. sugar program keeps the price of sugar about twice as high in the United States when compared to the rest of the world, making the cane sugar too expensive to use for ethanol production. With increased support for sugar-to-ethanol production, the process can be more competitive. Hawaii already is moving to increase ethanol production from cane by requiring that gasoline there include 10 percent ethanol. Sugarcane ethanol probably is never going to be as big in the US as Brazil, but with lower sugar prices and greater incentives, more cane sugar would be used for ethanol production.

One opportunity to move sugar-to-ethanol production in the United States forward is to use sugar mixed with starch from corn during fermentation, thereby increasing the overall yield of ethanol production. This strategy has been proven to work in the past when the price of sugar was low. Another path forward is by combining fermentation of sugar with the cellulose of the rest of the sugarcane plant. Today, this material often is considered waste but improved cellulosic ethanol production would increase sugarcane ethanol productivity and lower its cost. Locating ethanol production close to where cane is grown and creating ethanol production co-ops in these areas also keeps costs low and helps build viable businesses.

RELATED TREND

Finding coproducts from sugarcane plants in addition to ethanol can allow more money to be made from the same amount of crops, potentially reducing the number of plants needed to get started. Academic, government, and industry researchers around the world are finding creative ways to use parts of the sugarcane plants to make other products.

The barriers to making ethanol from cane sugar in the United States may seem daunting, but they are no more daunting than the obstacles standing in the way of other transportation solutions. Sugarcane ethanol can be produced economically, as Brazil has demonstrated. What is blocking the U.S. market is government policy, not science or technology. The same cannot be said of cellulosic ethanol (See Opportunity 5) or hydrogen fuel-cell cars. Policy may seem immovable, but it's not written in stone; it can change, and a chink in the armor already may be developing. One provision of the North America Free Trade Agreement

(NAFTA) of 1994 stipulates that Mexico can export unlimited sugar to the United States starting in 2008. Under current sugar policy, the U.S. government may be obligated to buy hundreds of millions or even billions of dollars worth of sugar to maintain current price supports and then sell it at a steep loss to ethanol producers.

INDUSTRY INFO

For the sugarcane industry's perspective, see the American Sugar Cane League (amscl.org).

Types of sugarcane-to-ethanol opportunities include:

- Creating ethanol production co-ops
- Mixing sugar with other ethanol fermentation
- Selling sugar coproducts
- Investing globally in sustainably produced sugarcane ethanol
- Combining cellulosic and sugar ethanol production

We often are looking for "the solution" to our energy needs, the one answer that provides low-cost energy without polluting, degrading cropland, raising food prices, destroying habitat, or contributing to climate change. Cane sugar might not ever supply all of our energy needs, or provide the solution for everything, but entrepreneurs supplying ethanol from sugar can build a good business with the right conditions in place. With the continued pressure to increase our energy security and fight climate change, a shift in U.S. policy to encourage the production of ethanol from sugarcane might be just around the corner.

Breaking the Cellulosic Ethanol Barrier

The Market Need	Cellulosic ethanol still is not a cost-effective business
The Mission	Make cellulosic ethanol cost effective
Knowledge to Start	Farming, distribution, fermentation
Capital Required	$$$$
Timing to Start	Years
Special Challenges	Research needed for commercial production

In the race to produce biofuels, production of corn ethanol consumed about a third of the corn grown in the United States in 2007 and displaced about 5 percent of the gasoline used (*The Economist*, December 6, 2007, also, Energy Information Administration). The U.S. government has set a target of reducing anticipated gasoline use by 20 percent by the year 2017 and 30 percent by 2030, an aggressive goal that creates a huge opportunity, but corn ethanol alone is not going to get us there. The price of corn already has doubled as a result of competition between fuel and food, raising food prices and stirring global protests. Producing more biofuel requires other solutions, and the big money is betting on cellulosic ethanol, which is produced by converting the cellulose in plants into ethanol. Entrepreneurs who can make the cost of cellulosic ethanol production competitive with other fuels will realize an even larger opportunity than corn ethanol.

Fermenting corn for ethanol uses only the corn itself; microbes convert the starch in corn into ethanol, like wheat is fermented to make beer or grapes for wine. This leaves the stalks, stems, and cobs made of cellulose behind. Cellulose is the most abundant biomolecule on our planet, but although it's made of sugar, most animals cannot digest it. Cellulose-eaters, such as cows and termites, rely on microbes to break down the cellulose into useable sugars. Whoever finds a clean and economical way to unlock the energy of cellulose will fuel the next biofuel revolution.

The Department of Energy, other parts of the U.S. government, and additional groups too numerous to list are funding cellulosic ethanol research. Researchers are looking at every step in the process: growing the plants, harvesting them, breaking up the plant material, breaking down the cellulose into sugar, and converting it into ethanol. All of this can already be done but needs to be done better to produce cellulosic ethanol cheaply enough to compete with gasoline. Companies like Novozyme of Denmark are making enzymes that can break down cellulose. Startups like Mascoma and Verenium, both in Massachusetts, are looking for new enzymes that release the sugar from cellulose. Pilot plants for industrial production of cellulosic ethanol already have been built by companies like Iogen of Ottawa, Canada, and more pilot plants are on the way. We know we can make ethanol and use it as fuel. The only question is whether we can do it cheaply enough to compete with other fuels and in a way that makes sense for the environment.

There is not one business opportunity in cellulosic ethanol but many. Corn-based ethanol is paving the way for cellulosic ethanol in many ways, but there isn't a system yet for harvesting and collecting the material that would be used to make the new fuel. For example, if switchgrass, a perennial, is a solution, then farmers will need new ways of harvesting it, and businesses will need to collect the material and transport it. What other material can be used to produce cellulosic ethanol? Potentially, every different crop will require different processing and a variation on getting sugar and ethanol out of the plant material. Growing different crops for fuel creates unique opportunities wherever you live.

Today, most ethanol is produced and sold in the Midwest and in states such as California that have mandated that ethanol be mixed with other fuels. To reach the U.S.

RELATED TREND

A related opportunity is for companies to find creative uses for coproducts. For example, if waste heat is produced, it should be captured. Compounds called lignins, which are released from cellulose, might have their own use. Companies such as Lignol Innovations in Canada already are starting to look at these opportunities.

RELATED TREND

With so many small companies getting involved in ethanol production, and a lot of money being invested, consolidation is expected to occur along the road to commercialization. Driven by the pressure for more research and to produce a cheap commodity, opportunities for mergers, acquisitions, and partnerships will spring up.

government goals set for 2017 and beyond, production needs to increase from between 5 and 6 billion gallons to 20 and 30 billion gallons in less than a decade. Regional producers across the country are producing corn ethanol, and if cellulosic ethanol is perfected, there will be massive expansion of this market.

Starting a business in ethanol production sees stiff competition, significant research investment, and no immediate payoff. However, the opportunities are not just for fuel production but exist at every step in the supply chain, including distribution and storage. Ethanol is corrosive and absorbs water from the air, making corrosion worse. The more ethanol takes off as a fuel, the more we need better ways of moving and storing it.

The glut in ethanol that depressed prices in 2007 was not because of excess ethanol production, but because production exceeded the distribution capacity to move the ethanol from the Midwest to other parts of the country (*New York Times,* September 24, 2007). With billions of gallons of ethanol being produced and far more planned, eco-entrepreneurs developing innovative ways of handling and distributing ethanol will find ready opportunities. Today, ethanol is distributed by rail and truck, although it would be more efficient to transport via pipelines. Finding a way to build

IN THE LONG RUN

While ethanol has several important factors in its favor—such as all the experience people have producing it, and it is known to work in many cars—it's not perfect. That's why bio-butanol is another fuel being developed as an alternative. Produced by engineered microbes, bio-butanol has a longer carbon chain than ethanol, helping bio-butanol absorb less water and giving it higher energy content. But bio-butanol still can work in our existing infrastructure. ⚘

pipelines that can handle ethanol is one option. Another is distributing the biomass to regional fermentation facilities where ethanol can be produced.

Types of cellulosic-ethanol opportunities include:

- Finding technologies and strategies to reduce the cost of cellulosic-ethanol production
- Distributing ethanol
- Finding improved ethanol-storage solutions
- Growing, harvesting, and processing new crops for ethanol
- Developing sustainably farmed and produced ethanol
- Finding uses for ethanol coproducts

The investments in cellulosic ethanol are large, but the potential payoffs are huge. Producing cellulosic ethanol on a large enough scale to make a significant contribution to our fuel needs is a big challenge, but we will never know if we can reach the scale unless we try. No matter what happens, at least we will be further down the road to a cleaner and more secure future.

OPPORTUNITY 6

Solar Cookers and Barbeques

The Market Need	Traditional cookstoves are too polluting
The Mission	Provide nonpolluting solar cooking in the developed and developing worlds
Knowledge to Start	Design, business
Capital Required	$ to sell; $$ to develop new products
Timing to Start	Weeks to months (to sell models produced by others)
Special Challenges	Need marketing and education in the United States

Cooking is universal. People everywhere cook, even if the foods they cook are vastly different. Every day in hundreds of millions of homes, food is prepared on stoves burning wood, dung, charcoal, coal, and other biomass. Burning wood for cooking in regions where wood is not abundant leads to further deforestation, long walks, and great expense for those without money to spare. Eco-entrepreneurs who encourage better ways of cooking are solving multiple problems at once.

Cooking with wood or other biomass is bad for the environment and for the health of millions. The smoke from indoor traditional cookstoves leads to respiratory diseases killing 1.6 million worldwide (WHO World Health Report, 2002). There is also a significant risk of fire in cramped living areas. In urban areas, cookstoves contribute to pollution and perhaps even climate change. Each cookstove is small, but with billions of them the smoke becomes a significant problem.

A variety of organizations have worked to bring cooking alternatives to the developing world, including Africa, India, Central and South America, as well as China. More efficient cookstoves have achieved some success, with hundreds of thousands of new stoves in Africa and millions of stoves deployed in China. These stoves still require biomass for cooking, but direct more of the produced heat to the food, and burn the fuel more efficiently with less carbon monoxide and smoke in the home.

That said, solar cookers are a cleaner way to go. Reflecting sunlight onto a small surface, they focus enough heat to cook food or heat up water. By avoiding the need for fuel, solar cookstoves save money that can be spent on education or other fundamentals. The designs and materials used in solar cookers seem almost limitless, ranging from simple homemade designs (such as a cardboard box covered with aluminum foil) to sophisticated parabolic mirrors. The expense of solar ovens reflects the materials and design. Parabolic cookers are efficient and able to heat food to temperatures as high as 400 degrees F. Box cookers, such as the Sport Solar Oven, can heat food up to 300 degrees F, plenty for most cooking needs. With a broad range of possibilities, there is still room for innovative new

RELATED TREND

Solar cookers also help purify water by heating and distilling it, another important need in many parts of the world.

designs that can attract the attention of consumers in different parts of the world.

Social entrepreneurs such as Solar Household Energy, Inc. (Chevy Chase, Maryland), Solar Cookers International (Sacramento, California), and the Solar Oven Society (Minneapolis, Minnesota) are working to bring solar cookers to the developing world. Acceptance of the ovens varies, and introducing solar cookers across the globe requires an understanding of the local culture and economy. Many early efforts to bring solar cookers or efficient cookstoves to the developing world resulted in sticker shock as people were unaccustomed to costs higher than a few dollars. The needs for lower costs and an understanding of local markets are good reasons for local eco-entrepreneurs to be involved in the production and selling of these ovens. For example, if buying an oven is not cost effective, eco-entrepreneurs help locals by selling materials and providing instructions to their fellow citizens; setup local co-ops to produce the solar ovens and sell the needed materials they will need; and work with microfinance organizations to support this eco-friendly micro-entrepreneurial drive (see Opportunity 26).

In the developed world, consumers are starting to take a fresh look at backyard barbeques. A backyard barbeque produces smog, particularly from the lighter fluid and charcoal used; solar cookers are a clean, green alternative for summer barbeques. Solar cookers can cook burgers as well as any grill, without all the flames, smoke, and carbon dioxide, not to mention the flame-broiled carcinogens. A variety of models are on the market, like the Sun Cook from Sun Baked of Toronto, Canada. Founded by Stephen Kerr, Sun Baked sells solar ovens and other solar products. Mirrors on the Sun Cook focus heat on to a black surface, where insulation and a glass-covered chamber hold it in so that cooking food takes only one or two hours. Solar cookers have not made propane or charcoal obsolete yet, but as growing environmental concerns cause some to reevaluate their backyard

> **INFORMATION RESOURCE**
> To learn more about efforts to increase the use of solar cookers in the developing world, visit solarcookers.org.

barbeque, eco-entrepreneurs may be able to market solar BBQs at local home-products stores.

The opportunities in solar cooking include:

- Increasing use in the developing world
- Selling kits and materials to build solar cookers
- Designing new models of solar cookers
- Marketing solar cookers to increase knowledge and drive sales
- Selling solar grills as alternatives to backyard barbeques

The main problem with solar ovens isn't whether they work. It is relatively straightforward to design, build, and sell solar cookers online, at fairs, or wholesale to green retailers. The problem is acceptance. The prevalence of solar cookers in the developed world has been low so far, but with increasing numbers of green consumers such as LOHAS (lifestyles of health and sustainability) and so many others diving into green gadgetry, the market finally may be ripe for solar ovens. They are not just for greenies eating tofu burgers and veggies, but are also great for manly green carnivores grilling meat. Entrepreneurs of solar ovens need creative marketing to help change preconceptions and show customers that solar cookers work well, making great food.

ECO-TIP

Home-built solar cookers are fun, but the cardboard and aluminum foil models won't get hot enough to cook meat, and an undercooked meal is no fun at all.

Customers need to see a solar cooker not as a curiosity but a product they want at home. Perhaps a Rachael Ray solar-grill revolution is needed. If you can get Rachael or Oprah cooking with your solar grill on TV, you've got it made. The greener things get, the cooler the solar barbeque will be. Hip and trendy solar grills may be coming soon to a backyard near you.

Microbe Electricity

The Market Need	New sources of energy and ways to treat wastewater
The Mission	Generate electricity from wastewater
Knowledge to Start	Microbiology, engineering
Capital Required	$$$ to $$$$
Timing to Start	Years
Special Challenges	Research to optimize design and find applications

Here's a little secret about the energy shortage—there isn't one. Energy is everywhere, but most of it is in forms we cannot readily use. The trick is figuring out practical ways to convert the energy that already exists all around us into forms we can use. In our cars, we burn gas molecules to convert chemical energy into heat, and the engine converts the heat again to move the car forward. Microscopic organisms like bacteria harness energy that we currently throw away in energy-rich sewage, garbage, or other biomass and convert it into electricity and other forms of energy, unlocking new possibilities in power production.

Life itself depends on capturing energy and converting it to other forms. Plants take energy from the sun and convert it to chemical energy found in sugars, lipids, and proteins. Animals take the chemical energy of plants and convert it again to other forms like heat, sugars, and movement to survive. Microbes are exceedingly skilled at the energy game. These powerful microscopic critters do a variety of tricks with energy that "more evolved" organisms, such as humans, can't. This allows microbes to live in just about every corner of the earth, and to produce energy from the tons of organic material we throw in dumps, burn in agricultural fields, wash into rivers, and flush down toilets. Instead of leading to poisoned rivers, overflowing landfills, and expensive waste-water treatment plants, this wasted chemical energy can be converted into useful energy.

Some of the energy in waste is captured by burning it and generating electricity using turbines. Another way to capture the wasted energy is to convert it to some other form that can be burned, just as microbes digest cow manure to produce methane and generate electricity (see Opportunity 72). Incineration is not always the answer though; in the case of solid waste from sewage, burning in incinerators is often out of the question. While a fire releases energy explosively and loses a lot of energy as heat into the surroundings, microbial fuel cells provide clean and efficient power generation without the pollution produced by incinerating waste. Microbial fuel cells produce energy directly by pushing electrons through a wire while eating waste.

Bacteria called "iron-eaters" eat organic compounds like acetic acid, pushing electrons to create an electrical current, generating power. Derek Lovley at the University of Massachusetts at Amherst has produced microbial fuel cells using iron-eating bacteria that are almost 80 percent efficient in capturing electrons to produce power, far more efficient than previous efforts to build microbial fuel cells or burning waste. Dr. Bruce Logan at Penn State has coaxed more garden-variety microbes into producing energy from wastewater and is working to demonstrate the process at larger scales. These academic breakthroughs may pave the way for businesses developing microbial fuel cells and applying them as a new form of renewable energy.

INFORMATION RESOURCE

For more about how microbial fuel cells work, see the websites of Dr. Bruce Logan (engr.psu.edu/ce/enve/logan.htm) and Dr. Derek Lovley (bio.umass.edu/micro/faculty/lovley.html).

One way to use microbial fuel cells is to generate electricity at wastewater treatment plants. We produce a lot of wastewater, and in the United States, getting rid of it consumes about $25 billion per year and 1.5 percent of our electricity (*Mechanical Engineering* magazine, 2004). The material contained in wastewater holds a lot of energy; it just needs to be unlocked and harvested safely. Waste treatment takes the organic matter in sewage and aerates, filters, and settles it to degrade organic material and remove dangerous microbes. Nothing useful is done with the energy in the waste. The process leaves behind a solid material called sludge that contains a lot of chemical energy but can be difficult to dispose of. One solution for sludge is to incinerate it, but sludge often contains pollutants such as heavy metals that can be released by burning. Microbial fuel cells could greatly improve the efficiency of water treatment, particularly where it is already costly.

The challenge of harnessing microbes to produce power for humans is often getting the microbes to convert energy into a form we can use, such as electricity. The next trick is making this process commercially viable. To build a microbe-power business, start by understanding the current state of research. Ask academic experts and their tech transfer offices at universities if intellectual property is available to license. Building electrodes with greater surface area is one field of practical research. According to Dr. Logan, the key challenge for commercialization of microbial fuel cells is "making it economical in terms of cost of materials and scaling it up."

One niche application is for the creation of environmental sensors. Sediments in oceans, rivers, and lakes contain organic material that can fuel a microbial fuel cell. Dr. Leonard Tender at the Naval Research Laboratory has developed a Benthic Unattended Generator (BUG) that gets its power from a microbial fuel cell to gather and report data on water and air conditions at sea. As the technology continues to develop, eco-entrepreneurs may use microbial fuel cells to build self-powered municipal water-treatment systems, home septic tanks, or even self-powered portable toilets.

For eco-entrepreneurs who are not afraid to get their hands dirty and are ready for a challenge, microbial fuel cells might pay off. New strains of microbes, conditions for fuel cells, material for electrodes, electrode shapes, and food for microbes are areas where ongoing research may open new doors and applications. When it comes to the amazing microbes, anything is possible.

RELATED TREND

What other devices are there where users would not want to change batteries? These are candidates to use fuel cells instead of batteries for power. They will still need some type of food for the microbes, but otherwise microbial fuel cells could have a wide range of applications.

RELATED TREND

Microbial fuel cells also can produce hydrogen from wastewater, helping to fuel the hydrogen economy from wastewater in the future (Bruce Logan, Penn State).

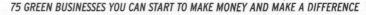

Summarizing microbial fuel cell opportunities:

- Identifying new fuel cell technology to license and commercialize
- Collaborating with researchers to develop new technology, optimizing the microbial strains, electrode shapes, and electrode materials to increase power and reduce costs
- Applying fuel-cell technology in novel areas like replacing batteries and powering portable toilets
- Using microbial fuel cells to improve the efficiency and reduce the cost of wastewater treatment

OPPORTUNITY 8

Fuel Cell Backup Power

The Market Need	Replace noisy, polluting diesel generators with better solutions for emergencies and remote locations
The Mission	Provide fuel cells for backup power, emergency power, and mobile power
Knowledge to Start	Business (to sell and distribute)
Capital Required	$$
Timing to Start	Months to years
Special Challenges	Finding a product to sell and distribute, and targeting the right market

Having a constant supply of electricity may once have been a luxury, but now it is an essential part of life. When our electricity fails, the consequences range from an inconvenience to life-threatening. When the power fails, it can mean lost work on the computer, lost food in the refrigerator, or a dangerous loss of power for medical equipment. Electricity has proven unreliable when weather, fires, and equipment failures strain an aging power-distribution grid. With the U.S. grid in desperate need of investment and power demand threatening to outstrip supply, the power supply will remain precarious for some time to come. Eco-entrepreneurs are addressing this need by providing clean backup power from fuel cells.

To avoid power interruption, businesses, hospitals, and many others have invested in backup generators. According to ABI Research, the market for generators in 2007 was more than $6 billion worldwide. Anxiety about an uncertain power supply is expected to drive continued growth for generators from 3 million units in 2006 to 7.1 million by 2011, according to market research group SBI. The market for generators includes backup generators; generators that provide power at remote locations and construction sites; and mobile generators. Engine-based generators running on diesel fuel are loud, polluting, and require constant maintenance to ensure they are ready to go at a moment's notice.

Fuel-cell technology to generate electricity is well-established. Fuel cells generate electricity directly from chemicals such as hydrogen by drawing the electrons from the fuel and pulling electrons through the system to create a current. Unlike diesel engines that are noisy and burn fuel to produce energy, fuel cells are quiet and shuttle electrons around to produce energy. Even better, when hydrogen is used as fuel, water is the only exhaust. Despite a great deal of talk and big expectations about fuel-cell cars, fuel cells are appearing more quickly in backup power generation.

In general, fuel cells still are an expensive way to produce electricity, which is one of the factors limiting their use in cars. For bulk power generation in the United States, such as using fuel cells as the main source of power for a home or business, fuel cells have a hard time competing with the price of electricity from the grid. But for backup power, fuel cells don't need to compete; they are on only when the grid is down. That makes backup power a nice niche to start with.

Fuel-cell generators won't replace diesel generators only for backup power; they will open new markets as well. You cannot run a diesel generator indoors without risking

COMPETING TECHNOLOGIES
Different fuel-cell technologies being developed and marketed include hydrogen and methanol fuel cells. Hydrogen's storage and supply are not yet routine, leading those in the small-generator markets to continue developing alternative systems that do not require hydrogen gas.

asphyxiation, but this is not a problem with some fuel cells. The Federal Bureau of Reclamation has compared several backup options—including ultra-capacitors, flywheels, batteries, and engines—and found that only fuel cells provide all the desired characteristics. The ability to use kilowatt-size generators in residential homes, office buildings, and other indoor settings will reach millions of additional customers who were previously not part of the generator market.

Many fuel cells are powered by hydrogen as a fuel. Hydrogen has many advantages as a fuel. However, the storage and distribution of hydrogen as a compressed flammable gas is not routine. Most homeowners are probably not ready to store compressed-hydrogen tanks inside their homes. Power Air Corp. in Livermore, California, and other companies are searching for hydrogen alternatives, such as zinc fuel cells, that lack these concerns. Power Air's fuel cells turn zinc pellets into zinc oxide to supply electricity without emissions. In addition, Power Air plans to recycle spent zinc oxide into new zinc pellets, closing the loop. As long as the Power Air system has zinc and air, it keeps producing power and can run indoors without a hitch. Competitively priced fuel cells that can run indoors without hydrogen will find a ready market.

Some industries produce hydrogen, making the fuel basically free. HydroGen Corporation of Cleveland, Ohio, is planning megawatt-size fuel cells powered with waste hydrogen from industries such as steel. FuelCell Energy of Danbury, Connecticut, also is developing large, industrial-scale fuel cells with a different chemistry, using molten carbonate.

Markets for sales of fuel cells to provide emergency power will include applications that put a premium on uninterrupted power. These would include hospitals, fire stations, police, communications systems, cell phone networks, banks, and information systems. In the paper "The Future of Fuel Cells" (*Electrical Construction and Maintenance*

magazine, March 4 2005), the economics affecting the uptake of fuel cells in the emergency power are discussed, projecting that fuel cells must provide power at $1,000 per kw to achieve sales to more customers, a goal that is fast approaching. According to Wintergreen Research, the market for stationary fuel cells could grow to $17 billion by 2012, as costs decline with increased production volume ("Stationary Fuel Cell Market Opportunities, Strategies, and Forecasts, 2006 to 2012," Wintergreen Research Inc. 2006, wintergreenresearch.com).

The opportunities in fuel-cell backup power include:

- Developing new technologies
- Distributing new fuel cells being produced
- Licensing technology to sell and adjust to new uses, targeting a specific market niche, such as fuel cells for office use, cabins, etc.
- Leasing fuel cells and renting them on a short-term basis as mobile power for special events (think green music events and festivals)
- Marketing in urban areas worldwide where electrical power is uncertain
- Suppling backup power to crucial computing and communication systems
- Providing power for emergency response
- Setting up cogeneration for fuel cells that produce significant heat, capturing both heat and power to increase efficiency

For all of the fuel-cell technologies, cost is an issue, and reducing costs will open up new possibilities. As long as our power supply remains uncertain, the great number of potential customers afraid of getting left in the dark ensures a bright future for fuel-cell backup power.

> **RELATED TREND**
>
> Fuel cells also might replace batteries for mobile uses, such as laptops. Methanol fuel cells are a problem to use on airplanes since methanol is flammable. There is an opportunity to invent a fuel cell for laptops using a nonliquid, nonflammable fuel that does not raise objections for airplanes.

Negawatt Installation and Verification

The Market Need	Increased energy efficiency
The Mission	Use markets to stimulate energy efficiency
Knowledge to Start	Mechanical, engineering, energy efficiency, green trading
Capital Required	$$
Timing to Start	Months to years
Special Challenges	The market for negawatts (white tags) is just getting started

As the economy grows, consumption of electricity also grows steadily, triggering the construction of new power plants and fierce debate about the best plants to build: nuclear vs. wind, natural gas vs. solar, and coal vs. just about anything. There is another answer though, one that often is overlooked: reducing the amount of energy we need in the first place. By most accounts, the United States wastes at least a third of the power it produces while other major economies use power far more efficiently. Entrepreneurs helping consumers waste less energy are freeing up much-needed electricity, saving money, and creating new markets in conserved energy.

These gigawatts of wasted energy are a big problem, but they are also a big opportunity. Robert Wilder of Wildershares Investments (Encinitas, California) has said, "We have Saudi Arabia-sized oil reserves under our feet in America through energy efficiency." Renowned efficiency expert Amory Lovins coined the term "negawatts" for this often-neglected energy resource. Eco-entrepreneurs who turn wasted energy into negawatts of saved energy may unlock the next Saudi Arabia.

DEFINITION TIME

One negawatt equals one megawatt of energy conserved for one hour.

Consumers and utilities are partners in wasted energy. Consumers often don't take advantage of even the easiest ways to stop wasting energy and money, such as changing light bulbs. Utilities generally have made money by selling power, and the more power they sell, the better off they are financially. In this scenario, with little or no motivation for the utilities to encourage conservation, it should not come as a surprise that energy efficiency has not received the attention it deserves.

Conservation can be increased, however. Since the 1970s, the state of California, along with the California Public Utilities Commission (CPUC), has worked with utilities to encourage conservation rather than consumption. As a result, Californians now use about half as much electricity as other Americans. The same measures that increased efficiency in California can work elsewhere; given the right financial incentives, utilities and customers can work together to improve how we use energy.

Realizing we waste energy is the first step, but how can we convert this knowledge into action? The problem does not require waiting for new technologies to be developed. We already have the light bulbs, insulation, double-pane windows and the many other efficiency measures needed to replicate the energy efficiency of California nationwide. What is missing is the right incentives. We need more carrots.

How can eco-entrepreneurs tap into the demand for more efficient energy use? One model is being adopted by demand-response companies such as EnerNOC in Boston, Massachusetts. The price utilities pay for energy can vary dramatically, from $.05 per kilowatt-hour (kwh) to four

MEETING POWER DEMAND WITH DEMAND RESPONSE

Demand-response companies coordinate power use by large energy users to help utilities meet the uneven demand for electricity. Demand-response companies include relatively large companies, such as Comverge of East Hanover, New Jersey, and small upstarts such as U.S. West Energy Solutions (Wenatchee, Washington). Also called load management, more and more utilities are turning to demand response to even out the demand for power and avoid brownouts and costly electricity for peak energy demand.

times as much during peak energy-consumption hours. EnerNOC does not produce or sell power. EnerNOC enrolls energy users into a network and asks them to cut back on use when consumption exceeds the utility's ability to supply power or when the peak price is too high. Users are paid for enrolling in the program and are paid more if they curtail power when asked.

Another way to encourage energy efficiency is a market-based approach. Things don't have value unless someone can buy or sell them in a market. If people can take the energy they save and sell it, they may be more willing to invest in energy efficiency. Energy efficiency certificates, or "White Tags," are being developed as a green trading mechanism to encourage energy efficiency. Each White Tag represents one megawatt-hour of electricity conserved over the course of a year, giving value to the energy that is *not* used, not just what is consumed. If a business saves energy by implementing efficiency measures, it can get the savings certified and receive White Tags for the negawatts it sends back into the grid. Originating in Europe, White Tags have been implemented in the United Kingdom, Italy, and France, and, as of 2007, are spreading to the United States, starting with Connecticut, Pennsylvania, and Nevada. Utilities are required to buy White Tags in these states, and several more states are likely to follow, creating a growing market for trading energy-efficiency certificates.

This is not the first time that market mechanisms have been used to work toward green goals. Acid rain was addressed in the United States using a similar trading mechanism. Sulfur dioxide produced by industrial sources, such as coal-fired power plants, causes acid rain. Rather than impose a restriction for each individual generator of sulfur dioxide or telling users how they must fix the problem, the government imposed a cap on the overall production of sulfur dioxide and let the market find the most cost-effective solutions. Companies that emitted less sulfur dioxide received credits to sell to those who did not reduce their emissions. This market-based solution for acid rain reduced sulfur-dioxide pollution faster and more cheaply than originally expected by allowing the market to find the best, most cost-effective solution. Similar trading of carbon emissions is under way in Europe and the United States.

Although the concept of negawatts has been around for a while, creating a viable market has taken some work. Companies such as Sterling Planet are helping to create markets for White Tags, encouraging future energy efficiency. According to Kelly Bennett, vice president of White Tags at Sterling Planet: "We serve as an intermediary in the marketplace, a retailer. We buy White Tags from owners of efficiency projects and match them up with buyers such as utilities that are required to purchase energy-efficiency certificates." Other buyers include individuals who want to buy offsets, or corporations or colleges that have set greenhouse-gas reduction targets and want to use market tools to help meet them. Creating their own efficiency projects is the best place to start reducing greenhouse gases, but White Tags can help them have even more of an impact in a cost-effective manner.

Bennett observes that the White Tag market is early in its development, but that it is "very much a growing market in response to our need to curtail additional generation, make individual homes and businesses more efficient and productive, and reduce carbon. Carbon is one of the big drivers." The growth of White Tags does not depend entirely on government action, it is also growing through voluntary use by those who want to do the right thing for the environment. "No matter what happens on the compliance market," Bennett says, "with the rules in place,

INFORMATION RESOURCE
See more about how White Tags work at sterlingplanet.com. The site also has a wide range of information about energy markets, including renewable-energy credits and offsets.

ECO-ISSUE
Sterling Planet has designed software to measure and validate the energy savings required to receive White Tags, solving one of the biggest obstacles keeping this market from taking off.

IN THE LONG RUN

A general concern is that if White Tags are implemented on a state-by-state basis, they will be difficult to trade because the rules will vary. Having a single, large market determined by federal rules would help this market grow and make it easier for markets to work. The experience of states starting to implement White-Tag markets can help regulators and industry leaders fine-tune future White-Tag efforts.

there is an appetite in the voluntary market to use White Tags in the same way as renewable-energy certificates."

RELATED TREND

In states that already are implementing White-Tag markets, there is nothing preventing homeowners from certifying their efficiency measures and selling white tags. For this to work, a large number of small projects need to be grouped together by an aggregator who could then deliver the tags to the marketplace.

One accessible opportunity is with an energy services company, which makes efficiency modifications in buildings and industrial settings. Knowledge of mechanical and building systems is needed. Projects start by auditing buildings and businesses, suggesting a plan for saving energy, and carrying out this plan. Similar opportunities exist in verifying and certifying efficiency projects. White Tags are a unique product; when you pay someone for not using power, the verification of projects is crucial. Finally, an opportunity that grows with the increasing size of the market and volume of transactions is facilitating market transactions from business to business, or business to other organization. "There will be lots of middlemen in all of these transactions," Bennett observes.

The opportunities for negawatt installation and verification include:

- Implementing efficiency as an energy services company
- Verifying efficiency projects
- Certifying efficiency projects
- Serving as on aggregator of smaller efficiency projects to deliver them to the market

It's still early days for White Tags in the United States. Everybody wants energy efficiency, and harnessing markets with White Tags might help make it happen. By selling White Tags, businesses can more rapidly pay off the investment they make in energy efficiency and justify the improvements more easily based on the rapid return on investment, a hurdle often encountered on the path toward energy efficiency. The growing trading market for White Tags will change minds about the value of energy efficiency and transform how we use energy—being negative can have a very positive impact on the environment and business.

> **GREEN LEADER**
> Peter Fusaro of Global Change Associates, New York, New York, is an expert on green trading, including White Tags and Green Tags, and the many successes and challenges of these markets. See his classes for in-depth knowledge about green trading (global-change.com).

OPPORTUNITY 10

Solar to Go

The Market Need	Mobile power, freeing people from the power grid
The Mission	Build solar into a ubiquitous mobile power source
Knowledge to Start	Solar, electrical, design, engineering
Capital Required	$$
Timing to Start	Months to years
Special Challenges	Finding a specific need and designing the right product for the market

Many people today are always connected electronically, never without an iPod, smart phone, or other gizmo in their ear or face. I suspect they sleep plugged in, their dreams piped in electronically. The older end of this group has their BlackBerry mobile e-mail always on, always on the go. In the United States and other countries, many have abandoned a regular phone line, using instead a cell phone as their main telephone number.

With electronic gear increasingly integrated in our lives, electrical cords have become our lifeline. The horror of running out of juice looms large, and we worry about getting our next hit of electricity. Next time you are at the airport, notice those feverish power junkies clustered around stray electrical sockets with their phones and laptops.

Now imagine a life free from the constraints of this umbilical connection to the electrical grid. Solar solutions set us free. Mobile solar panels in a variety of formats are being developed and marketed to provide power for laptops, iPods, cell phones, and other electronic devices.

Who is the market for this solar-powered gadgetry? Young, urban, and on-the-go is one group—electronic devices are an integral part of their lifestyle, and the more integrated the power can be, the better. Outdoors enthusiasts are another group. They also have their mobile global positioning system (GPS) devices, radio, cell phone, and other devices that need a charge. As new solar technologies such as high-efficiency flexible panels or organic solar emerge, so will the opportunities to license these technologies to provide mobile power.

> **RELATED TREND**
>
> Maybe the Climate Savers Computing Initiative will solve the laptop power problem, encouraging the development of more energy-efficient laptops that can run with 30 watts or less. The less power that laptops need, the better solar chargers will work with them.

Another market being addressed is laptop chargers—most laptops still have limited battery life, defeating the idea of a mobile computer. Imagine being able to take your laptop anywhere without worrying about running out of juice? The Solaris solar charger from Sierra Solar Systems is one solution, providing 15 or 22 watts of power, enough to charge a battery or run a low wattage computer.

One challenge is to get enough watts out of a charger to supply a laptop. The wattage supplied by a solar-power system depends on its size, efficiency, and how much light is hitting it. Because the amount of power collected is proportional to the surface area exposed to the sun, mobile solar panels are often designed to fold out to open to the sun. Solar power systems usually are rated according to the maximum level of energy they can supply in strong daylight. Typically laptops need 60 watts of power, so running a laptop from the charger would require at least this much. Panels are still expensive, and there is some pressure for mobile chargers to be small, so current solar laptop chargers usually generate 30 watts or less. A system like this can charge the battery given enough time but is not strong enough to power the computer. Either the chargers need to get stronger or the laptops need to use power more efficiently (or both).

Integrating solar power into electronics is one business opportunity. Sometimes this is as simple as matching solar panels and electronic devices together and selling them as a package. In other cases, integrating solar into electronic devices will take some design work. Keep your eyes and ears open, and your Google skills sharp, to find and sell great new solar gadgets before everyone else.

Smaller devices are easier to charge because they require less power and therefore smaller, less expensive solar chargers. The iSun is an iPod charger, and Solio (Berkeley, California) makes a popular cell-phone charger. Powerfilm of Ames, Iowa, already makes the R15-600 9 watt, 12V solar charger (hey guys, I think you need to work on its name) using a thin film technology. As a thin film, this charger is flexible and can be rolled up to make it easier to carry.

Taking mobile solar power to the next level may require new technologies, such as flexible thin films; using these a new generation of flexible thin-film solar can be built into clothing, briefcases, bags, and bikes. Thin films still are expensive for your roof, but for niche electronics applications, the cost of the panel is less of a factor. New technologies with higher efficiencies

INNOVATION TO GO

One opportunity might be using solar-concentrator technology in the mobile solar-charger market. Using a reflective surface to capture more energy might keep the cost down, minimizing the amount of actual photovoltaic material required, solar concentrators are gaining interest for other applications and might be useful here as well. ❦

probably will be more expensive when first introduced and may find their first uses in electronic devices rather than rooftop solar panels.

One limitation for mobile solar chargers is that they will require users to pack another item adding weight and complexity to the trip. Who wants to carry another bag with your laptop? What really makes consumers go gaga is an innovation that makes power a given, something they do not have to think about, something built right into the device. Integrating solar in a device means never having to say your battery is dead. Calculators have been this way for a long time; why not your blender or other household appliance? More and more items that today are powered by batteries or plugged in with a cord will run off solar power in the future. Think LED (light-emitting diode) flashlights with solar panels on the handle. Because you usually don't use a flashlight every day, having it charge slowly may be enough for it to be ready when needed (as long as it is not in a drawer or closet).

A few of the opportunities for mobile solar power include:

- Developing solar bags and briefcases
- Integrating laptop solar chargers with high-efficiency laptops
- Using small solar panels in electronics and small appliances
- Retailing solar gadgets

Ultimately, power should be so integrated that it just happens without any thought. Batteries never run out because solar recharging is built into the devices. Going green in this case means freedom—freedom from the grid, and freedom to use gizmos whenever and wherever you want. As long as the sun shines and the urban WiFi never fails, you can sit in the park Googling all day long.

Seeding Entrepreneurial Green Careers

Being entrepreneurial is more than starting your own business. It's about taking charge and trailblazing a path forward, and this can happen anywhere. Employees work as entrepreneurs inside businesses or government, taking risks and innovating to create change. The evolution of the modern economy forces us to be entrepreneurial in our daily work. Globalization, out-sourcing, telecommuting, the internet, and the flattening

of hierarchies have hastened the evolution of the company man of the 1950s into the one-man, mobile work force of today. We can't rest on our laurels, slowly rising up the career escalator based on our years of service. Today to survive, we must get out in front and live the change we want to see in our organization and our world.

Eco-entrepreneurial individuals in government, business, and nonprofits are engineering sustainability from the inside out, but what starts as an inside job need not stop there. The evolution of work blurs the line, and the green wave you start in your company may soon carry you to start your own business.

One place where eco-entrepreneurs are engineering change is in our schools, remodeling them inside and out (Opportunity 11). More efficient and healthier school buildings are just the start. Teachers are using green schools to prepare kids for a greener world ahead.

Eco-entrepreneurs also are working inside corporations in every industry, helping businesses ride the green wave. More and more businesses are finding environmental issues to be such an important challenge, and opportunity, that they are creating the position of chief sustainability officer (CSO) to lead the way (Opportunity 12). The CSO ensures the corporation complies with environmental regulations; deals with risks from climate change and pollution; looks for opportunities to save money through improved efficiency; and finds growth opportunities that the green revolution creates. The CSO cannot fake it or just go through the motions. When creating a vision for how the company will look in the green future, the successful CSO expresses his/her sincere vision of a sustainable world.

Another center of green change is the nonprofit world. Environmental nonprofits are not new—they have successfully moved policy, regulation, and action on many occasions. Now climate change has re-invigorated environmental activists, but at the same time, some are questioning if nonprofits are as effective as they could be. The proliferation of small groups with a fragmented, disjointed effort may not be effective in meeting a global problem such as climate change that requires decades or even centuries of effort.

Helping nonprofits to be more effective, measuring their outcomes, and investing funds with the most productive methods will ensure that philanthropy delivers results (Opportunity 13).

Government stands smack in the middle of the green wave, creating laws and regulations about how we interact with the natural world. Some people wish government would get out of the way, while others wish it would do more. Governments at the local, state, and regional level in the United States have crafted plans to address climate change, and action at the federal level seems inevitable. We need sound government action that addresses these problems even as it encourages robust economic growth. Green lobbyists shape legislation and regulation on environmental issues at all levels of government (Opportunity 14).

We associate the green movement with clean flowing water, pristine mountain peaks, and solar panels. Lawyers may not be the first resource that comes to mind when thinking of the environment, but many green battles often are fought with legal papers. As companies increasingly become motivated to do the right thing, there are fewer battles, and opportunities abound for green lawyers working as partners with businesses to address environmental issues upfront (Opportunity 16).

The dramatic upswing in green business also has led to an upswing in the demand for innovative solutions that eco-entrepreneurs can use in their businesses. Universities are a key source of innovation, with university tech-transfer groups (Opportunity 15) ensuring that academic inventions don't stay academic, but continue to seed the green businesses that will drive continued long-term economic growth.

Opportunities for entrepreneurial individuals to do right and do well are not limited to these; they are everywhere. Answers often lie right in front of us. Even if the first step is small, do something green at work today. Plant a seed of change, care for it, and watch it grow. Don't worry about what people will say; before long, they will be joining in as the opportunities grow from the seed that you planted. That's being entrepreneurial.

OPPORTUNITY 11

Green Schools and Teachers

The Market Need	Teaching kids to work and live in a green world
The Mission	Work as a green teacher and build green schools
Knowledge to Start	Education, sustainability
Capital Required	$ (to start as a teacher), $$$$ (to start as a school)
Timing to Start	Months to years
Special Challenges	Being a green teacher or providing green supplies happens quickly; building schools takes time

Kids are merciless. When they learn something at school and bring it home, they won't let it go until they are satisfied that their families get it. Take recycling. The little ones learn about it at school, and next thing you know, they are telling us how to recycle and asking why we aren't doing more. I thought I was reasonably conscientious, but the energy, purity of vision, and openness of children puts me to shame. They believe they can do anything. They are right. Green teachers and schools are helping them get started on the path to a green future.

Kids need to learn the basics, and to apply the basics in order to help build a healthy economy, society, and planet. It's like working with a computer, learning a language, or picking up good nutritional habits. If learned early, such things become second nature to us, woven right into our fabric.

Landmark schools are part of a developing movement to green schools inside and out. The U.S. Green Building Council (USGBC) is supporting the greening of school facilities, helping schools save money, create a better learning environment, and teach what it means to go green. In 2006 the USGBC estimated that a school can save $100,000 per year on its utility bill by going green—dollars that could

INFORMATION RESOURCE

To learn more about what is being done to build greener school buildings, visit the USGBC green schools website at buildgreenschools.org.

be spent on salaries and books. The upfront cost of building green schools has been estimated to be as little as 1 to 2 percent more than traditional schools—money that is recouped quickly through lower power bills ("Greening America's Schools, Costs and Benefits," A Capital Report, 2006). Schools around the country are making this change, with 10 percent of school construction expected to go toward green approaches. Schools dating from the baby-boomer era are now so old that they need replacing, creating an opportunity to construct better buildings. Going green also can help the morale of staff and teachers, provide a better work environment, and help staff connect with students behind a common purpose.

Having a green school building leads the way to renewed programs inside, teaching about energy efficiency, waste reduction, and renewable energy by using the school itself as a learning tool. Reading about these topics is great, but learning firsthand how to install a solar panel can change how a young person sees the world. Green schools help kids relate to and get excited about physics (how do solar panels produce electricity?), biology (how are biofuels produced?), and ecology (what services do ecosystems provide for us?). Students who ask the proverbial "Why do we have to know this stuff?" can simply look around their school for the answer, seeing each application in action.

The staff at the Bertschi School in Seattle has been greening its facilities and using these steps as a starting point for learning about sustainability, working with the green schools consultant, Meredith Lohr, to involve teachers, parents, and administrators. With a background in the environmental and earth sciences, Lohr blends her teaching with work to add sustainability to the curriculum at Bertschi. The school now has solar panels, a water reclamation system, composting, and gardens with plants native to the region.

"The curriculum at Bertschi has always emphasized diversity and social responsibility, and we have built upon this foundation over the last few years," Lohr says. "The

RELATED TRENDS

As the green-schools movement grows, perhaps there will be a green certification program and a green curriculum that will establish minimum course requirements. Maybe kids and teachers can have their sustainability quotient (SQ) tested, rather than their IQ.

students study neighborhood gardens and tend the small plots on the school's urban campus. They study ecology, through visits to local wetlands and watersheds, and participate in restoration projects in local parks." Students get involved in tracking wasted water and energy at the school, and find ways to do better. The curriculum includes visiting an organic farm in the second grade, reducing their garbage at school and at home in the third grade, conserving water in the fourth grade, and learning about renewable energy provided by the building's solar panels. The students learn how their lives, their school, their community, and the living world are connected. "We find that when presented with real connections and left to draw their own conclusions, children will make choices that benefit all living things, in the present and the future," Lohr says.

INFORMATION RESOURCE
See the Alliance to Save Energy's website at ase.org and click on the section about education for more information.

For eco-entrepreneurs interested in education, one opportunity is to grow their own green private school like the Bertschi School. Those who start out as green teachers can develop a green teaching program or even their own school. To be effective, a green approach is not layered on top but built into the foundation of the school. Green schools need to cover the same material as other schools, but have the advantage of a unique and valuable perspective about the environment that parents won't find at most other schools. Schools such as the Bertschi provide a model for how to build a green school that others can adopt.

Another opportunity for eco-entrepreneurs is to provide schools with green supplies, curriculum materials, food, janitorial services, and so on. Green schools want cafeteria food that is consistent with their beliefs, opening the way for school chefs to work with local food, food service providers, and distributors of food supplies for green schools. Green schools need recycled paper, and lots of it. The growth of green schools will create a market for more materials for projects such as fuel cells and solar energy.

In working to make new and old schools greener, teachers and administrators need to be entrepreneurial, taking the initiative and risk to create change. But there is a lot of help out there. The Green Schools Program of the Alliance to Save Energy is promoting green schools (Kindergarten through grade 12) around the country, setting up programs to teach about energy, save energy, and spread the word. The program provides curriculum materials like the "Energy Hog Challenge." Local programs, such as the San Francisco Green School-yard Alliance, are also getting involved, providing more ideas and materials to encourage schools and teachers to go green.

RELATED TREND
Another great opportunity is a green summer camp, such as Planet Energy run by Strategic Energy Innovations in Marin County, California (seiinc.org).

Green schools do not stop at the K–12 level. Colleges, universities, business schools, and many others are going green as well. Second Nature of Boston, Massachusetts, is a nonprofit group encouraging sustainability in higher education. Many schools have pledged to improve their environmental performance, including a pledge by the American College and University Presidents Climate Commitment to go carbon neutral. Courses and majors related to sustainability are popping up everywhere, and business schools and product-design schools are rising to meet the demand for those who want their work to reflect their commitment to a new way of working and doing business.

Opportunities for green teaching and schools include:

- Starting a green school
- Getting involved in building green school facilities
- Providing healthy and green food to students
- Providing green school supplies
- Founding a green summer camp

As the green economy grows, so does the need for people who can continue building green businesses for the future. The lessons kids learn shape their lives and their world. Someday, they will tell stories to their kids of how crazy things were before we all learned to live a better, greener way. I warn you though, once you get going as a green teacher and unleash kids on greening the world, they will prove unstoppable. Kid power is the ultimate form of renewable green energy.

OPPORTUNITY 12

Chief Sustainability Officer

The Market Need	Businesses need to understand and act on risks and opportunities of environmental issues
The Mission	Guide businesses to compete and succeed in the new green playing field
Knowledge to Start	Business, sustainability
Capital Required	$ (as a job in a company); $$ (to start a small consulting business)
Timing to Start	Weeks to months (to create a position)
Special Challenges	Motivating corporate commitment and action

There is a green-business revolution under way, and businesses are working hard to understand what it means for them. What risks does it expose them to? What opportunities does it create? Company executives have spent their careers focused on other issues and often don't know how to react to the pressures of the green wave. To lead them through the risks, challenges, and opportunities in the brave new green world, many businesses are creating a new position in the company: the chief sustainability officer (CSO). Whether it is called the chief sustainability officer, chief environmental officer, or chief green, this position is an opportunity for the right person to help companies ride the green wave to success. It can also lead to a new business working as a consultant helping others to go green.

Green issues are not limited to green companies producing solar power, organic food, or organic clothing, and if business is going to be green, the change cannot be limited to businesses whose main focus is the environment. Major corporations such as DuPont and Wal-Mart are changing how they do business to reduce their carbon footprint, and cut down on waste and pollution. DuPont has taken the initiative to reduce its carbon footprint 72 percent since 1990, and is selling green products in fields such as solar power and fuel cells. The largest retailer in the world, Wal-Mart, is investing hundreds of millions of dollars to increase energy efficiency, reduce packaging, and produce renewable energy. Wal-Mart also is driving its immense chain of suppliers to make similar changes. These changes are not always easy, and they would often not happen without strong environmental leadership within the company.

Ensuring company compliance with regulations is one responsibility of the chief sustainability officer. Compliance includes dealing with existing regulations to reduce pollution, such as the Clean Air Act and the Clean Water Act, and addressing future legislation. Some businesses still are assuming a wait-and-see attitude about climate-change legislation in the United States, but those that get started early will be ahead of the game when legislation finally arrives, giving them a competitive advantage.

The responsibilities of the chief green extend far beyond sticking to the letter of the law. Business leaders are realizing that being green is something they want and need to do to build a better world and a better business. Reducing a company's carbon footprint is the right thing to do and may be essential to stay competitive. Investors are asking businesses to outline their business risks related to climate change, and how the business contributes to the problem. Revealing this risk may even be required in the United States under the Sarbanes-Oxley Act of 2002, U.S. government legislation about the rules of financial disclosure. Businesses also are being asked to describe their climate footprint and what programs they have in place to offset that footprint. Businesses without a good handle on their environmental footprints may lose customers.

The chief green is responsible not just for cutting back on greenhouse gas emissions, but also for helping the business to attend to the old-fashioned bottom line: making money. Businesses that consider green factors are finding opportunities in a changing world and using them to create

MOVING BETWEEN WORLDS

Those not ready to create a green position within a company or small companies or those that cannot afford a full-time position devoted to green issues may turn to external consultants, experts with experience moving companies toward sustainability (see Opportunity 61). The roles are related and individuals may work as a green chief in their career and later perhaps move to consulting. ❦

good business. Does your company produce a great deal of waste and pay others to dispose of it? Cutting back on the waste will save money. How can you help eliminate wasted energy or develop economically attractive options for using renewable energy? What does your company make or do? Can you reduce packaging? Can you green your office? If you are in plastics, can you produce bio-plastics or find creative ways to encourage recycling?

RELATED TREND

As part of the Climate Savers Computing Initiative, Google's Bill Weihl and others are developing computing systems to be more energy efficient. PCs consume a surprising amount of energy, a lot of which is wasted. The more pervasive computers become, the more important it is that they be as efficient and green as possible. "There are a few efficient PCs on the market, not many yet," Weihl says, "but in the next three or four years, they will be the norm."

Going green is a big opportunity, but there are risks the move will be seen as "greenwashing," seeking the appearance of greenness while lacking substance. The green community increasingly is skeptical of the growing chorus of companies suddenly proclaiming their greenness, suspecting they are hoping to capitalize on a trend. To avoid this, implement the initiative first, and then let the public know about it—not the other way around.

Bill Weihl is the green energy czar at Google and helped to negate Google's carbon footprint in 2007 through a variety of measures. He sees the position of chief sustainability officer position becoming increasingly common and more important. Google may not be your average company, but like many, it is working to use energy more efficiently and create a more sustainable economy. For Weihl, the CSO understands and implements best practices across departments to "get out in front [by] pushing these issues." A green chief also helps companies shape legislation and make the most of opportunities created by climate legislation like AB-32 in California requiring a 25 percent reduction in greenhouse gas emissions by 2020. For Weihl, "Success will be to put myself out of business"—the day when being green is not an extra effort but part of daily business.

To be the chief green, you need to understand environmental issues. A growing number of schools have programs related to sustainability, producing a cadre of graduates trained to lead the way. Having an advanced degree may help, but it's more important that you be eager and open to learn, and make use of experts from a wide range of backgrounds. Topping those with the experience to minimize environmental risks, deal with compliance, and capitalize on green business opportunities will help achieve those goals.

The opportunities include:

- Working as the chief sustainability officer in a larger business
- Taking on environmental responsibilities as an employee in a smaller firm
- Developing independent consulting business, working as an external advisor in various aspects of going green (see Opportunity 61)

While being green is not always easy, it can be done. The harder the choices, the more important it is that a chief green be on board to make the changes happen. The most important qualities for a chief green are having the commitment, drive, and passion to keep moving forward. There are enough challenges and opportunities ahead to keep many chief greens busy for a long time to come.

> **ECO-TIP**
>
> A word of warning: Keep your job title professional. It might be fun, but Jason Kovak of WorldatWork, an association of human resources professionals based in Scottsdale, Arizona, advises against using the "Doctor of Green," or other titles that might be hard to take seriously. Try telling your new job title to your friends and see if they can keep a straight face before you print your business cards.

OPPORTUNITY 13

Green Philanthropy Management

The Market Need	Green philanthropists are well-intentioned but may not always accomplish their goals
The Mission	Improving how green philanthropic money is invested, ensuring that the money makes the greatest possible difference
Knowledge to Start	Business, finance, philanthropy
Capital Required	$$ to $$$
Timing to Start	Months to years
Special Challenges	Research to measure nonprofit effectiveness and acceptance by donors of those measures to guide donations

Philanthropy is a hot business. Bill and Melinda Gates have given more than $30 billion to their foundation and Warren Buffett is adding another $31 billion. This high-profile philanthropy may signal a new age, eclipsing even the era of Rockefeller, Carnegie, and Mellon. While the Gates Foundation funded grants worth $1.4 billion in 2005, it is not the only source for funding. Americans gave $260 billion to charitable causes (Giving USA estimates for 2005). One focus of giving today is environmental causes, and green philanthropists increasingly want to see that their money is well spent.

Sir Richard Branson has committed $3 billion to fight climate change, and the Clinton Climate Initiative is committing additional billions to the fight. Google has created a foundation that is promoting a next generation of automobiles—such as plug-in hybrids using biofuels—and investing hundreds of millions of dollars to drive the price of renewables down to the cost of coal. In 2005, green philanthropy accounted for $8.9 billion (Giving USA), and this

GREEN LEADER

One nonprofit organization committed to fighting climate change is StopGlobalWarming.org, founded by Laurie David, a Hollywood producer. There are countless others committed to a wide range of environmental issues.

number is increasing steadily as concern grows about climate change and other issues. Some donations are large and from well-known names, but more come as small donations from millions of people.

How can people making donations ensure that their money makes a difference? Green philanthropists don't want to just throw money at the problem and walk away, hoping for the best. They hope to leverage their wealth to make lasting changes in the lives of millions or even billions of people, but with large sums of money at stake and big goals in mind, philanthropists need to ensure that their money is well spent. While giving money to worthy causes is inherently rewarding, nobody wants to see money wasted or misused. The more money there is at stake, the greater the risk of wasting money, particularly in the absence of the economic pressure toward efficiency that is ever-present in the business world. "Billions are wasted on ineffective philanthropy," says Michael Porter, of the Harvard Business School. "Philanthropy is decades behind business in applying rigorous thinking to the use of money" (*The Economist*, February 3, 2006).

The new philanthropists often are called "social entrepreneurs," attacking social and environmental problems with the zeal and rigor of the business world. The salary may not be as large in the nonprofit world, but making a difference in the lives of millions may prove even more rewarding in other ways. Using the lessons of the business world allows green philanthropists to produce the greatest environmental impact per dollar invested.

Foundations and social entrepreneurs need to measure success to keep track of how well they are doing. Making this work requires a nontraditional accounting system, in which the value created is not measured in profits but in the value to society. Nonprofit "portfolio managers," "philanthro-capitalists," or "venture philanthropists" track how investments in non-profits perform. Professionals from other industries also are getting into the nonprofit act, including management consultants, venture capitalists, and bankers.

INFORMATION RESOURCE

One group of philanthro-capitalists is New Philanthropy Capital in London, England, a non-profit that advises donors on how to make the most of their donations. The group's report, titled "Green Philanthropy," describes nonprofit efforts in the environment.

One model establishes a firm to guide money toward the most effective environmental nonprofits. To start, the performance of nonprofit groups needs to be measured and compared to each other. How many tons of greenhouse-gas emissions were avoided per donated dollar spent by each group? How many lives were improved and by how much? Simply measuring the percent nonprofits spend on overhead is not enough to judge how effective investments in a nonprofit are; overhead says nothing about how efficient an organization is. In fact, the ongoing emphasis on lowering administration costs for nonprofits may be hurting their effectiveness in the long-run, creating well-intentioned but poorly funded management. By measuring how much organizations achieve with their expenditure money can be guided to the organizations and strategies that work best.

GREEN LEADER

The Center for Effective Philanthropy in Massachusetts (itself a non-profit) is working to help foundations measure success and be more effective (effectivephilanthrophy.org).

Once data on nonprofit performance is available, the firm helps guide philanthropists, large and small, toward the best and most effective places to donate their money, helping them get the most bang for their buck. Once the money is invested, you can track the performance of donations and nonprofits year after year. By putting a value on a nonprofit's work, the organization is pressured to do better and get as much done as possible with donated money.

Getting the venture started on the road to guiding and improving the results of green philanthrophy requires research to evaluate the performance of nonprofits. Nonprofits have not always been transparent about how money was spent or how well projects work. More effective nonprofits may be eager to cooperate and have the quality of their work validated by an independent "auditor." Another challenge will be to decide whether to form a nonprofit or to pursue a for-profit structure to analyze nonprofits and guide donations. The nonprofit does both the analysis and grant-making. A for-profit enterprise might provide the service and access to research for a fee. If your service is launched as a small independent firm, partnering with one or more financial-service providers would allow your service to integrate with investment, tax, and estate planning to reach existing customers.

GiveWell—a nonprofit founded in 2006 by two former hedge-fund managers, Holden Karnofsky and Elie Hassenfeld—works to fund charities based on how effective they are, not on the size of their overhead or the pictures in a brochure. Karnofsky and Hassenfeld got their start with a group of friends looking for charities to give to and were motivated by their frustration with the lack of good information about how effective charities really are. For each cause GiveWell takes on, it reviews grant applicants in depth, analyzing how effective the applicants are for the money they spend, and then funds organizations accordingly. Although not currently targeting environmental issues, Hassenfeld says, "The causes we cover are a function of what our donors ask us to analyze, and our interests and passions." Environmental issues may be part of their future. Some critics are skeptical of GiveWell's approach, but according to Hassenfeld, "Many in the nonprofit sector agree with our principles." To move change forward, Karnofsky and Hassenfeld plan "to keep saying what we think, asking others to engage us in conversation if they think that we're wrong." Sounds reasonable to me.

While most envision a clean divide between the for-profit and nonprofit worlds, others are blurring the worlds of business and organizations advancing environmental causes. Google.org is a for-profit philanthropic enterprise, investing in startups rather than granting money. Operating as a for-profit means that Google.org is subject to taxes but allows a greater range of activities. If an investment is successful, Google.org can create a business around it to ensure that the investment realizes its environmental, social, and financial value.

Renowned venture capitalist Vinod Khosla has decried the whole idea of charity, insisting that a for-profit enterprise is the only effective route to making a difference. The competing models pursued by social entrepreneurs will uncover the process that works best, and others can follow.

The opportunities include:

GREEN LEADER

For more about GiveWell's story, how it is working, and the latest news with its projects, see givewell.net.

- Forming a nonprofit organization that rates green nonprofits based on their performance and makes grants based on these rankings
- Establishing a business that researches the effectiveness of environmental nonprofits and sells information for a fee
- Working as a consultant for environmental nonprofits, helping them adopt best practices in business and environmental fields
- Working as an auditor of reports from environmental nonprofits, verifying their environmental impact claimed in reports
- Integrating analysis of nonprofit performance with other financial services as part of estate and tax planning

The scale of environmental problems can seem overwhelming, but there are great opportunities to improve our world. Ultimately, the greater the effectiveness of those fighting environmental challenges, the greater donor confidence and the greater contributions will be in the future, making it in everyone's best interest to make sure this happens.

OPPORTUNITY 14

Green Lobbyist

The Market Need	Businesses and society need green interests represented for regulation and legislation
The Mission	Ensure effective government action on the environment
Knowledge to Start	Government, law, environment
Capital Required	$ (as a job); $$ (to start a small independent lobbying firm)
Timing to Start	Weeks to months (to find or create a position); months to start a business
Special Challenges	Making connections, getting your voice heard

Our government and the environment are inextricably linked. Landmark legislation in the United States, such as the Clean Air Act and the Clean

Water Act, has helped protect the public from pollution and slow the rate of degradation of our natural resources. How governments regulate food, pesticide use, transportation, energy, water, and parks affects all of us. With the upswing in concern over environmental issues, support for groups lobbying the government on behalf of environmental causes also has surged.

A 2007 BBC poll showed 76 percent of Americans would make significant changes to their lifestyle to help prevent climate change. State and local governments have enacted climate-change legislation, with California passing AB-32, The Global Warming Solutions Act of 2006, to mandate reductions in greenhouse-gas emissions to 1990 levels by 2020 and suing the Environmental Protection Agency (EPA) to control greenhouse-gas emissions from cars. In response to these changes, it is commonly believed that the U.S. federal government will soon act on climate change. Lobbyists are helping to shape the important steps that are being taken.

Now endorsing federal action toward climate change are representatives of many industries, including the United States Climate Action Partnership (us-cap.org) with industrial members such as Ford, GE, and DuPont working together with environmental organizations, such as the NRDC (Natural Resources Defense Council). While there has often been an adversarial relationship between industry and the environmental movement, representatives of both are coming to view the other as an essential partner in dealing with environmental problems and are working together to find solutions that work for everyone. Both sides share the desire to do the right thing and, perhaps, a practical desire to simplify the developing patchwork of inconsistent state regulations across the United States. If climate-change legislation is inevitable, companies want to influence the action to ensure it does not hurt their business.

Karen Wayland is the legislative director at the NRDC, working to steer government toward environmental solutions that work for everyone. "We are comprised of lawyers, scientists, policy-specific experts, and some economists," Wayland says, describing the variety of backgrounds of those working at the NRDC. However, additional skills may be

GREEN LEADER

One of the groups the NRDC works with is Environmental Entrepreneurs, or E2, a nationwide group of businesspeople who believe we can protect the environment and build a strong economy at the same time.

even more important. "To be effective in shaping policy, one needs an under-standing of the policy process, politics, and Congress itself," Wayland says. "Astute people skills are a must, as is the ability to be a persuasive speaker."

With increasing concern about climate change and other environmental issues, support for groups such as the NRDC and receptiveness toward their messages have increased dramatically. According to Wayland, the NRDC staff uses a variety of strategies to get their message across. Approaches include direct lobbying, promoting a message through the media, as well as mobilizing activists and influential individuals on the NRDC's behalf. These efforts seem to be working. Wayland cites a discussion with a senior staffer in the Senate who has worked with a 20-year senator: "He had never seen such a dramatic shift on an issue in such a short amount of time. [The] NRDC is much busier on [Capitol] Hill than it has been in years."

Not ready to move to Washington, DC? Look closer to home, lobbying your state and local governments. Not so well-connected to start your own green lobbying firm? Join with someone who is, and your network will swell quickly. Those who work at lobbying may start their own firm, building on their experience and connections. There is no license or certification required to be a lobbyist, although registration with the government is required.

ECO-TIP

Green lobbyist Roger Ballantine has offered advice for green advocates of climate-change legislation: Don't over reach. The fear is that by going for the most aggressive legis-lation, green efforts may backfire and get nothing at all.

Once climate-change legislation is secured, the work is not over. Climate change will require consistent action for decades and even centuries, work that cannot be abandoned with changing political events. And, while climate change is the uber-environmental issue of today, it is far from the only challenge we face. What will be the government's future role in other environmental issues, such as waste disposal, auto effi-ciency, home-building standards, renewable energy, habitat preservation, and oil exploration? Whatever happens with climate change, the govern-ment will keep legislating and regulating, and green lobbyists will make their clients' voices heard. That's what I call job security.

Opportunities for green lobbying include:

- Working as a green lobbyist in an existing firm, lobbying for environmental nonprofits or for industry
- Establishing a new lobbying firm at the state or local level
- Creating firms that provide tools, technologies, and processes for lobbyists to mobilize activists and promote their message

OPPORTUNITY 15

Green-Tech Transfer

The Market Need	Green companies need innovation to compete
The Mission	Help entrepreneurs move green innovations from patent to product
Knowledge to Start	Technology, patents, business
Capital Required	$ (as a job); $$$ (as an intellectual property broker)
Timing to Start	Weeks to months (to find or craft a position)
Special Challenges	Not only to license technology, but also to help technology build successful businesses that make an impact

The green economy is booming with cleantech companies developing technologies that solve environmental problems in water, energy, and other fields. If green companies are to keep up their blistering growth and avoid being a fad, they must continue to innovate or get left behind in the fast-moving global economy. Breakthrough technologies in biofuels, solar, wind, fuel cells, water purification, and other areas are essential for cleantech to green the economy, but these companies cannot produce all of the innovation. Luckily, they don't have to. Eco-entrepreneurs are taking cutting-edge research at universities and using it to build green companies; careers and businesses moving patents to products through technology transfer are rewarding in more ways than one.

University and government research sites have been the source of many of the great innovations that industry has commercialized in recent decades. Many of these innovations can be traced back to the Bayh-Dole Act of 1980, which allows universities to patent research funded by the federal government, and to help move inventions from the research stage to products that can be sold. The billions of dollars in economic growth created by this act makes it "possibly the most inspired piece of legislation to be enacted in America over the past half-century," according to *The Economist* in 2002. The number of cleantech patents has been growing by about 5 percent a year, with 4,094 U.S. patents issued in 2006 in areas such as energy, air, water, and waste reduction (Lux Research and "State of Green Business 2008" report by Joel Makower and the editors of Greenbiz.com).

Green clusters, developing in places such as San Francisco, California; Seattle, Washington; and Boston, Massachusetts, are invariably focused around leading universities, in part because of the opportunity to capitalize on the innovation found there. Entrepreneurs founding companies in biotech and information technology often are based on work in university labs, funded by venture capitalists. As in other sectors, this is happening again in cleantech/green tech.

Major research universities in the United States and many other countries have technology-transfer offices devoted to advancing technologies from academic labs to commercial enterprises. Inventions that stop in academic labs might make for great science but have little effect without application in the real world. The staff at a tech transfer office works with faculty members to ensure any promising findings are properly protected by patents and then connects intellectual property with companies eager to move it forward.

ECO-TIP

For tech-transfer opportunities in green tech, one place to look is in major green business clusters, but don't stop there. Green innovation is not limited to schools near these clusters, and "green" includes a great variety of strategies, processes, and products that help the environment. There is innovation everywhere. Some of the best opportunities may be found in less obvious places where others have yet to look closely.

One of the nice things about tech transfer is that every-body wins. The university wins with revenues from intellec-tual property. In many cases, academic researchers do well financially, sometimes even choosing to follow their inven-tions to new companies formed around the technology. Entrepreneurs win through access to a steady stream of inventions. Investors win access to opportunities at an early stage.

Cleantech has seen rapidly increasing research and sky-rocketing funding. According to some, tech transfer is a misnomer. A more accurate description is catalyzing com-mercialization—not just licensing intellectual property, but assembling the people, money, and alliances to take inven-tions and patents from lab to marketplace.

One sign of the times for green-tech transfer is in stu-dent business-plan contests. Business schools run such con-tests every semester in some cases, and as the green economy booms, student-generated plans are more focused on cleantech than ever. It's not unusual these days for the winners to put funding together and start a company. That's what happened for the founders of Aurora Biofuels, which originated at the U.C. Berkeley Business Plan Competition. Matt Caspari, the CEO of Aurora of Berkeley, California, was going to business school at U.C. Berkeley and looking for ideas. Together with other stu-dents, he put together a plan for an algae biofuels company and entered the contest. They won, and have moved from contest to corporation in a matter of months with the help of investors.

According to Caspari, "Tech transfer is a good place to go for entrepreneurs wanting to start a business." Aurora Biofuels is an example of the kind of company that can come out of universities. One way they help is with a rich

INFORMATION RESOURCE

To get a sense of the scale of inno-vation at universities, look at the University of California, one of the world's largest university systems. The University of California has active technology transfer at all its campuses. The 2006 annual report "UC Tech Transfer" (available online at ucop.edu/ott) describes the full range of inventions available at UC campuses, with hundreds of patents issued in a single year and thou-sands of inventions available to license.

GREEN LEADER

Aurora Biofuels is developing algal production of biodiesel, a hot field. The company is using low-tech farming methods to keep costs low, and large, open ponds with seawater, selectively evolving the algae to produce as much fuel as possible.

network of connections, including relationships with those holding that magic stuff that grows visions into businesses: money. Working in a cluster like the San Francisco Bay Area, tech-transfer groups have access to venture capitalists, angels, and other investors. Caspari says people working in technology transfer "definitely know VCs [venture capitalists], know other people, set up introductions, and want to be helpful in getting companies out the door." Venture capitalists know a good investment when they see one and know that university tech transfer is a rich reserve of green innovation. Venture capitalists attending a business-plan contest or acting as judges can find seeds of future businesses, and pick and choose the ones to take on and grow.

There are some practices that those working in tech transfer should avoid when helping companies get off the ground. Tech transfer should be as simple and straightforward as possible, avoiding bureaucracy. It is best if the transfer is rapid, standardized, and as assembly-line oriented as possible. Entrepreneurs putting together a business have enough on their hands without being slowed down by unnecessary complexities.

Beyond universities, there are other entrepreneurial opportunities to build business around tech transfer. One is to be a tech-transfer broker, acquiring intellectual property from universities, moving this research closer to a product, and then re-selling the products to others who specialize in commercialization, production, and marketing. Similar business models have worked in biotech-related technology commercialization. By working independently, you can consolidate intellectual property from a range of schools and build a portfolio focused around one particular field, such as batteries or biofuels. With green patents scattered at so many institutions, it can be difficult to find relevant opportunities. Another opportunity is to consolidate all the information in one database, evaluate opportunities, and make the consolidated information available for a fee!

RELATED TREND

Cleantech clusters attract investor communities, such as CONNECT in San Diego, California. This brings together inventors, academics, investors, legal representatives, and businesspeople. Businesses are propelled by making the right connections; helping to make these connections is a business all of its own.

To work in tech transfer or create a business, a law degree is not essential. Understanding of intellectual property would be a must, since patents and the law around them are essential in this field. Many classes are available for non-lawyers to learn about technology transfer. However, those in the business should be able to read patents and understand what they say, with some level of technical proficiency. The "FLC Technology Transfer Desk Reference" from the Federal Laboratory Consortium for Technology Transfer in May 2006 (federallabs.org/pdf/T2_Desk_Reference.pdf) provides a useful overview to see what is involved in the field.

Working in green-tech transfer ensures that the great minds of academia are tapped to solve real-world problems and that businesses are built around these solutions. Basic research is fun and intellectually rewarding, but using that knowledge to build a greener world provides emotional and financial rewards for all involved. The amount of work is increasing steadily, and the need for innovation will never go away.

Opportunities in green-tech transfer include:

- Working as a career in tech transfer in a university setting
- Establishing a business as an intellectual property broker, aquiring patents and technology to advance and sell
- Forming a consolidated database of green patents and selling access to the database for a fee

OPPORTUNITY 16

Green Lawyers

The Market Need	Being green involves playing by the rules
The Mission	Provide excellent legal advice and legal services to support green businesses and environmental causes
Knowledge to Start	Law, environment
Capital Required	$ (as a job); $$$ (to start a firm)
Timing to Start	Weeks to months (to find or craft a position)
Special Challenges	Emerging legal framework regarding climate and the environment

Despite stereotypes to the contrary, the green movement is not all Toyota Prius® drivers, hippies, or any other one single group. The green umbrella covers many different people. It even includes great opportunities for lawyers—possibly Prius-driving lawyers.

Being green often involves legal work—particularly at the regulatory junction between government, industry, and the public—so it makes sense that green lawyers are at the heart of the action. Those growing healthy, green foods must deal with laws and regulations for organic produce, such as the California Organic Foods Act and FDA regulations. Those providing green buildings must deal with the legal framework surrounding the building industry, as well as understand the issues unique to green construction methods and verification. Businesses that are coming to terms with climate change and other environmental issues need solid legal advice.

Traditionally, green lawyers worked as watchdogs to ensure that businesses adhered to regulations, using litigation as a threat and tool working for nonprofits, such as the NRDC or Earthjustice. Innumerable groups, large and small, labor for myriad causes, as described by Paul Hawken in his book *Blessed Unrest*. One opportunity for green lawyers is to join such groups and work for their many causes.

The relationship between business and environment is changing, with many businesses eager to stop fighting environmental law and do the right thing. Bill Sloan is working the green wave from San Francisco, as part of the Cleantech Practice of the global law firm Morrison & Foerster. The firm's Cleantech Practice has represented clients in a variety of environmental areas, including biofuels, climate change, green building, clean water, and waste reduction. Before joining Morrison and Foerster and its more than 1,000 lawyers around the globe, Sloan worked in the watersheds of the Ganges River in India, at the EPA, and at a small boutique firm specializing in environmental law. He has seen the relationship between business and government undergo a seismic shift in the last ten years. "Companies now have sustainability reports. They are now recognizing that green business can be good business, changing the rules of the game," Sloan says. "More and more, when we are representing industrial or business clients, we get phone calls where the client says, 'Our funding plan is to do something good for the environment and make sure we don't slip up.'" The last thing anyone wants is to make well-intentioned investments in carbon offsets to reduce the greenhouse-gas emissions of others, only to realize, after the fact, that the offsets did not have the desired effect.

> **INDUSTRY INFO**
>
> For more about the Cleantech Practice at Morrison & Foerster, see mofo.com.

Environmental lawyers understand and deal with emerging legislation affecting climate change and how businesses can reduce their carbon footprint. "We are at the birth of a new legal regime," Sloan says, and everybody is coming to terms with what this means for them and how they can do something environmentally beneficial. Offsets are a popular mechanism that individuals and businesses are using to reduce their carbon footprints. But without standardization, companies often need help understanding offsets. The Federal Trade Commission (FTC) is working on standards relating to what companies must do to be truly green and avoid greenwashing. The Securities and Exchange Commission (SEC) is getting involved, checking if companies with large carbon footprints need to disclose risks and strategies for dealing with the problem.

Smaller law firms are going green as well. Wendel, Rosen, Black & Dean in Oakland, California, has 60 attorneys, several of whom are working in the Green Business Practice Group. Using their expertise in green building, food regulation, and other areas of business law, these attorneys help businesses stay smart, legal, and green. In addition, to show the firm's commitment to the green cause, in 2003, Wendel Rosen became certified as a green business, the first law firm to so. To be certified as a green business, the staff focused on energy efficiency, recycling, reducing paper waste in a paper-intensive business, and using post-consumer recycled paper.

LEGALLY GREEN

To see how a smaller firm became a certified green business, see more about the green efforts at Wendel at wendel.com.

The work is not limited to the United States. Carbon knows no national boundaries, and the whole world is working to deal with climate change. Projects can span continents, with businesses in the United States or Europe sponsoring projects to reduce emissions in China, for example, through Kyoto Clean Development Mechanisms. Across the board, and around the world, environmental lawyers and businesses are charting new territory together. Sloan finds himself increasingly working on climate-change projects with "implementation organizations in Europe, investors in the United States, and project locations in Asia." Work in biofuels is following a similar path. Environmental lawyers with a strong international practice will be best placed to address these opportunities.

For lawyers concerned about the environment, there is an opportunity to change the focus of their work or even start a practice focused on environmental law. For those in law school, or considering a move in that direction, a career or business working to help the environment is waiting. The opportunities in environmental law are not just for lawyers. Environmental law firms or non-profits like Earthjustice have people from a variety of backgrounds working to do the right thing.

Opportunities for green lawyers include:

- Working in a law firm helping nonprofits and business work together for better environmental outcomes

- Forming an international practice advising business and transactions related to climate change around the world
- Establishing a green law firm, focused on environmental law
- Going green at any law firm by greening office and practices

This is an exciting time in environmental law, helping all parties involved come together to find solutions. With everybody on board and often wanting the same thing, the time is ripe for action. Business is booming: Sloan says the Morrison & Foerster Cleantech Practice is "really seeing it take off." That's not bad, either.

Building Green Homes and Businesses

Most of us spend more time indoors than outdoors, but our buildings are seldom as healthy and efficient as they could be. They often have been designed and built to pass minimum performance hurdles, just getting past building codes. About 76 percent of our electricity is used in buildings (Architecture 2030), and billions of dollars are wasted. A 2007 report from the McKinsey Global Institute, a research group in

McKinsey & Co., found that the United States could save a third of residential power use with fixes such as more efficient appliances as well as heating, cooling, and lighting systems, saving $900 billion annually by 2020. Entrepreneurs at the forefront of the movement for greener building methods are finding great business opportunities.

One problem that green buildings address is climate change. About half of the electricity in the United States comes from coal-fired power plants (Energy Information Administration, U.S. Department of Energy), and coal is the main culprit behind climate change, releasing more carbon dioxide than any other fuel (Architecture 2030). The group, Architecture 2030, led by green architect Ed Mazria, is promoting a silver bullet for climate change, working to eliminate the need for coal with more efficient buildings. Mazria and his group are calling for all new buildings to reduce their fossil-fuel consumption by 50 percent in 2008, with new construction growing steadily more efficient until new buildings are carbon neutral, producing no net carbon dioxide.

In addition, green buildings are saving water, saving money, saving resources, and providing healthier, more productive places to live and work. In some cases, the initial cost of green buildings is no greater than any other building, and green buildings give back to their owners and inhabitants through energy savings and quality of life as long as the building stands. The U.S. Green Building Council (USGBC) is setting standards for green building with the Leadership in Energy and Environmental Design (LEED) rating system. The USGBC has set the goal that by 2010 there will be 100,000 LEED-certified green commercial buildings and a million homes, and that these numbers will grow ten times by 2020.

California provides an example of what can be done with energy conservation. The California state government has created incentives since the 1970s for people to save energy and use it more wisely. To do this, the state has rewarded utilities for conservation—not just for selling

INFORMATION RESOURCE

Go to architecture2030.org for more information about the impact of climate change on all of us, how our buildings are part of the problem, and how more efficient buildings are part of the solution.

more electricity. As a result, California's energy use has stayed flat while electrical consumption has doubled in the rest of the United States. This puts California's energy efficiency more in line with green countries such as Denmark. Give people the right incentive and they will fix things; nobody loves wasting electricity, and we love wasting money even less. Entrepreneurs who seek out the waste and provide solutions will continue to do well.

Beyond constructing new green buildings, there are millions of existing buildings loaded with opportunities to increase energy efficiency. Entrepreneurs are installing cool roofs that reflect heat rather than absorb it (Opportunity 17). Entrepreneurs are designing, producing, and installing energy-efficient modular homes with slick green designs (Opportunity 18). Eco-entrepreneurs are working together to design and install energy-efficient lighting (Opportunity 19) and fix leaking air ducts in heating and cooling systems (Opportunity 20). Arming homes with sensors and customers with knowledge helps consumers make smarter decisions and leads to a variety of new business opportunities (Opportunity 21). Entrepreneurs are capturing wasted heat energy in homes and businesses, and putting it to good use (Opportunity 22). The growth of the green building industry creates the need for businesses that can provide efficient verification of green buildings (Opportunity 23). For others, the opportunity is to examine a home to improve health and efficiency (Opportunity 24).

The more entrepreneurs look, the more opportunities they find to improve homes and other buildings, making them healthy, productive, and inviting spaces to live and work. All it takes is a different way of looking at our buildings and their effect on our world, and a commitment to get into action.

OPPORTUNITY 17

Cool Roofs

The Market Need	Cost to cool buildings rises when roofs absorb a lot of heat
The Mission	Design, produce, and install cool roofs to save energy
Knowledge to Start	Roofing, cool roofing products
Capital Required	$$ (starting small)
Timing to Start	Months
Special Challenges	Regulations vary from state to state

The roofs over our heads give us security as well as protection from wind, rain, and snow. With the exception of termites, hurricanes, or the passage of time the traditional roof does this part of its job reasonably well. But it generally fails in the energy-efficiency perspective. There are millions of roofs that need improvement, and cool roofers are stepping up to the challenge.

The first part of a building that sunlight encounters is the roof, and traditional roofs absorb a lot of the sun's energy, converting it into heat. On a hot summer day in the southwestern United States, roof-surface temperatures can soar to 180 degrees F. This heat flows down into the rest of the building, costing energy and money for air conditioning to pump back out again. Hot roofs even help create urban "heat islands" in which the heat absorbed by concrete, roofing, and streets makes cities between 4 and 8 degrees hotter than surrounding regions (Heat Island Group, Lawrence Berkeley National Laboratory). Before joining Morrison and Foerster and its more than 1,000 lawyers around the globe.

To prevent this temperature spike, new roofing materials keep the heat out of the building in the first place. A reflective roof can be far cooler, staying just above ambient air temperature, and studies have found that buildings with more reflective roofing materials can consume between 20 and 70 percent less energy for cooling (Environmental Protection Agency). On commercial buildings with tens of thousands of square feet of rooftop, this can mean thousands of dollars of saved energy each year. Whatever opinions people have about climate change, or whatever their political leanings, everyone likes to save money.

INDUSTRY INFO

To learn more about the Cool Roof Rating Council see coolroofs.org.

A variety of products is available for cool roofs. The Cool Roof Rating Council (CRRC) is an independent group that tests and certifies products for reflective roofing, and makes this information available to consumers and those who work in the roofing industry. In addition, some cool-roofing products help buildings get certified as part of the USGBCs LEED system. One type of cool roof uses reflective coatings—such as those from Endurance Building Systems, Houston, Texas,—that are applied like paint, reflect light and heat, and contain no or low volatile organics (VOCs), making them healthy for crews, building occupants, and the environment. Another type of cool roofing—supplied by Carlisle Syntec of Carlisle, Pennsylvania—uses membranes applied to flat or low-slope roofs for waterproofing and heatproofing.

INDUSTRY INFO

See Endurance Building Systems at endurancebuilding.com and Carlisle Syntec at carlisle-syntec.com.

Overall, about 10 percent of the commercial-roofing market is estimated to be in cool roofing materials (USPA, "Cool Roof Product Information"), and this percentage is growing. According to the ChemQuest Group consulting firm in 2007, the market for cool-roof coatings is about $440 million. Regulatory requirements in some states are helping to drive the market toward increasing use of cool roofs. In California, Title 24 (Energy Efficiency Standards for Buildings) now requires cool roofs for new construction or re-roofing of commercial buildings (the requirement does not yet apply to homes).

As the general manager of Dinyari Inc., a company specialized in cool-roof installation, Bill Shevlin has ten years of experience using reflective coatings to increase the efficiency of buildings and help customers cut down on their cooling costs, "putting money back in their pockets." According to Shevlin, cool roofs are no more expensive than the nonenvironmental choice, and "a cool roof is like stepping on grass under a tree compared to asphalt on a hot sunny day."

"In spite of the economy, we've done pretty well," Shevlin said in late 2007. "Initially when we started ten years ago, we had 10 people and now we've grown to 120." Working with nontoxic material, cool-roofing companies expose workers to fewer hazards than those who work with asphalt, making for healthy and productive workers. That's good for business, too.

Combining roofing experience and green materials allows companies to work on the whole roofing system and building envelope—not just one aspect of the problem. For example, many buildings still do not have adequate insulation, which is easily remedied and cost effective.

California has led the way in cool roofs with Title 24 and the Cool Roof Rating Council, but states such as Florida are likely to start mandating cool-roof standards. "A lot of other governments and entities are looking to California to see what it is doing," Shevlin notes. The increasing incorporation of cool-roofing standards nationwide, and in other countries, will benefit entrepreneurs focused on cool roofing.

Another opportunity is in the spread of cool roofing from commercial to residential buildings. Some companies are starting to provide lighter-colored, more-reflective asphalt shingles on residential roofs, and Carlisle Syntec's Ecostar is working on rubberized roofing shingles that are made from recycled material but have an attractive appearance and improved efficiency. With the market for residential cool roofs just getting started, this is an area that is wide open for eco-entrepreneurs.

You have to understand roofs of all types, in and out, before working to convert roofs to cool roofs. If you are already a roofer or run a roofing business, you are more than half the way there. If you are not already working in roofing, learning some background in the field is important. Roofing Contractor (roofingcontractor.com) has a wealth of information about roofs and starting your own roofing business. Training and certification in general roofing provides a strong foundation, which can be added training in the unique aspects of cool roof installation.

RELATED TREND

Other ways of cooling homes include ventilating air from the attic. To be more green, use a solar-powered fan.

Another developing field is covering roofs with living plants. The roof is waterproofed, then soil and plants are installed, blocking the sun, and cooling the roof. The California Academy of Sciences in San Francisco, and the Chicago (Illinois) City Hall have been remodeled with planted, green roofs, insulating the roof from heat as it grows. Green roofs save energy in the same way as reflective roofing, fighting the heat-island effect.

For the future, new products are being researched and developed. At the Oak Ridge National Laboratory (Oak Ridge, Tennessee), Bill Miller and Jan Kosny have developed advanced materials that can be sandwiched in reflective-roofing materials, absorbing heat during the day to keep even more heat out. With a combination of good attic insulation and new innovations, customers save money—paying for the system—and prevent the need for heating and cooling.

Opportunities for cool roofing include:

IN THE LONG RUN

Look at Google maps with the satellite view and zoom in anywhere. The number of white, reflective, cool roofs you see is not a large percentage, suggesting that the cool-roof market has only just started. The regular roofing market is mature, to say the least, but it will be a long time before we run out of opportunities for installing cool roofs. 🌱

- Specializing in cool-roofing installation on commercial buildings
- Working in the emerging residential cool-roofing field
- Distributing or selling cool-roofing supplies
- Developing or commercializing new cool-roofing materials

Part of the interest in cool roofing reflects the growing concern about climate change and the need to take action, but as Shevlin notes, "Whether you believe in climate change or not, or are in it for the environment or not, cool roofs are still the way to go." This is one green-building trend without a real down side. If you can provide roofs that are reasonably priced, pay for themselves through improved energy efficiency, increase building performance and building values, and fight climate change, a cool roofing business may open up some doors—and roofs. The logic is hard to beat. In the future, we may see cool roofs extend to cool walls, cool streets, cool sidewalks, and cool parking lots, turning urban heat islands into islands of cool.

RELATED TREND

You may also consider selling new supplies to existing roofers and training them about the advantages of new approaches. Education (and regulation) are driving this market.

OPPORTUNITY 18

Fab Green Prefab

The Market Need	Green homes, and lots of them
The Mission	Design, produce, and install modular green houses "out of the box"; some assembly required
Knowledge to Start	Architecture, building trades
Capital Required	$$ (for assembling homes)
Timing to Start	Years
Special Challenges	Trend in green prefab is just taking off

In the world of green building, it seems there are as many ideas about green homes as there are people building them. Homes can be made of straw bales, tires, rammed earth, adobe, logs, structurally insulated panels; the list goes on. All materials have enthusiastic advocates and are green in varying ways, but not all are readily suited to construct millions of homes. In the multitude of green building ideas, green prefab buildings are rapidly gaining steam and have the potential to fundamentally improve how we build.

Prefab houses may sound like a blast from the past, but these are not your 1950s-style prefab trailer homes. In the new prefab wave, houses are sleek, energy efficient, sustainably built, low in waste, and steeped in zen. Seeing one of these green modular homes in action helps you appreciate its potential.

At the 2007 West Coast green building conference, the MKLotus house designed by Michelle Kaufmann of Michelle Kaufmann Designs in Oakland, California, was displayed in the Civic Center Plaza in front of the San Francisco (California) City Hall. Manufactured by XtremeHomes of Oroville, California, the home was shipped to the site and assembled in just three days, complete with landscaping while surrounded by towering urban concrete, stone, and glass. Built completely from green, healthy materials that are good for the environment and do not emit toxic chemicals, the MKLotus home generates all the power it needs and conserves water. Built smartly, the home can make the most of natural ventilation and lighting. A seed of change, this little green house is a sign of the growing movement in modular homes.

Kaufmann started designing modular homes in 2003, responding to her own housing situation. While using traditional methods to build a home of her own design called Glidehouse, she was working on the prefab, factory-assembled version of the same design. The modular version of Glidehouse won the contest, hands down, and was completed far more rapidly and with fewer headaches. Seeing

ECO-TIP

Some prefer to call these homes modular to avoid the image sometimes associated with terms such as manufactured homes or prefab.

GREEN LEADER

Michelle Kaufmann has a variety of prefab designs available on her website—mkd-arc.com. There is also background about how prefab works, how it is more sustainable, and work her company is doing.

the client's and builder's perspective showed Kaufmann the need for a better way to build green homes and the promise of prefab.

Factory-built houses can be put together on-site in a month, while traditional homes can take a year (or longer) to build. As much as a third of the material in landfills is from home construction. Because prefab homes are manufactured to fit precisely, they produce between 50 and 75 percent less waste than traditional wood-frame construction on-site, and any excess pieces or remnants produced at the factory can be reused in other products rather than getting dumped in landfills.

Prefab green homes are also more energy efficient. Every home is built precisely to the architect's design—something that can be more easily accomplished in the controlled conditions of the factory than on-site. And the cost? The rapid and efficient assembly of prefab homes helps to reduce their final cost. Prefab homes cost between $200 and $250 per square foot, comparable with normal construction costs for homes, while high-end homes built on-site can range as high as $300 to $400 per square foot.

Enertia Building Systems in North Carolina sells its own line of prefab homes. The Enertia building method, invented by Michael Sykes, enables homes to take care of most of their heating and cooling by engineering in smart-air circulation and storing heat in the building, thereby requiring less money to be spent on energy. The homes are created with channels that carry air through the walls from the exterior and basement, drawing hot air out through the top of the building.

The opportunity for green-home designers is clear, but there are also opportunities for other entrepreneurs throughout the process. Green prefab homes need suppliers of fixtures and materials for manufacturing. Builders will need workers skilled in the on-site assembly of these unique homes, skills that are in some ways distinct from those used in the traditional construction trades. For prefab green homes to make it really big, they will need developers who adopt customizable modular homes for whole developments.

Opportunities for green prefab include:

- Designing homes
- Manufacturing homes in factories
- Transporting homes to sites
- Assembling homes on-site
- Producing fixtures and materials targeted for prefab

There is a wave of interest in green prefab homes, the number of completed homes is steadily increasing, and the trend is just getting started in the United States. In Sweden and Japan, prefab homes are common, and given their rapid construction, low waste, energy efficiency, and other benefits, they seem destined to continue growing in popularity. Are people ready for fab green prefab? If owners get a great home at a great price, most are not going to complain. These are not just green homes. These are great homes that just happen to be green. If the public is ready and builders are on board, we may see large numbers of efficient, healthy, bright green homes.

OPPORTUNITY 19

Lighting the Future

The Market Need	Inefficient lighting wastes electricity and money
The Mission	Bring more efficient lighting systems into homes and businesses, saving money and energy, and reducing carbon-dioxide emissions
Knowledge to Start	Electrical, lighting applications
Capital Required	$ (as a green electrician)
Timing to Start	Weeks to months
Special Challenges	Keeping up with rapidly evolving technology and products

Thomas Edison invented the incandescent light bulb in the late 1870s, and it has remained the mainstay of lighting in the home since the dawn of the age of electricity. Since this time, we have flown men to the moon and gone through the computer revolution, but we are still using almost the same incandescent light bulb. In its defense, it's a simple invention and it works. Put a current through a filament in a partial vacuum, and it glows white hot, giving off light. Unfortunately, incandescent light bulbs waste 90 percent percent of their energy as heat rather than light, adding to the cooling needs of buildings (Rocky Mountain Institute, Home Energy Brief #2: Lighting). We use about 25 percent of our electricity for lighting in the United States, and most of it is wasted. The need for more efficient lighting creates opportunities for businesses that can deliver it.

Fortunately, the incandescent bulb, halogens, and others are not the only light bulbs available. Compact fluorescent light bulbs are three to four times more efficient than incandescent bulbs at converting electricity into light and can last up to ten times longer—about 10,000 hours (*New York Times*, January 2, 2007). Compact fluorescents are so much more efficient that Australia is banning sales of incandescent bulbs by 2010, and other locales are following suit. Each incandescent bulb replaced could keep 450 pounds of carbon dioxide from being released into the atmosphere and save the consumer between $30 and $50 during the life of the bulb. Save money, save energy, and save the planet. It sounds like a great deal; problem solved, case closed.

Not so fast. The acceptance of compact fluorescent bulbs has been slow. Despite the advantages of compact fluorescents, only about 6 percent of U.S. homes are using them (*New York Times*, January 2, 2007). They aren't doing anyone much good on store shelves. The failure to change every bulb in the country to more efficient lighting is also an opportunity for entrepreneurs who can capture the value of this wasted energy and wasted money.

How can a business make money by making it easier for the customer to get the bulbs installed? In the United States, $40 billion is spent on lighting each year, most of it on older lighting technologies. In 2007, Wal-Mart achieved its goal of selling 100 million compact fluorescents, but such bulbs are not perfect. One sticking point is the cost. They cost more than incandescent bulbs as much as eight fold more for some designs. Costs have decreased as production has increased, but compact fluorescents are still initially more expensive than incandescent bulbs. Also, the compact fluorescent bulbs contain mercury that must be disposed of properly, they take a moment to warm up, and not everyone loves the color of the light some of the bulbs produce. Finally, some just don't like the appearance of the coiled tube in many bulbs.

To increase the use of energy-efficient lighting, businesses need to improve consumer acceptance with marketing. New green brands might help efficient lights bulbs to take off. Another option to help change the lighting in businesses and homes is to bring the bulbs to the people. Some utilities give the bulbs away at lighting-exchange events and still are only scratching the surface. If financed by a local utility, you could go door to door to increase use. The utility

> **ECO-TIP**
>
> When installing and financing solar energy systems, it might also be the ideal time to make improvements in lighting efficiency. Consumers investing in solar should be motivated to make the energy they produce go as far as possible. Packaged with solar power, the cost of changing light bulbs becomes relatively small.

IN THE LONG RUN

The next product beyond LEDs is already on the horizon: OLED, organic LEDs—with flexible surfaces that light up—are in the works to open a different set of applications. Sony is marketing an OLED video screen, and more products are likely to follow.

could pay based on the number of bulbs installed and the conservation achieved. Further supporting the market for more efficient lighting, the 2007 U.S. Energy Bill includes a phase-out of incandescent bulbs from 2012 to 2020, requiring a 70 percent increase in bulb efficiency by 2020.

LEDs (light-emitting diodes) are another rapidly emerging technology that may provide the next generation of energy-efficient lighting. LEDs are even more efficient than compact fluorescent bulbs and last up to 100,000 hours (10 times longer than compact fluorescent bulbs and 100 times longer than incandescent bulbs). LEDs also allow a range of colors, light up quickly, don't contain any mercury, and look pretty cool. They are now the cutting edge of lighting.

Although LEDs are still expensive for regular lighting applications in homes, their unique capabilities are driving their rapid uptake into specialty applications, such as Coast Guard buoys, traffic signals, flashlights, and architectural installations. Businesses are starting to market LED street-lamps—solar-powered in some cases to be extra green. LEDs can be useful in almost any application where it is difficult to change a bulb or where a burned-out bulb might create safety issues. A commercial display can contain hundreds of bulbs in hard-to-reach places, and one burned-out bulb can mar the whole display. One smart application Wal-Mart is pursuing with vendors is putting LEDs in refrigerator cases, to avoid adding heat and the need to change light bulbs inside a chilled cabinet. One LED application that's proven popular with consumers is Christmas-tree lights, which last far longer, use 10 percent of the energy of old lights, and avoid annoying burnouts.

RELATED TREND

As LEDs take off, there is the opportunity to build LED fixtures. Because LEDs last so long, they allow creative, programmed, changing colors in displays. Try doing that with Edison's bulbs.

The cost of LEDs is expected to decrease rapidly while their range of properties improves, constantly opening new applications. Greg Thorson—founder of Environmental-Lights, San Diego, California, engineer, entrepreneur, and fix-it guy—expects LED technology to continue improving rapidly, following Haitz's law that the light output of LEDs per watt will double every 18 months—the same type of rapid innovation that drove the computer revolution not so long ago. Thorson is using LEDs to fix our lighting. "LED lighting can and should change how we light everything," Thorson says, focusing on color, brightness, and the ability to dim the lights are the key issues, and always paying attention to quality. With such rapid improvements in quality and falling prices, it is expected that we will see more LEDs in the next few years. The small LED manufacturer Polybrite of Naperville, Illinois, already is producing LEDs with the goal of replacing bulbs in more standard light fixtures, and is expecting to move its product into stores in 2008.

Glenn Wade (glennwadelights@gmail.com) has decades of experience in the lighting industry—ranging from work with the Rolling Stones to architectural installations—and has seen lighting technologies come and go. Wade also has seen an exponential increase in the use of LEDs. In addition to their increased efficiency and durability, Wade notes that the unique capabilities of LEDs are leading them to replace other lighting applications, such as neon lights. By packing LEDs together and controlling them individually, they can be used to create images, replacing large video-projection systems.

Electricians are faced with the opportunity to specialize in and start a green-lighting business. Open the Yellow Pages and you'll find electricians fighting to distinguish themselves with bigger ads or cheaper prices. How many green electricians are there? Every home will have energy-efficient lighting someday, but we are a long way from that point, creating an opportunity for entrepreneurial electricians.

Opportunities in green lighting include:

- ◉ Becoming a green electrician
- ◉ Selling lighting efficiency door-to-door
- ◉ Designing LED lighting fixtures
- ◉ Exploring new applications that LEDs make possible

GREEN LEADER

Greg Thorson's online store on the internet at environmentallights.com has one of the widest offerings of energy-efficient lighting you'll find.

INFORMATION RESEARCH

People such as Michael Siminovitch at the California Lighting Technology Center, U.C. Davis, are lighting the way forward with ongoing innovation and promotion of lighting improvements, and another resource for information (cltc.ucdavis.edu).

KID'S FUNDRAISING SUGGESTION

Maybe the Girl Scouts or other youth groups can sell energy-efficient lighting instead of cookies. What more potent sales force is there than an army of bright young faces selling you a light bulb to save the world? They would be unstoppable. The same applies to schools. Have kids make money with weather-stripping and compact fluorescent bulbs and save the planet while they raise money. It would be better than wrapping paper and chocolate bars for all involved. ❦

Meanwhile, industry and government researchers continue developing new lighting advances, with an ever-increasing range of colors, brightness, and efficiency that will open new opportunities for entrepreneurs to invent and adapt around LED technology. Anywhere lighting is used is a candidate for change, and new applications will emerge with newer technologies. With $40 billion in the lighting business, there is a lot of business to go around.

OPPORTUNITY 20

Duct Repair

The Market Need	Leaking air ducts for heating and cooling waste energy
The Mission	Plug leaks, save customers energy, and make some money; everybody wins
Knowledge to Start	Heating and cooling
Capital Required	$
Timing to Start	Weeks to months
Special Challenges	Educating homeowners and selling the service

Air ducts may not be the sexiest thing around, but they do important work. Hidden away in walls, attics, and/or basements, ducts carry air forced through air conditioning and heating systems. It all sounds simple enough in theory. In practice, though, ducts can lose between 25 and 40 percent of the energy used to heat and cool air, and the average American home wastes hundreds of dollars each year on leaking air ducts. With more than 100 million homes in the United States, leaky air ducts cost hundreds of millions of dollars a year— money that can be captured by businesses addressing this problem.

Duct repair was never high on most to-do lists, but duct cleaning seems to have caught on, with customers motivated by nasty images of dirty, dusty ducts. However, there don't seem to be any corresponding hideous images of leaking ducts to get people on the phone with a repair company. I have inquired about help with leaking ducts myself, even with heating and cooling contractors, but mostly have encountered a lack of interest. Perhaps selling a new heater is quicker and easier.

It is possible for consumers to repair ducts themselves, but duct tape is not the right tool. Getting in the attic and sealing joints with mastic will often take care of things. Part of the problem though is that most of us just don't do it.

ECO-ISSUE

In addition to leaking air and losing energy, faulty air ducts can allow outside air to flow in, sucking dust from the attic into the house, causing health problems.

VARIATIONS ON A BIZ-THEME

One way to go is to specialize in air ducts. Another approach is to address them in the overall efficiency of homes, a holistic approach like that of Sustainable Spaces (See Opportunity 24).

Out of sight is out of mind, and who wants to go up in the cramped, hot, dusty attic?

Others have realized the market need for duct repair. The City of Anaheim, California, is paying for people to have their ducts inspected and giving them a rebate to pay half the cost for repairs. Once again, the best source of energy is the waste we avoid through efficiency: negawatts are the energy source of tomorrow. The energy saved in duct repairs makes them one of the most cost-effective energy-efficiency options available.

Given the low profile of air ducts, education might be essential to form a business in air-duct cleaning to provide a convenient, lasting, and cost-effective solution. Showing the cost effectiveness of this work is a great start, but you have to get homowners' attention. Because heating and cooling companies may not be interested, but are in the right place at the right time, try partnering with an existing company to sell a package—change your heater plus clean or repair your ducts.

Creating a business as a duct-sealing contractor requires some knowledge of heating and cooling systems—understanding the whole system to improve how it works. Industry associations for heating and cooling contractors, such as the PHCC (Plumbing-Heating-Cooling Contractors Association, phccweb.org) can provide helpful information about getting started in the field. There are building codes and regulations about air ducts that a contractor needs to know about and training courses that are available to help, including distance learning on the internet, such as courses for HVAC (heating, ventilating, and air-conditioning) for technicians at online-education.net.

GREEN MARKETS

If air ducts had to be inspected and sealed when homes are sold, this would increase awareness of the problem and the business opportunity.

Aeroseal (Carrier Aeroseal, a division of Carrier, Syracuse, New York) has developed a different solution for leaky ducts: sealing the ducts from the inside. A material is sprayed into the interior of the ducts and sticks to the edges of leaky spots to close up gaps. This may be the only solution for ducts that are built into walls or other inaccessible

IN THE LONG RUN

Hiding all of the ducts, plumbing, and electrical lines behind the drywall looks clean with everything hidden, but it's dangerous, inconvenient, and inefficient. The only way to get at these systems is by ripping the walls open. Some homes are now being built with plumbing and wiring in conduits, allowing for easy repairs and upgrades. One part of building sustainably is allowing for future change so buildings don't have to be ripped apart for rewiring. 🐞

spaces. Many contractors around the country are licensed to work with this product.

Another problem is air-duct design. Homeowners often complain that their heating or cooling is uneven from room to room because the ducts are poorly designed, producing uneven air flow and environmental control. In looking at a customer's ducts, go beyond the sealing work and take it to the next level: building better air handling.

Opportunities for air-duct repair include:

- Creating a business specializing in air-duct repair
- Partnering with heating and cooling companies
- Improving duct systems to produce more even flow
- Developing and commercializing improved ducts and vents that do not leak, are efficient and create even airflow in buildings

To seize the opportunity in duct repair, first make people aware of the problem. Find a way to show people digital images of their own duct problems, glowing-red, infrared images, perhaps. Advertise in the green pages, such as the Co-op America National Green Pages (coopamerica.org/pubs/greenpages). Can people do it themselves? Some will, which is great, but plenty of people won't. Leaking air ducts are some of the low-hanging fruit in the energy-efficiency world, ripe and ready. It's time they were picked by more people.

OPPORTUNITY 21

Smart Homes and Informed Consumers

The Market Need	Lack of understanding causes wasted energy
The Mission	Provide better information and tools to homeowners and structures
Knowledge to Start	Electrical skills, information technology
Capital Required	$$
Timing to Start	Weeks to months (for low-tech applications such as room sensors)
Special Challenges	Lots of potential for long term; lower tech, accessible solutions available today

When you get your power bill each month, do you know where the money is going? Even if you take the time to sort through the bill, what does it mean to you? Whether at work or at home, energy consumers generally have a difficult time connecting the bill and decisions they make about electricity use. It's like when your dog poops on your carpet. If you scold him a month later, it's too late. Immediate feedback is needed to improve our energy efficiency. Entrepreneurs may consider helping people see where their energy goes by monitoring energy use.

The average house in the United States with the average occupants consumes $480 for heating each year, $300 for its water heater, and $197 for cooling (according to the Rocky Mountain Institute, a nonprofit studying resource issues, rmi.org). But knowing the story of Mr. and Mrs. Average does not tell consumers much about specific things they need to improve in their house. How much electricity are *you* using right now? How much is it costing you? Most of us don't have a clue, and that is a big part of the problem, as well as an opportunity to provide consumers with better, more detailed, and more rapid information about where their energy and money are going.

Smart meters that utilities are rolling out around the country are a step in the right direction. The old meters, the dumb ones, just spin around tallying up how many kilowatts are used. Smart meters track how much electricity is used and when it is used. The cost of power for utilities varies greatly from hour to hour and month to month. Like any commodity, electricity costs more when it is scarce, when it is in high demand. This means electricity costs far more on a hot summer afternoon than during a gentle spring night. While the utility pays more for power in the heat of the summer day, consumers pay the same rate no matter what time of day the power was used, giving them little incentive to throttle back on the air conditioner.

Charging consumers a price that reflects the true cost of electricity provides more valuable feedback to consumers. But they still need more rapid feedback to guide their energy decisions moment by moment. Demand response systems are another piece of the energy puzzle connecting information with smart energy use (See Opportunity 9).

Once a smart meter is in place, another step forward is to provide the meter's feedback directly to the consumer. Smart meters generally are enabled to communicate consumption information to the utility, so sending this information to the consumer is possible. With real-time information sent to their computer, consumers could see their moment-by-moment power use, along with the money they just saved by turning off the lights (don't leave your PC on when you're not using it though). This information will allow homeowners to better manage their electricity use. Studies have seen a 10 to 15 percent reduction in power use with real time feedback (Parker and Hook, Florida Solar Energy Center, and Meier and Brown, LBNC, "How Much Energy Are We Using? Potential of Residential Energy Demand Feedback Devices").

ECO-TIP

Those producing solar power at home also benefit from smart meters, since solar panels produce the most electricity when it costs the most (summer afternoons) and these consumers get paid by the utility for power sold back at this higher rate.

WATCH YOUR UNITS

Information provided to users about energy use is ideally expressed in terms of money, not watts or kilowatts. To most of us, kilowatts don't mean as much as money does.

One of the hot green business trends for 2008 (Sustainable Industries, January 2008) is providing information about energy use to consumers in order to change their behavior. The Lucid Design Group of Oakland, California, provides a software solution, the Building Dashboard, which displays energy use on a consumer's computer and focuses on devices that consumers can readily control. In addition, tech-savvy eco-entrepreneurs are developing small wireless devices to provide a real-time readout of current power usage and relay the information to consumers. Talon Communications of San Diego, California, is producing refrigerator magnets able to receive short-range wireless communication (the wireless technology is called Zigbee) about electricity use. With internet-enabled devices, users can even check their home's power use on the internet from work and control appliances remotely.

Good information helps people make good decisions and opens doors to new opportunities. How much energy are appliances consuming in standby mode when they are turned off? Once people see where their energy is being used, they are more motivated to make changes. What if a monitoring system shows consumers that their home is burning a lot of power on backup systems when nobody is around all day? Then, consider Greenswitch, which provides a wireless connection of outlets to a master switch and can cut off standby drains when the home is empty. By monitoring consumption of the house as a whole, entrepreneurs can develop integrated solutions for consumers.

The green homes of the future may be smart homes that make their own energy decisions. Rather than waiting for a human to see what the smart meter has to say, light switches with occupancy sensors like those from Watt Stopper of Santa Clara, California, turn lights off in a room when nobody is around, for example. That's the first step toward a smart home. If being green is strenuous, it becomes hard for people to keep up, like a diet. The easier the solution and the more it takes care of itself, the better.

Opportunities in smart homes include:

- Installing home-occupancy sensors and automated switches
- Auditing homes for standby power drains
- Developing and marketing devices to provide real-time power use and cost information
- Marketing home-automation products

There are opportunities today for businesses that can install existing technology. Straightforward experience in electrical work can allow you to create a business installing sensors in home-lighting systems to turn lights off when nobody is around or to reduce lighting in stores when natural light is bright enough. We have the technology today to remove phantom power loads created by electronics on standby, another opportunity for businesses to improve home-energy efficiency. Connecting to vendors who supply these systems and working as a local distributor and installer is another way to get started. Home automation will continue growing more sophisticated in the future, allowing the technology to be more broadly implemented and creating a variety of new opportunities for entrepreneurs who develop and commercialize these systems. Home automation will allow heating and lighting systems to follow homeowners through the house, to make blinds open or close, and to turn off the air conditioner when windows are open. Creating homes and technology that take care of energy without human action is the best long-term opportunity for entrepreneurs, making energy conservation automatic.

INDUSTRY INFO

Watt Stopper sells a large variety of lighting controls to make homes and businesses more energy efficient. See wattstopper.com.

RELATED TREND

Home automation is a big field. To see some of the latest products and think about where technology is going, check out smarthome.com. Another place to look is homeautomationforum.com.

OPPORTUNITY 22

Recycled Heat

The Market Need	Heat is discarded in one place while energy is burned to create heat
The Mission	Put waste heat to work
Knowledge to Start	Plumbing, heating, cogeneration
Capital Required	$$ (To install products)
Timing to Start	Months to years
Special Challenges	Some applications require new construction or major remodeling

Heat is universal, but not always where we need it. We spend a lot of energy and money heating buildings and generating heat for industrial processes, while spending more money and energy getting rid of heat in other places. A coal-fired power plant uses only about 35 percent of the coal's energy to produce electricity and loses the rest as waste heat (Union of Concerned Scientists, ucsusa.org). Released into a nearby river or ocean, that waste heat can disrupt lifecycles of fish and anything else growing there. Meanwhile the building down the road burns natural gas for warmth. All in all, this is a losing proposition, wasting heat and money, harming the environment, and contributing to climate change. There is a better way to go: cogeneration.

FOR EXAMPLE

Your car uses cogeneration. When you turn on the heater, your car takes heat from the engine and uses it to heat the car interior. Otherwise, engine heat is just wasted and disposed of to the air outside.

This path to energy enlightenment is to put wasted heat to good use. One large-scale application of this can be found with power stations. In some cities power stations are designed to treat the heat they produce as another useful product, using the waste heat to produce steam, hot air, or hot water that heats buildings or is used in other ways. This process is called cogeneration. By capturing this waste energy, cogeneration dramatically increases the efficiency of power plants—as much as 200 to 300 percent in some cases (United States Clean Heat and Power Association, uschpa.org).

Whole sections of cities are involved in large-scale cogeneration called district heating. The steam pipes running under the streets of Manhattan are the world's largest example of cogeneration of power and heat while district heating supplies a significant portion of the heating needs in parts of Iceland, Denmark, Sweden, and Poland. A system such as this can greatly reduce the carbon footprint of an urban area by avoiding the need for separate heating systems, such as those powered by natural gas.

If you've ever walked barefoot on asphalt on a hot sunny day, you know how much heat roads can absorb. This heat can be captured and used. The Dutch Company Road Energy Systems is developing technology to lay pipes beneath roads and use the heat for nearby buildings. The road heat might also be able to cool buildings through condensers in trigeneration systems.

Cogeneration can take place on a smaller scale as well. Wherever there is heat, there is an opportunity for cogeneration. Small power units in apartment buildings, commercial buildings, or industrial settings can be used to produce on-site power and capture heat, often with microturbines powered by natural gas. Other technologies used for small-scale cogeneration include Stirling engines, fuel cells, and solar power. Stirling engines use external heat and a difference in temperature to generate power. They have been proposed for power generation in homes.

Heat pumps can also take heat from the environment. They work in a similar way to an air conditioner but in reverse, taking heat energy from outside the house and moving it in. They can even do this when it's colder outside

VARIATION ON A BIZ-THEME

Another variation on this theme is trigeneration. A trigeneration plant produces power, heat, and cool air, by using heat to power condensers. Trigeneration can further increase the efficiency of overall energy use.

INDUSTRY INFO

For examples of companies producing microturbines, see Capstone MicroTurbine (Chatsworth, California, microturbine.com) and Elliot Energy Systems (Stuart, Florida, elliotmicroturbines.com).

RELATED TREND

Fuel cells are one emerging cogeneration opportunity. Some types of fuel cells create a lot of heat, which either needs to be disposed of or used. Better to use it.

than inside, and better heat pumps keep moving heat inside even when the temperature outside falls below freezing. Despite improvements in heat pumps, most heating contractors are used to working with furnaces burning natural gas or heating oil, and are not familiar with or don't understand heat pumps. If you can get a good grasp of heat pumps, there is an opportunity for enterprising heating contractors to move this field forward.

Hot water in your house also takes heat down the drain along with the water. This heat can be recycled to heat up cold water. According to Renewability Energy of Ontario, Canada, writing in 2002, $40 billion of wasted heat goes down the drain each year. Renewability Energy's Power-Pipe uses the hot water going down the drain to heat water going into the hot water pipe and heater. There is also comes in a scaled-up version of the Power-Pipe for use in commercial or industrial settings for even bigger savings.

Another opportunity to save wasted heat in homes is in clothes dryers. The clothes dryer produces a lot of heat that gets piped out. However, condenser dryers dry clothes without venting the hot, moist air. They heat air, pass it over the clothes, and then send the hot, wet air over a cold condenser to remove the water vapor. The same air is then heated again, repeating the process. If the condenser uses air from the surrounding room, the air will heat up. This might not be so bad in the winter, but finding a way to divert the heat in the summer would be wise. Unfortunately, condenser dryers use about 15 percent more electricity than vented ones, although this does not reflect savings from the recycled heat. Think globally, act in your laundry room?

Opportunities in recycled heat include:

◉ Introducing industrial and commercial cogeneration with microturbines, fuel cells, or other technologies combining heat with power

- Distributing and installing systems such as Power-Pipe to save heat from hot water
- Working as a heat-pump contractor
- Developing innovative ways to save wasted heat from clothes dryers

Creative opportunities in cogeneration are everywhere, large and small. To find the right opportunity for you, put on your infrared goggles and follow the heat, then find a way to put it to use.

OPPORTUNITY 23

Green Building Certification

The Market Need	As the number of "green" buildings grows, their true effect on the environment needs to be measured
The Mission	Rate green homes and buildings
Knowledge to Start	LEED professional accreditation, or knowledge of other green rating systems
Capital Required	$
Timing to Start	Months to years
Special Challenges	There are still relatively few green buildings, although the number is growing quickly

Green homes and buildings are sprouting everywhere, with billions of square feet already in place and more going up all the time. The U.S. Green Building Council (USGBC) is hoping to see 100,000 LEED (Leadership in Energy and Environmental Design) commercial buildings by 2010, almost 100 times more than had been certified by the end of 2007. From there, the USGBC hopes for another ten-fold increase by 2020, to 1 million LEED-certified commercial buildings. A similar trend is developing in green homes. Attendance at the USGBC Greenbuild Conference has grown from 85 people at its first meeting a few years ago to more than 25,000 at the 2007 meeting in Chicago, Illinois. Green buildings save money, fight climate change, increase productivity, are healthier for their inhabitants, and provide spaces in which people enjoy living and working. Green buildings also are a fast-growing business opportunity.

What makes a building green? Green is a big word these days, and sometimes green is in the eye of the beholder. What seems green to one person can appear downright gray to someone else. To ensure buildings are as green as people say they are, independent verification and certification of homes and buildings is needed.

To provide this independent certification green-building groups have developed rating systems. The LEED green-building rating system was introduced by the USGBC in 2000. Since then, LEED has expanded to include LEED for Retail, LEED for Homes, LEED for Schools, LEED for Health Care, and other categories tailored for specific building needs. In the LEED system, points are given for energy efficiency, production of renewable energy, siting, water use, and use of sustainable materials, and a ranking of "certified, silver, gold, or platinum" assigned. There now are more than 43,000 people who have taken courses, paid a fee, and passed an exam to become LEED accredited professionals.

INFORMATION RESOURCE
To see a description of what it takes for a building to be LEED certified visit the USGBC website at usgbc.org.

LEED is the leading system for the certification of green buildings in the United States, broadly adopted as the standard by the burgeoning green-building community that filled the USGBC conference. But as a pioneer in the certification process for green buildings, LEED also has been the subject of criticism. Auden Schendler, the Executive Director of Community and Environmental Responsibility at Aspen Snowmass Ski Resort in Aspen, Colorado, has commented that LEED "has become expensive, slow, confusing, and unwieldy." LEED has been criticized for not emphasizing energy efficiency enough, while giving too many points for small factors such as having a bike rack. Another criticism is that by trying to cover all geographic regions, LEED may not be sensitive to varying priorities. Water conservation is far more important in Las Vegas, Nevada, than in

Seattle, Washington, so perhaps LEED certification should be weighted to account for this. A sophisticated system, LEED also can be expensive and complex, requiring documentation of each point. The USGBC is continuing to adapt LEED to address these criticisms, but some project managers have opted to skip LEED certification to save the money and difficulty.

GREEN LEADER
You can find Auden Schendler's comments posted on Grist, one of the leading environmental journalism and blog sites, at .grist.org (search for Schendler and LEED).

If dealing with the paperwork or the online forms to document LEED points is slow and costly, one entrepreneurial opportunity is to specialize in taking care of the process for others. By making documentation more efficient, you can reduce the cost of this step and pass some of the resultant savings to clients. With reduced costs, builders and building owners are less likely to skip the LEED certification. Developing this opportunity requires knowing LEED and its certification system, and knowing a little about information technology to improve document management. As the USGBC continues to evolve LEED and streamline it to address concerns, your system also can adapt and business can keep on growing.

Another growing opportunity is for commissioning of green buildings. Part of LEED certification is commissioning, in which a third party reviews the building to ensure everything is functioning as planned, similar to the shakedown cruise of a ship. The commissioning team checks heating and cooling systems, air quality, lighting efficiency and water use—both on paper and in the actual building. Engineers and others are needed who understand these systems and can critically evaluate their performance. Once the building is occupied, another opportunity is for the builder and/or commissioning team to train new facilities managers about the building systems to get the most from the green investments.

LEED is probably the best-known green-rating system, but it's not the only one, especially not for homes. Another comment about LEED is that it generally targets elite green buildings but does not address the broader movement to make all homes greener, if not platinum-green. A rating sys-

IN THE LONG RUN

Look for these other systems to complement, not displace, the LEED system. LEED is not perfect, but it has a lot going for it and quickly has become the dominant player. It will evolve and grow, but it is not likely to go away.

tem developed by the group Build It Green is Green Point Rated, which focuses on the needs of California. Simpler then LEED to implement, the Green Point Rated system also addresses a broader cross-section of homes. Verification through the Green Point system is provided by Green Point Raters, who can offer this service as one of several. Other local systems are taking root nationwide. These more accessible, green-rating systems for homes may prove a necessity for owners who want to market their house as green. In the future, part of the home-inspection process for selling and buying a house could be the "green" report. Even in a challenging real-estate market, green homes in places such as San Francisco, California, have done well, proving the value of building and certifying green homes.

Opportunities in green building certification include:

- Creating a business helping green builders through the LEED certification process
- Developing a business commissioning green buildings
- Training teams to maintain green commercial and industrial buildings
- Performing inspections and creating green reports for homes when they are sold

Green buildings are not a fad, but a healthy response to long-term issues we all face. The pressing need for better buildings should ensure the value of green buildings on the market, but having a trusted and working system to rate green buildings will make selling them easier. Today, these efficient and healthy structures are still relatively few and far between. Hopefully there will come a time when all buildings are green, and that means a great number of buildings will need to be inspected and certified.

Home Energy Efficiency Consulting

The Market Need	There are millions of inefficient, uncomfortable, and unhealthy homes in the United States
The Mission	Make existing homes healthier, comfortable, and more energy efficient
Knowledge to Start	Building systems, energy efficiency
Capital Required	$$
Timing to Start	Months
Special Challenges	Reluctance to invest in energy efficiency

America, along with the rest of the world, is coming to terms with climate change. Factors contributing to climate change often originate in our homes. While sexy, new, green homes get a lot of attention, millions of existing homes remain the bulk of the problem. For every green concept home in a magazine, there are a million not-so-green homes currently wasting gigawatts of energy. Worldwide, buildings use 40 percent of our energy. There are more than 110 million homes in the United States (U.S. Census Bureau), and of these, 70 million are owner-occupied single-family homes that create 21 percent of our carbon footprint. Americans waste billions of dollars every year on heat that escapes through cracks, poorly insulated attics, old inefficient light bulbs, leaky air ducts, and inefficient appliances. Entrepreneurs fixing these issues are realizing a big opportunity.

Improving energy efficiency does not really require new technology. We have solutions but don't always use them, leaving us all to pay the price. We know how to insulate homes, and there are a variety of insulation options, some greener than others. Yet half or more of the homes in the United States are underinsulated. We know how to put weather strips on doors and windows, and it costs little, but this does not mean it always happens. The same goes for air ducts, lighting, and other parts of the home.

INDUSTRY INFO

To reach the market, Sustainable Spaces staff has found it important to get out in the community with education, outreach, and local events, as well as to use broader marketing approaches, such as those available through the web.

Governments in some areas are starting to require improved efficiency of existing buildings. In many cities—including Santa Monica, San Francisco, Berkeley, and Oakland—homes are being required to have energy-efficiency retrofits when they are sold; this avoids carrying forward old inefficiencies and improves standards. As governments adopt efficiency standards, the need grows for businesses to implement efficiency.

Sustainable Spaces in San Francisco is providing home-performance solutions that look at the whole home rather than just one piece of it. According to Sustainable Spaces CEO and founder Matt Golden, the solutions start with the "low-hanging fruit"—such as insulation and duct repair—and range all the way up to major systems—such as heating, cooling, and renewable energy. Too often, people forget that buildings are systems in which all the pieces must work together, and focus on one solution while leaving other questions unanswered. Installing a new ultra-efficient furnace does not make a lot of sense if the air ducts are still leaking 30 to 40 percent of the air. Spending a lot of money to put solar panels on the roof while still using inefficient appliances and light bulbs also might not be the best approach, Golden observes. By taking a holistic approach, Sustainable Spaces provides efficiency solutions that make all-around sense.

RELATED TREND

Buildings also may contain high levels of environmental toxins that require remediation, another service that Sustainable Spaces offers. The Environmental CheckUP1 tests levels of carbon monoxide, volatile organics that can be emitted from building material, and other material that can contaminate indoor air.

A key part of the Sustainable Spaces model is building a relationship with the client. Sustainable Spaces's energy auditors thoroughly examine each home and test its performance, then produce a comprehensive report outlining all opportunities for improvement. With the report in hand, the auditors sit down with each client to see what plan of action makes sense. Improving home performance is not about one change, Golden says, but more about "providing a pathway for customers to approach the goal over time, taking it down a road over a period of years, if necessary, to build a long-term relationship." Golden and his staff work at "getting people comfortable to have maximal value for any budget," and prioritizing the work to remove one of the reasons people give for not making these changes: they think they cannot afford it. The holistic approach considers not just buildings but the people who live in them.

IN THE LONG RUN
To really work at the scale needed, the efficiency of whole neighborhoods needs to be addressed. An urban-efficiency business could be the new patriotic way to serve your country.

Opportunities in home energy efficiency include:

- Performing audits of home energy-efficiency performance
- Implementing energy-efficiency projects for buildings
- Working with home remodelers to improve home performance at the same time homes are remodeled for aesthetic reasons

With more than 110 million homes in the United States, and millions of commercial and industrial buildings, there is a lot of inefficiency waiting to be fixed. Golden confirms that while existing buildings have not yet received enough attention in the green-building movement, his company is working to change this. Sustainable Spaces grew from 9 to 24 people in 2007 and has plans for future growth. There is plenty of business across the country to fuel industry growth, and the pressure to act grows more urgent all the time.

Investing Green Money

With more businesses going green all the time, the green economy is growing quickly, now more than $200 billion in 2005 (Natural Marketing Institute). One thing doesn't change though: green businesses still need money to get started, grow, invest in research, and pay their bills. For some, their green business is providing loans, investments, or financial advice. In other cases, the power of finance is being used to fight climate change through mechanisms such as green trading markets. Either way, money makes green businesses go. Green businesses working on the financial side are growing as fast as the green economy, fueling its continued growth.

Fortunately for eco-entrepreneurs, the growing recognition of green business has increased the availability of capital. A green startup finance broker (Opportunity 25) helps budding eco-businesses find capital. Environmental microfinance enables similar efforts by small eco-entrepreneurs in the developing world, with small loans that can make a big, environmentally sustainable difference in people's lives (Opportunity 26).

Businesses and individuals working to reduce their greenhouse-gas emissions often need additional tools to become fully carbon neutral. One such tool is offsets, which fund reductions in greenhouse-gas emissions by others. Some offsets produce genuine results, reducing greenhouse-gas emissions in ways that would not otherwise occur, while others have a questionable effect. Helping businesses choose the right offsets through investigation and verification is a service whose time has come (Opportunity 27).

Another way that finance and the environment are linked is through green trading markets. Just as market mechanisms were used to reduce sulfur emissions and fight acid rain in the United States, many activists, economists, and politicians see trading of greenhouse-gas emissions through carbon markets as the key to fighting climate change. Carbon markets resulting from the Kyoto Protocol to address climate change are already functioning in Europe, and voluntary trading of greenhouse-gas emissions is taking off on the Chicago Climate Exchange. The 2007 carbon market reached between $60 to $70 billion, according to the International Emissions Trading Association, and the new round of coordinated global action on the climate is starting to take shape based on the 2007 United Nations meeting in Bali. International and the United States action to deal with climate change will further boost the carbon market (Opportunity 28). More traditional investors also are seeing the value of green stocks and mutual funds. However, such a surge in interest carries the risk of a green investment bubble, creating the need for investment advisors to help investors find solid green investments that will pay off (Opportunity 29).

Moving the business world to a greener place requires big changes, including changing how businesses measure success. If a business cuts down a forest, makes money selling the wood, but leaves the land barren and eroded, was a profit really made? By conventional accounting, the business may be seen as a success regardless of its impact on natural resources, which are also called "natural capital." Today we see that to develop a sustainable economy, we must consider the value of nature in our business dealings. Pressure from investors, business partners, activists, and governments is driving the need for environmental accountants who track, audit, and report the environmental impact of businesses (Opportunity 30).

There are parts of the green world where money is still a bad word considered synonymous with the forces that have created the environmental problems we face, but they are dwindling. Money is neither good nor evil; money is money. It's what you do with it that gives it value. Harnessing the power of money to create a brighter, more sustainable, and healthy future is a good thing indeed.

OPPORTUNITY 25

Green Startup Finance Broker

The Market Need	Many entrepreneurs need help finding money to succeed
The Mission	Match eco-entrepreneurs with financing to move their vision forward
Knowledge to Start	Finance, business, connections
Capital Required	$ (investing money of others)
Timing to Start	Months
Special Challenges	Finding companies with solid, competitive business plans

Emerging eco-entrepreneurs come loaded with vision, passion, and commitment. The opportunities are everywhere, and having a vision is important, but sometimes vision is not enough. When it comes down to reality, starting a business usually requires at least some money. Rich in commitment, some eco-entrepreneurs are low in cash, limiting their ability to develop their vision into a business. To address this gap, work as a green finance broker to secure funding for entrepreneurs.

Some entrepreneurs may realize their green-business dream with money from savings, friends, and family. Others, however, need additional capital but may prefer to focus on building their company than on raising money. Even if an entrepreneur does not mind making the rounds, he or she may not be skilled at it. The skills required to sell a vision and secure investors are often not the same skills needed to manage a business. A green finance broker complements the skills of an entrepreneur and helps him or her secure needed funding.

Green finance brokers work with green entrepreneurs to access capital from a variety of sources, including venture capitalists (VCs), banks, angels (wealthy individual investors), grants, and even philanthropic groups, such as Google.org. To succeed you need a thick address book full of connections to the right people who can provide a wide range of financing options. You need to be creative financially, have business experience, and provide feedback to entrepreneurs to sharpen their business plans and pitches. You also will help VCs, angels, and others by prescreening investment opportunities and promoting only those that make sense.

Now that business skepticism about green businesses has largely evaporated, it is easier to raise money. Billions of dollars are pouring into green businesses, which receive routine coverage in *BusinessWeek*, *The Economist*, and *The Wall Street Journal*. According to "CleanTech Venture Capital: How Public Policy Has Stimulated Private Investment," a 2007 report on cleantech by Environmental Entrepreneurs (E2, a community of business people in the NRDC nonprofit) and the Cleantech Venture Network (an organization supporting cleantech development based in San Francisco, California)

North American venture firms invested $2.9 billion in cleantech in 2006, 78 percent more than the previous year. Renowned VCs such as Vinod Khosla are betting that the green revolution is the wave of the future, and he has good company. Al Gore joined the venture firm Kleiner-Perkins in 2007, determined to change the world by promoting investment in biofuels, solar technology, wind companies, and other clean ventures. VCs are eager to invest but flooded with ideas, so having a finance broker with the right connections can move an entrepreneur's business plan to the top of the pile.

Not everyone will receive funding from VCs, but they are not the only source of money. In 2006, cleantech investment totaled $48.3 billion with money from government and corporations—that's in addition to $2 billion from VCs (Lux Research and "State of Green Business 2008" report, Joel Makower). Government grants are available at the state, federal, and local levels. Another source of money is from "angels," wealthy individuals who take on riskier, earlier-stage companies by using smaller investments than VCs.

Community banks, such as the New Resource Bank in San Francisco, California, are another option. New Resource is a pioneering bank helping entrepreneurs grow businesses in areas such as green building, organic farming, and renewable energy. The first commercial green bank in the United States, New Resource opened in 2006 and has rapidly grown, with investors and depositors attracted, in part, by its support of green entrepreneurs. "We look to add value to green businesses through our focus and knowledge of sectors such as organics, green buildings, and clean technology," says Rosita Nunes, marketing and business operations officer at New Resource. The bank provides a full panel of financial services, but its support for green businesses does not stop there. "Green is not just a small and token part of our overall portfolio," says Nunes, "it's part of our DNA." Helping clients and working in the community, the New Resources staff furthers the green-business movement. "As the awareness of living and

> **INFORMATION RESOURCE**
> To see the State of Green Business 2008 report, visit Greenbiz.com.

> **GREEN LEADER**
> For more about the pioneering work at New Resource Bank, see newresourcebank.com.

INDUSTRY INFO

The Green Business Loan Fund from the Initiative Foundation targets small loans for green companies and is looking for viable companies to invest in. This is not a charity, but the fund does try to support the development of businesses that contribute to sustainability.

working sustainably grows, so does the market share for green entrepreneurs," says Nunes.

Peer-to-peer lending provides another emerging funding option. In peer-to-peer systems, individual lenders and borrowers connect directly. Sometimes these lending systems stem from social networking sites, which connect people with related interests, thereby giving entrepreneurs access to networks that are broader than the more traditional lending systems. At Prosper.com, borrowers make their credit reports available and describe what the loan is for, and lenders bid a loan at varying interest rates based on how much risk the lender thinks the borrower presents. The lowest rates offered win the loan.

Small eco-entrepreneurs who are rich on ideas but low on cash will increasingly look for partnerships with large corporations that have the opposite problem. The finance broker can connect companies that want to invest time, energy, and money to collaborate on the development of the business.

Opportunities for green startup financing include:

- Creating a business as a green startup finance broker, helping entrepreneurs secure capital
- Consulting with green businesses to help them with business plans, grant applications, and presentations needed to secure funding
- Opening a peer-to-peer lending system targeting green entrepreneurs

Helping businesses by securing financing and brokering deals will assist many startups over the first few hurdles and keep them from running out of money early on. For the finance broker, having an equity stake in the company might provide an incentive to stay involved and keep the company moving forward. Helping eco-entrepreneurs get the financing they need could be a rewarding way for those with a financial background to join the green revolution.

OPPORTUNITY 26

Environmental Microfinance

The Market Need	Microenterprises in the developing world can have a significant environmental impact
The Mission	Support development of environmentally sound microenterprises
Knowledge to Start	Finance, sustainability
Capital Required	$$
Timing to Start	Months to years
Special Challenges	Influencing the direction of large numbers of microenterprises

Surprisingly small amounts of money can make a substantial difference in people's lives. With loans as small as $100, people in the developing world can start their own business and move out of poverty. Far from a fringe endeavor, such lending is getting a lot of attention. By supporting environmentally sound microbusinesses, green microfinance is mobilizing a grassroots green revolution in the developing world while also spurring green business in the developed world.

Microfinance lends small amounts of money to men and women for their modest business dreams. For example, a farmer can get money to invest in harvesting tools to increase his productivity. A well digger can borrow money to buy better tools for digging, helping him work faster and helping those around him get clean water. A seamstress can buy a sewing machine to work more quickly than sewing by hand. A produce seller or farmer can buy a refrigerator to keep food products fresh. Whatever their business focus, these small businesses can affect the environment.

Conventional wisdom has been that lending such small amounts of money makes bad business sense, posing a high risk of not being repaid. As it turns out, conventional wisdom is wrong. Microfinance works, and the rate of repayment on microfinance loans is high. Grameen Bank in Bangladesh, and its founder Professor Muhammad Yunus, received the Nobel Prize in 2006 for work with microfinance, validating that it can change the lives of the entrepreneurial poor. While some have pointed to the high interest rates on some microfinance loans as a potential downside for borrowers, the majority of the news from microfinance remains positive.

In addition to affecting lives, microfinance affects the environment. Cookstoves save lives and help the environment, but if they are to be successful in the developing world, they are best produced locally and cheaply by microenterprises. Small loans provided by microfinance can get such businesses started. Environmental microfinance can allow microenterprising people to buy a solar water pump and sell water to their neighbors, or to buy a solar panel to set up a micropower system in a village. The impact of projects like these ripples through the community, spreading hope.

Some examples in which microfinance can help the environment include:

- Building sustainable agriculture, allowing small farmers to avoid expensive chemicals and grow higher-value crops
- Establishing small, local businesses that support ecotourism
- Funding low-tech local entrepreneurs digging wells, storing water, and purifying it in clean water systems
- Using forests for products other than timber, to support local economies and preserve the forest as an economic support system
- Bringing small solar- and wind-power systems to rural regions, establishing renewable energy

One microenterprise on its own is not likely to affect the environment much, but with millions of microenterprises, the impact adds up. If a microenterprise that builds cookstoves also releases toxic metals into the air or soil, the long-term environmental and health cost will negate any short-term economic benefit. Similarly, if increased farming provides an initial advantage but depletes the soil, the long-term benefit will be lost. A wide range of microenterprises need to be steered in a green direction, or else they risk short-term economic gains at the cost of long-term depletion of area resources.

Green Microfinance, of Phoenixville, Pennsylvania (greenmicrofi nance.org), has been working to encourage the development of environmentally sustainable microfinance since 2002. The vision of Green Microfinance "is that all microenterprises globally make a contribution to improving the natural environment." The president of Green Microfinance, Elizabeth Israel, cites the company's research that there is a strong demand for sustainable microfinance in the developing world. "The increased interest in financing green products and services for the poor in this short span of time is phenomenal," she reports. ESAF, for example, is a microfinance organization that caters to 250,000 clients in India with a range of services, including those related to conservation, promoting enterprises that generate income, and protecting nature. According to Israel, Green Microfinance is promoting environmentally sound microfinance by working with clients such as Fonkoze in Haiti and ESAF in India, and is establishing a nonprofit organization through which people in the developed world can support green microentrepreneurs.

The staff of Green Microfinance steers microenterprises toward sustainable development using the power of technology and money. "Our team of microfinance experts and energy engineers support clean energy—including solar, micro-hydro, micro-wind, and biofuel systems—using biomass that is not produced on productive forests, grassland, or cropland," Israel says. "By providing loans for environmentally sustainable products to their low-income clients, microfinance institutions will not only be contributing to greener communities, increasing their revenues, but most importantly, will also be growing and nurturing millions of green microbusinesses."

The opportunities are not all in the developing world. People in developed countries can work as consultants for green microfinance and as conduits for information, providing financial support, creating partnerships, and creating business models. Through research and work with academic researchers, green microfinanciers can determine which approaches work best, thereby avoiding pitfalls. Green microfinance businesses in the developed world can also support the production of goods and services that are imported for sale in the developed world. An organic tea company in the United States, for example, can support the development of a tea farmer cooperative in the developing world, helping farmers as well as his business. If the greening of microenterprises can have a significant environmental impact at a modest cost, then it's a sound investment all around.

Opportunities for green microfinance include:

- ⊛ Forming nonprofit organizations in the developed world that support microfinance efforts
- ⊛ Consulting and raising money to support the growth of green microfinance institutions in the developing world
- ⊛ Forming microfinance organizations that support environmentally-sound business practices in the developing world

Although many environmental challenges are global, the solutions need to allow for the unique conditions in each country, working with people rather than against them. Green microfinance has the potential to spread business seeds throughout the developing world that can bloom into green microenterprises. Helping people to help their economies grow in simple and sustainable ways ensures that we all grow closer to a green world.

OPPORTUNITY 27

Offset Investigator

The Market Need	Offsets help reduce our carbon footprint but vary in quality
The Mission	Validate high-quality offsets that people can trust
Knowledge to Start	Tracking, auditing, and certifying greenhouse gases
Capital Required	$ to $$
Timing to Start	Weeks to months
Special Challenges	Travel and footwork

Climate change is caused by the carbon dioxide and other greenhouse gases that we send into the atmosphere by driving a car, taking a plane, turning on the furnace, or using electricity produced with fossil fuels. We can reduce our carbon footprint by changing how we live, but for all the less-than-perfect environmentalists out there, offsets can help reduce our carbon footprint even further. Businesses creating and verifying well-validated offsets are growing while slowing climate change.

No matter how you or your business produces greenhouse gases, you can buy an offset, which means you give money to projects that are reducing greenhouse-gas emissions somewhere else. This reduces your net impact on climate change. For example, the next time you fly on business, just jump on the computer, find a carbon calculator on the internet, and see how many offsets you need to buy to zero out your contribution to climate change. You can still go on the trip but don't have to worry as much about whether you are worsening climate change. The same goes for businesses. Most businesses use energy—there's no way around it. If a business wants to green its ways, it can work to reduce its greenhouse-gas emissions and then use offsets to completely eliminate its

INFORMATION RESOURCE
Offsets are not mandatory, and are different from carbon credits or renewable-energy credits. For more about offsets, see the websites of one of the many offset providers, such as NativeEnergy, nativeenergy.com.

carbon footprint. For example, if you run an organic bakery, you might use the most fuel-efficient trucks available, but at the end of the day, the trucks will be responsible for some carbon dioxide. Buying offsets would allow the bakery to become fully carbon neutral.

Offsets have taken off since their inception only a few years ago. According to a 2007 report from New Carbon Finance, $91 million of voluntary offsets were sold globally in 2006. Early offsets often involved paying groups to plant trees. The more trees you paid to have planted, the more carbon dioxide the trees take in from the atmosphere as they grow. Since then, offsets have diversified into a broad range of creative and cost-effective ways to reduce the emission of greenhouse gases. Many offset projects reduce methane from livestock production. Methane is an even more potent greenhouse gas than carbon dioxide, and cows and pigs are big methane producers. Capturing the methane in anaerobic digesters keeps it from getting into the atmosphere and even can provide energy (See Opportunity 72). Offsets also are available through projects that invest in renewable energy, such as wind to reduce consumption of coal, or that keep forests intact when they otherwise would have been cleared.

CALCULATING CARBON

LiveNeutral (liveneutral.org) can measure your carbon emissions and calculate how much it would cost to offset emissions from your car or plane trip through companies on the Chicago Climate Exchange.

Offsets may sound innocent enough, but they have generated an amazing amount of controversy. To some, they are the modern equivalent of indulgences sold by the medieval church, buying your way out of sin rather than changing your evil carbon-emitting ways. Others say offsets are a sham or a waste.

Living a carbon-neutral life is a good goal, but it's not always easy. We live in a complicated world. Most of us have jobs and live lives where producing some carbon dioxide is inevitable. We wouldn't get very far if we couldn't ever drive a car, get on a plane, take a train or bus, or use almost any other mode of modern transportation. Let's face it—most of us are not ready to unplug from the grid. More consumers and businesses are choosing fuel-efficient cars, but most cars today still burn petroleum-based fuels. People can choose to avoid wasteful travel, but we can't eliminate necessary travel. For those working to reduce their carbon footprint, offsets are a valuable tool to achieve carbon neutrality.

The biggest problem with offsets is that they are largely unregulated, despite numerous schemes proposed and implemented in different areas. Not all offsets are created equal, and some have questionable value. If you are paying people to do something they were going to do anyway, then you have not really reduced your carbon footprint. Businesses buying offsets need to take care to fund only projects that provide additional carbon savings. In the offset world, this is often called "additionality," a key feature to look for. If a project pays for trees to be planted, but the trees are not cared for or are burned, then there is no overall benefit to the climate. Offset buyers also should look for transparency with all information about offset projects freely available, and verification of projects by independent third parties.

The problems with offsets also create opportunities. Those who produce high quality offsets, and can verify that they are making a real contribution to fighting climate change, will continue to find a market. Google is doing a great deal of work to support renewables, with some of the largest private investments in solar power (see Opportunity 12). Those such as Green Energy Czar Bill Weihl are working to improve their energy efficiency, but Google still produces carbon dioxide from the power they use. To eliminate the company's carbon footprint and become carbon neutral, Google invests in offsets, but not just any offsets. Company leaders find offsets that have a real impact, investigating and verifying the benefits of each project.

How can individuals and other business leaders know which carbon offsets to invest in? Here is an opportunity for eco-entrepreneurs to work verifying offsets for others. Not

MARKETING STRATEGY

One way to sell offsets may be through eBay. Pop!Tech (poptech.org), a social network and conference organizer, opened an eBay store in 2007 selling offsets related to its conferences. The Pop!Tech carbon initiative is supporting offset projects that provide both a social and an environmental benefit.

INFORMATION RESOURCE

Check out ecobusinesslinks.com for a survey of offsets and their prices. Prices vary widely.

GREEN MARKETS

Offsets sold on the Chicago Climate Exchange must be verified by third parties through annual desk and field work. Qualifying to verify these offsets is one way to get into the business. Third parties during the work of auditing projects are approved by the Exchange for different types of offset projects. ❦

every business has the time or money to investigate each offset project in detail. Provide an offset-verification service to sort through such projects. While others work to establish standards, help is needed for the field work. To do this you need to be knowledgeable about the developing standards for offsets, ask questions, get good answers, and keep good records to document the climate benefit from offset projects. You also should be willing and able to travel and get a little dirty. The details of offset verification will vary depending on which standard is being applied.

To create a business providing carbon offset verification as a service, it is important to know the standards being developed for each type of offset scheme (methane capture, tree planting, forest preservation), and the developing protocols for their verification. For consumers and businesses to trust offsets, verification and certification must have teeth, and for it to have teeth, verification needs to have clear rules and full access to information. Perhaps customers will trust offsets more if they can see more directly how their offsets make a difference, perhaps by linking them to images or data about a specific part of a project that can be viewed on the internet. Since verification should be performed by an independent third party, your offset verification business cannot have direct business ties to the projects that are being verified.

Another business opportunity is to create high-quality, cost-effective offsets. High-quality offsets are not necessarily the cheapest, but they will produce cost-effective reductions in greenhouse-gas emissions that would

SETTING A STANDARD

Six major nonprofit groups have joined forces to form the Offset Quality Initiative, working to ensure offset quality:

1. The Climate Trust
2. California Climate Action Registry
3. Environmental Resources Trust
4. Greenhouse Gas Experts Network
5. Pew Center on Global Climate Change
6. The Climate Group

not have been achieved otherwise. NativeEnergy is one high-quality offset provider—a privately held American Indian energy company. The Climate Trust of Portland, Oregon, is another offset provider with a diverse portfolio of projects, including internet-based carpool matching, rainforest restoration, and reducing carbon emissions from making concrete. Some of the key factors that make these offset providers stand out are their verification and clear additionality (see Related Trend). With verified high-quality offsets, buyers trust that they are making a difference.

A variety of standards have been proposed, and many groups are pushing for government regulation of offsets, but such changes have not yet happened in the United States. As of 2007, not all offsets are certified, and those that are go through a variety of certification mechanisms. One form of certification is the Kyoto Clean Development Mechanism. Another is to have each project certified independently by experts, rather than one centralized authority. For example, offsets used to create tradable green securities

RELATED TREND

Renewable-energy credits present a similar opportunity. It is convenient for businesses that want to reduce their carbon footprint to buy renewable-energy credits, meant to encourage further investment in renewable energy. As with offsets, additionality is a big issue and some dispute whether these credits really cause more renewable energy to be built.

are certified by the Chicago Climate Exchange; Environmental Resources Trust certifies renewable-energy offsets.

Opportunities for carbon offsets include:

- ◉ Creating, and selling high-quality verified offsets
- ◉ Working in offset verification and certification
- ◉ Packaging offsets with products to reduce their carbon footprint
- ◉ Linking offsets to images and data about specific projects on the internet

At the end of the day, the choice is up to each of us. We should all work to reduce our greenhouse-gas emissions by whatever means available. If offsets are certified and genuine, creating and selling high-quality offsets, and helping others to find the best offsets are good ideas. When taking on a project as big as climate change, you need all the tools you can get.

OPPORTUNITY 28

Carbon Trader

The Market Need	Slowing climate change requires putting a cost on carbon-dioxide emissions and a value on reducing them
The Mission	Reduce greenhouse-gas emissions through green trading
Knowledge to Start	Trading, finance
Capital Required	$$
Timing to Start	Months to years
Special Challenges	Carbon market is just starting

People around the world are building businesses that mitigate climate change in many ways. Some help build wind farms, others develop and market electric cars or plug-in hybrids. For some, the business is at their computers, trading greenhouse-gas emissions in green trading markets.

Throughout human history, until current concerns of climate change arose, the emission of carbon dioxide or other greenhouse gases has been free. The only cost for burning coal was for the coal itself. Harnessing market-based approaches to reduce greenhouse-gas emissions is broadly accepted as a solution. As part of the Kyoto Protocol, emission credits for greenhouse gases can be traded to promote further reductions over time. If a cement plant or a utility reduces its emissions, it can sell corresponding carbon credits in the market. The Emissions Trading Scheme (ETS) is now operating in the European Union to trade emissions credits created by Kyoto. The International Emissions Trading Association estimated carbon-emissions trading between $60 and $70 billion in 2007, up from $30 billion only one year earlier, with even larger growth expected in the future.

> **INDUSTRY INFO**
> The International Emissions Trading Association is developing green trading markets around the world. To learn more, go to ieta.org.

In addition to the ETS, another rapidly growing contributor to green trading markets is credits earned under Kyoto's Clean Development Mechanism (CDM). In a CDM, a company in a developed country can pay for projects reducing greenhouse-gas emissions in other parts of the world to earn carbon credits. In the United States, the Chicago Climate Exchange was launched in 2003 for the trading of carbon credits from voluntary reductions, with more than 200 companies signed on to reduce their carbon footprint. Members of the exchange include major emitters of greenhouse-gas emissions, such as utilities and Fortune 100 companies.

Although joining the Chicago Climate Exchange is voluntary, one benefit to joining is that members will be better prepared for future changes, with already-low emissions and skills in operating as part of a green trading system. The Regional Greenhouse Gas Initiative (which includes several states in the northeastern United States) is creating an emissions trading system, and other states, such as California, are likely to join. Action by the U.S. government is only a matter of time. By getting into the carbon market ahead of the game, companies reduce their risk of future costly reductions

INDUSTRY INFO

See *Carbon Finance* for news
about emissions markets at
carbon-financeonline.com.

in greenhouse-gas emissions, become leaders in a developing field, and demonstrate their commitment to environmental progress.

The carbon markets are growing rapidly but also encountering challenges. *The Economist* has reported that European companies are not yet using carbon markets to their advantage (August 2, 2007). Companies often hold credits too long rather than selling them, thereby losing out on potential revenue, in part because the decision to sell is left to the company's environmental rather than financial experts. This lost value signals an opportunity for more savvy emissions traders to help companies get more value out of the credits. The better the markets work, the greater will be their impact on climate change and the more the business world will get out of the emissions markets.

The more open and liquid the markets are, the more trading occurs, and the more comfortable traders are with the markets, the better the markets will function. CantorCO2e is a financial-service provider based in San Francisco, California, and London, England, that is building a global presence in this market. To move markets forward, the Intercontinental Exchange (ICE) and the Chicago Climate Exchange have pioneered electronic internet trading of emissions credits. Futures and options contracts of emissions provide a variety of products in addition to emissions credits.

Those with a background in finance may want to get in on the emissions-trading field now. Brokers in emissions trading—such as Evolution Markets

IN THE LONG RUN

Personal carbon-trading schemes have been proposed, with individuals being given a certain amount of carbon dioxide they can produce, and then being required to buy or trade credits to stay within this limit. When you buy gas, or other applicable items on your credit card, the carbon credits could be subtracted automatically from your carbon account. 🌱

and Natsource, both of New York, New York—are emerging. In addition to handling transactions in emissions commodities, brokers can help clients capture opportunities in carbon markets and emissions reductions. Brokers also can integrate their services with other financial offerings. As the rapidly evolving emissions-trading field tests new ideas for emissions markets, it also generates ways for traders to drive environmental and business progress. If mandatory reductions in greenhouse-gas emissions take effect in the United States in a cap-and-trade system—as they are likely to—the market and value for carbon credits will grow. The opportunity will also grow for businesses that help others reduce their emissions, verify reductions, and trade carbon credits to cash in on their value.

INDUSTRY INFO

To learn more about brokers in a green trading market see Evolution Markets at evomarkets.com.

Becoming a carbon trader is a hot field for entrepreneurs looking for a way to make money and help the planet. Working at carbon-trading firms, traders can start out making $60,000 to $100,000 (NPR, *Morning Edition*, April 7, 2008) and come from a variety of backgrounds, including business, finance, and the power sector. Carbon traders can work at one of the emissions-trading brokerages that already exist or set out on their own creating innovative new businesses. Since carbon trading through mechanisms like the Clean Development Mechanisms established by Kyoto is increasingly an international business, one opportunity is traveling around the globe to arrange deals, matching buyers and sellers, and brokering transactions between them. Another business is to work as an analyst of the carbon market and other green trading markets, helping businesses understand and predict the future of the market and what it might mean for them.

Opportunities in carbon trading include:

- Consulting for businesses about green trading markets, helping them get the most value from carbon credits
- Developing an audit service for businesses to verify reductions in greenhouse-gas emissions

- Working as a green trading broker, trading carbon credits and other green trading instruments such as renewable energy certificates, energy-efficiency certificates
- Creating a financial services business brokering transactions through the Kyoto Clean Development Mechanism
- Analyzing and reporting the factors affecting the carbon market

Carbon markets already are starting to make a difference, reducing carbon emissions by about 88 megatons of carbon dioxide in 2007 (New Carbon Finance, and "State of Green Business 2008," Joel Makower and the editors of Greenbiz.com). This is a relatively tiny amount of carbon dioxide globally (a few hours of worldwide activity), but still it's a start. The action taken by the U.S. government and the world in the next round of climate talks is expected to drive the growth of carbon markets, making significant inroads in slowing climate change.

OPPORTUNITY 29

Green Investment Advisor

The Market Need	Investors are increasingly aware of, and make decisions based on, the triple bottom line of people, profit, and the planet
The Mission	Assist investors to make solid green investments
Knowledge to Start	Finance, investing, sustainability
Capital Required	$ to $$
Timing to Start	Weeks to months
Special Challenges	Identifying long-term value among the many green investment options

Even as the markets wobble and teeter on the latest economic news, investors and analysts seem to agree that green is good. The greener people get, the more they want their investments to mirror the rest of their lives.

THE BIG PICTURE

Green investing is a part of what is often called "socially responsible investing," in which investors look at the impact of businesses on the broader world. Socially responsible investing was estimated by the Social Investment Forum (socialinvest.org) to be worth more than $2 trillion in investments at the end of 2002. ❧

Being green is not just good for the planet, it's good for business. Evidence of this is seen as serious investors move toward green investments. Analysts and advisors at major investment firms are suggesting investment strategies to deal with the changing climate, energy, and other environmental issues. The more excitement there is for the rapid rise of green business, the greater the need for green investment advisors to help investors looking for the next big thing.

Some green investors are moved by the rising price of oil, which passed $120 per barrel in May 2008 with the probability of moving even higher. The price of oil affects the economy in many ways, not all of them good, but companies producing renewable energy and fuel-efficient cars are likely to do well as long as the price of oil is high. Climate change is another important factor driving green investment decisions. Climate change is not a fad and will not go away overnight. Government action at the state, national, and international level will drive long-term value in companies helping to mitigate climate change.

Investors are taking action in many ways. *Forbes* magazine reported in December 2007 that Richard Keiser, technology strategist of Sanford Bernstein, an investment firm of New York (bernstein.com), has identified cleantech, greenhouse-gas-reducing companies, as the place to invest during the next five years. In the same month *BusinessWeek*

INDUSTRY INFO
Many investment firms offer green mutual funds. One is Green Century (greencentury.com), founded and run by nonprofits, and offering no-load environmental mutual funds as a way to direct investments toward green companies.

GREEN LEADER

You can find more about Generation Investment Management at generationim.com.

featured the article "How to Cash In on a Warming Planet," describing climate-change-related investment strategies at Citi, HSBC, and Deutsche Bank. Al Gore and David Blood, a former Goldman Sachs CEO, launched the investment firm Generation Investment Management in 2004 to integrate analysis of sustainability with profitability and growth. Investors can choose from a proliferating number of green mutual funds and exchange traded funds containing green stocks. Investment in individual green companies is another way to go, either in companies focused on the environment, or businesses in other fields that are improving their environmental profile.

Investors get excited about high performance, and companies that pay attention to green and social issues have outperformed their peers on the stock market. The green "Waveriders" described in the 2006 book *Green to Gold* by Dan Esty and Andrew Winston outperformed the S&P 500 by a wide margin from 1996 to 2006. Maybe this is not just because green companies are doing the right thing, but because they are smart and efficient businesses. As Esty and Winston note, "A number of studies have demonstrated that environmental performance is a powerful indicator of overall management quality." The authors of the book *Clean Tech Revolution* (Ron Pernick and Clint Wilder, 2007) predict that four cleantech sectors they described (biofuel, wind, solar, and fuel cells) will grow from $55 billion in 2006 to $226 billion by 2016.

The areas in which to invest are not always obvious, and simply having a green label does not guarantee a company's success. With many investors jumping into green investments, the price-to-earnings ratios of some renewable-energy and biofuels companies have soared. Some investment analysts are concerned that the green investment field already is overplayed, that there is too much money chasing too few assets, and that a green bubble will develop. There may be some truth to this. Many renewable-energy companies

ECO-ISSUE

Activists are using investment as a tool to influence corporate action by encouraging shareholders to divest from non-green investments and using shareholder advocacy to steer decision makers. With $2 trillion in pay, activist investor influence can be significant and is encouraging companies to go green.

started 2008 with a downward slide (along with the rest of the market). With significant long-term growth expected in green industries, there still will be values to be found among the many companies involved. As solar power grows, it's not just panel producers who do well, but so will those producing inverters that convert DC (direct current) power from panels into AC (alternating current) that homes can use. A dip in the price of ethanol production might create a great buying opportunity if ethanol has the future many think it does. The ability to sort through all this to find long-term values makes the services of a green-investment advisor valuable for investors.

Financial advisors are paid either by commissions or fees. Advisors are increasingly receiving fees directly from clients for their services, helping to avoid any potential conflict of interest, as recommended by NAPFA (National Association of Personal Financial Planners, napfa.org). In the United States, investment advisors must generally pass two sets of exams to become licensed: the Series 66 Uniform Combined State Law Exam and the Series 7 Stockbroker's Exam. If you are just starting down the path to becoming an investment advisor, be prepared to spend long hours working and training at a financial planning firm. If you are already past these hurdles and working as an investment advisor and financial planner, forming your own green-investment advising company is less daunting—independent investment advisors are self-employed, run their own business, and can take advantage of tools and services offered to help in their business.

Opportunities in green-investment advising include:

- Becoming an independent green investment advisor
- Creating a green-investment newsletter
- Focusing on socially responsible investing

Being green is good business for many companies, but it's not magic. Investors need help finding the best values among all the green options. What are the fundamentals of these companies? Which young cleantech companies are

> **VARIATION ON A BIZ-THEME**
> One opportunity is to create the *Green Investment Fool* (like the *Motley Fool*), offering a newsletter with advice and critical insight into which green companies are good investments. The newsletter at Green Chip Stocks provides an example of this (greenchipstocks.com).

headed toward commercialization, and which are built on hype? Not every green company can come out on top, but if biofuel production, solar production, and other green companies really are poised to take off, they are going to transform our economy. Al Gore and David Blood wrote in *The Wall Street Journal* in 2006 that "sustainable development will be the primary driver of industrial and economic change over the next 50 years." If that is the case, then the upward climb of green investments in the stock market has only just begun.

OPPORTUNITY 30

Environmental Accountant

The Market Need	To measure how businesses affect the environment and track their bottom line
The Mission	Measure the impact of businesses on valuable natural assets
Knowledge to Start	Accounting, sustainability
Capital Required	$ to $$
Timing to Start	Months to years
Special Challenges	Field still developing

Business and nature are more interrelated than most of us think. As governments, activists, and investors look for environmental solutions, companies are feeling pressure to track and report their impact on natural systems. Environmental accountants helping businesses measure greenhouse-gas emissions and other environmental impacts are addressing a relatively new but rapidly growing market.

Accountants traditionally keep track of business performance by tallying up how much companies spend, save, invest, produce, and earn. But looking at money alone does not provide the whole picture. Stepping back, we see that gross domestic product (GDP), profit, and productivity have come with a hidden price: the cost to nature that economic progress often has taken. Natural systems everywhere perform essential services for humanity. We have taken these systems for granted and now are threatened by these changes. When economists tally up the value of services provided by nature, they find them to be worth trillions of dollars—probably more than all human economic activity (*Nature*, May 1997, "The Value of the World's Ecosystem Services and Natural Capital," Costanza et al).

Changing course to produce a sustainable economy requires the "second industrial revolution" as Paul Hawken, Amory Lovins, and L. Hunter Lovins described in *Natural Capitalism*. Businesses are part of the solution, but they are not going to reach environmental goals with traditional accounting methods that look just at money. To produce a sustainable economy, businesses need a new accounting method that measures the value of nature and natural capital in business transactions and performance.

Businesses can implement this accounting only if they have accountants who are trained in tracking natural capital. The System of Integrated Environmental and Economic Accounting (SEEA) is used by many countries to track how natural resources are used, how wastes are disposed of, and the net impact on the environment, in addition to more traditional measures of economic performance. Similar accounting systems are being adapted to track the impact of natural capital in individual corporations.

For a corporation, there are several motives to hire environmental accounting firms. One is that it's the right thing to do. Another is that tracking environmental impact is often good for business: find waste, reduce it, and save money. The environmental accountant can calculate the cost of disposing of waste and balance this against the cost

RELATED TREND

Many conservationists argue that conservation should focus more on the value of ecosystem services a habitat provides, and not just biodiversity. This is another area where environmental accountants can contribute.

INFORMATION RESOURCE

Natural Capitalism by Paul Hawken, Amory Lovins, and L. Hunter Lovins describes the importance of valuing natural systems in our business decisions, and how people are using information about natural capital to build more environmentally sustainable businesses in many areas.

REPORTING GREEN PROGRESS

More businesses are producing annual sustainability reports, including the environ-mental impact of their activities. These reports are often given in response to pressure from investors, business partners, and activists. Some reports adhere to a standard called the Global Reporting Initiative (GRI), working to make sustainability reporting as standardized and credible as traditional financial reporting. ❦

of preventing the waste. This includes carbon as a pollutant. Environmental accountants also can help with an alternative annual report, or a sustain-ability report, demonstrating the green measures taken to reduce a com-pany's carbon footprint. As the world puts a cost on greenhouse-gas emissions, companies will need environmental accountants to understand what this cost means for them.

Professor Robert Gray is the director of the Centre for Social and Envi-ronmental Accounting Research at the University of St. Andrews School of Management in the United Kingdom, and the author of *Accounting for the Envi-ronment: Green Accounting.* Gray writes that another opportunity lies in envi-ronmental reporting: "communicating an accurate, although much simplified

IN THE LONG RUN

The growing importance of carbon emissions to the business world will drive the opportunity for environmental accounting. Climate-change legislation in the United States is increasingly likely, and the round of global climate-change negotiations started in Bali also will affect the cost and importance of greenhouse-gas emissions for businesses. Tracking and reporting greenhouse-gas emissions is moving from voluntary to mandatory. ❦

overview of the organization's environmental interactions to stakeholders of the organization." While avoiding greenwashing, he writes, voluntary reporting on environmental impact is likely to be "substantial and honest, but partial and selective." Environmental accounting is required in some countries, including Denmark, Sweden, France, Australia, and South Korea. Others will follow. Where not yet

INFORMATION RESOURCE
The data from the Carbon Disclosure Project is available free online at cdproject.net.

required, some companies are performing voluntary environmental reporting to convey their commitment to environmental causes.

The value of tracking greenhouse-gas emissions is demonstrated by the growth of the Carbon Disclosure Project. The Carbon Disclosure Project represents institutional investors managing more than $41 trillion in assets, and sends companies an annual questionnaire requesting information about greenhouse-gas emissions as well as climate-change risks and opportunities. The number of companies that respond has steadily grown, with about 38 percent taking part in 2007. More companies are also creating sustainability reports, sensing the importance of transparency on these issues.

To track and audit an environmental impact, businesses are hiring accounting firms and others to inspect their business, identify green issues, and find opportunities to improve. Large established accounting firms, such as PriceWaterhouseCoopers, offer a green audit service to help clients understand the impact of environmental issues on their business. Smaller firms are also getting involved. The more serious companies get about greening operations, the more sophisticated the audits, tracking, and reports will become, creating more opportunities for environmental accountants.

A corporation increasingly is judged not just for its impact on the environment, but on people and societies as well. The value of people, their knowledge, experience, and productivity, is often called "human capital," and being green increasingly involves human capital as well as natural capital. If a corporation reduces its carbon footprint but harms people to do so, the net impact still may be negative. In parallel with financial and natural capital, businesses are increasingly concerned with their impact on human capital in the company, the country, and the world. Tracking business impact on social systems is difficult to judge at times, but look for increasing pressure on businesses to provide transparency on this issue.

Opportunities for environmental accounting include:

- Establishing a green auditing service, quantifying and verifying the impact of businesses on natural and human capital and finding strategies for improvement
- Quantifying the risk that climate change poses for businesses and strategies to reduce their risk
- Establishing an environmental accounting firm, helping companies track and report their carbon footprint, water use, energy efficiency, waste, and other factors
- Specializing in writing sustainability reports for the growing number of companies eager to satisfy stakeholders

In measuring a business's impact on nature, environmental accountants and their clients cannot afford to lose sight of the traditional bottom line, the one based on financial profit. An environmental accountant who reduces a company's carbon footprint but eliminates its financial profit will not be employed for long. Businesses need to find ways to make money *and* make a difference, not one or the other. It's a worthy goal for environmental accountants and a far cry from just counting beans.

Finding Business Solutions in the Living World

For hundreds of years, the industrialized world has worked hard to subdue nature and extract resources to drive economic growth. We have done well in this battle. Too well; nature is showing some serious wear. While man's efforts were once small compared with the magnitude of natural systems, the ecosystems that produce our clean air and water, and help control the climate, are now stressed and in danger from persistent mistreatment. This is not merely a concern for species such as the spotted owl. By endangering nature, humans endanger themselves. To find another way, eco-entrepreneurs are developing a sustainable green economy by learning from nature, finding business solutions that work with nature rather than against it. To further their work, eco-entrepreneurs are going back to school, studying nature, and using what they learn to build a business.

Nature has a lot to teach us. In her eloquent book *Biomimicry*, Janine Benyus argues the case for using nature as a model and mentor. My copy is well-worn. There are a few books that I return to over and over in my life, and this is one of them. "Biomimicry" describes a wide array of examples in which nature has proven more efficient and "greener" than human efforts, including those in manufacturing, energy production, food production, and medicine development. Evolution is a powerful creative force that has produced countless innovations humans can adapt and use. "Living things have done everything we want to do, without guzzling fossil fuel, polluting the planet, or mortgaging our future," Benyus writes in her book. Mussels produce an adhesive that works underwater better than anything human chemists have invented. For its weight, spider silk is stronger than steel. The abalone's shell is twice as tough as our high-tech ceramics, and produced without extreme heat and toxic solvents. The more we study nature, the more inspiration we find for ways to build businesses that are less wasteful, less polluting, and more vibrant.

At the Biomimicry Guild she co-founded, Benyus continues finding new natural innovations that the business world can adapt. In order to explain how biomimicry differs from traditional bio-based endeavors, Benyus offers the following definitions: One of the ways we interface with nature is bioutilization, in which a natural product is used by business, such as harvesting trees for lumber or using bamboo for floors. The second way we interact is bioprocessing, in which organisms are used to produce something else, such as yeasts making bread or bacteria cleaning wastewater. The third way business relates to nature is biomimicry, the focus of Benyus's work, "learning from and then emulating a natural design, a blueprint from the natural world."

Looking at biomimicry more closely, Benyus describes three different levels of emulation: mimicking a form, a process, or ecosystem. The forms (shapes and patterns) of organisms have evolved over vast stretches of time around functions they perform, and by studying how these forms work biologists and engineers can find more streamlined ways to build things. Mimicking processes can involve looking at the chemistry of living systems as the inspiration for more efficient and sustainable human equivalents. In ecosystems they can find a model for how businesses and economies can work sustainably on a large scale, reducing waste. While the industrial extractive economy has been based on depleting natural resources and creating mounds of waste, natural systems don't waste anything. There are no landfills or toxic waste dumps in nature. Whenever a plant dies, it is recycled back into the soil for new plants in future generations. Natural systems have evolved to be inherently sustainable, using resources in endless cycles of renewal.

When Benyus and the consultants at the Biomimicry Guild are approached by a business client with a problem, they frame the question on a functional level: "What do I want my design to do?" From there, they produce an "Amoeba to Zebra" report, looking through the scientific literature to identify all the solutions for the problem that natural systems have developed. For example, if a client is looking for an improved helmet design, Benyus and her staff will look at the many ways that organisms protect themselves against impact, including nutshells, skulls, and bark on trees. From the thousands of possibilities the consultants identify common approaches used by many organisms and suggest potential product applications. Working with the client, design engineers sit down with "biologists at the design table," do a feasibility study, produce one or two ideas to look at in-depth, and engage the biologists responsible for the original research.

In the end, the Biomimics hope not just to create solutions that mimic nature but also to create a more sustainable world. When finding solutions,

VARIATIONS ON A BIZ-THEME
The applications of biomimicry are many. For the 2004 Athens Olympics, Nike was looking for innovative clothing to keep athletes cool. Benyus and the Biomimicry Guild found 25 ways that nature keeps things cool and from these suggested product applications.

guild consultants try to reduce material use and the production of toxic material to create more sustainable products. They also work to create business models that help support the organisms that were the source of inspiration in the first place, "preserving the well-spring that gave rise to the great idea." Benyus says, "It wouldn't feel right without somehow saying thank you in a tangible way." That's why the the Biomimicry Institute (a nonprofit) offers companies a way to show their gratitude through the Innovation for Conservation program, which uses the funds to preserve the habitat of organisms that provided the original inspiration for products. What goes around comes around, and by taking care of nature, biomimicry supporters are providing for future inspiration for all of us.

One lesson from nature is its efficiency and creativity at the molecular level. Nature is the world's oldest and most inventive chemist. The same chemistry that man produces with extreme heat, pressure, and noxious chemicals, nature does at environmental temperature, at normal pressure, without waste, and with plain old water. By studying the chemistry of nature and learning from it, chemists are finding cleaner, less toxic, and less wasteful processes and products (Opportunity 31). Plastics are another opportunity. As useful as they can be, the millions of tons of plastics made from petroleum will sit in landfills for thousands of years after they are thrown away. Bio-plastics can be made using living organisms, or can be designed to mimic nature's polymer solutions. These new plastics are replacing petroleum-based products and are made from renewable resources, cutting down on pollution and waste (Opportunity 32).

In addition to living cleanly, without producing toxic waste, living systems have proven adept at cleaning. Humans' solutions for cleaning up toxic messes have often involved digging up and moving thousands of tons of dirt. This is an expensive and slow solution, and may not always work. A bio-assisted method to clean up toxic waste, called bio-remediation, uses plants and microbes to bind up toxins, prevent their spread, and convert the contaminants to less dangerous compounds. Eco-entrepreneurs are harnessing living systems to clean up human toxic waste and restore soil and water (Opportunity 33).

Diversity is a fundamental property of nature. The world is populated by millions of species, most of which have yet to be described. Within every leaf, within the microbes in each patch of soil, nature holds a vast repertoire of chemical diversity for us to learn from and use. The treasure trove already has provided aspirin, cholesterol-lowering drugs, antibiotics such as penicillin, pain-fighting drugs from cone snails, and diabetes drugs from gila monster saliva, among other examples. More treasures still are waiting to be found. Bio-prospectors investigate living things and the chemical secrets they hold, seeking new drugs or other useful surprises (Opportunity 34). Bio-prospectors are working against the clock, racing to make their discoveries even as habitats and species disappear. Done correctly, bio-prospecting provides the economic incentive to preserve habitats, biodiversity, and the future innovations they will inspire.

Living things have evolved to move air and water efficiently around and through their bodies by using smooth currents, rather than by creating turbulence as our machines often do. Evolution has built in the designs that produce smoothly flowing air and water moving through their veins, over their gills, and around their wings. In doing so, animals already have solved many of the problems that engineers and designers struggle with in building industrial products. If cars, airplanes, and trains can move through air as efficiently as fish move through water or birds move through air, human transportation will consume less fuel by wasting less energy on resistance. Studying and mimicking the forms of nature and how they function is helping entrepreneurs build more efficient products (Opportunity 35).

Take the time to go outside and look around. Leave your BlackBerry at home, and look at the pattern of the leaves. Bend down and look closely at the bugs, mushrooms, mosses, and ferns, and think about what they are doing. Take notes. If you feel a little humble, then maybe you are getting it.

But don't feel bad, natural systems have been perfecting their work for billions of years, and we are only just starting to learn.

One of the biggest lessons from nature might be the necessity of evolution. Learning from nature does not mean business must stop; it just means that businesses must evolve to do better. Businesses that fail to evolve might not be able to compete and survive against those that take the lead, just as natural selection removes species in the natural world. Learning from nature is not just clever; it is imperative. We can build vibrant green businesses, protect nature, and secure our own destiny. It's a lesson worth learning.

OPPORTUNITY 31

Green Chemistry

The Market Need	Chemistry produces countless products and trillions of dollars of economic activity but can be hard on the planet
The Mission	Find a cleaner and less wasteful approach to chemistry
Knowledge to Start	Chemistry, business
Capital Required	$$$ to $$$$ (to develop new products, processes)
Timing to Start	Years
Special Challenges	Research to find new products and processes, and ways to commercialize them

The chemistry business is worth more than $2 trillion a year in agricultural products, plastics, adhesives, fabrics, pigments, and other fields (American Chemistry Council, 2006, americanchemistry.com). The typical American home is loaded with products that chemistry helped make: electronics, paint, drugs, cosmetics, soaps, kitchenware, cleaning agents, and many types of clothing. However, modern chemistry does not have a great reputation with environmentalists concerned about health and environmental impact. The way chemistry is performed is changing to use "green chemistry's" products and processes that are more efficient, use fewer resources, and generate less waste and pollution.

Where a traditional industrial process may utilize large volumes of toxic solvent for a reaction and then discard the solvent afterward, green chemistry recycles the solvent, reduces the volume of the reaction, or uses water. In the traditional approach, a company might pay for the solvent twice, once to buy it and then again to dispose of it. This is costly and can entail occupational risks to chemical workers. More efficient chemistry is good for the environment and makes good business sense.

> **GREENING THE BOTTOM LINE**
> Hazardous-waste disposal can cost more than the original material cost, providing a significant incentive for chemistry to be greener.

Green chemistry also can open doors to new opportunities. Large chemical companies, such as DuPont and Dow, are developing new and greener products and ways of doing business. When chlorofluorocarbons were found to cause loss of ozone, the world was faced with a choice: we could either give up refrigerants altogether (no refrigerators, no air conditioners), or find greener, less damaging alternatives. DuPont and any consumers who have refrigerators produced in recent years chose the latter.

The great potential of green chemistry is highlighted by the winners of the Presidential Green Chemistry Challenge Awards Program awarded by the Environmental Protection Agency (EPA) each year. In 2007, one of the winners was Columbia Forest Products, recognized for developing a new formaldehyde-free process for producing plywood and particle board.

ECO-ISSUE

One goal for green chemists is the reduction of greenhouse-gas emissions. DuPont has taken voluntary measures to reduce its greenhouse-gas emissions by 72 percent since 1990, making real improvements (statistic from DuPont, 2006). If a mandatory cap-and-trade system comes into play in the United States, China, and India in coming years, the financial incentives for green chemistry will increase. 🌱

INFORMATION RESOURCE

The EPA has a green chemistry web-site describing opportunities for chemists, businesses, and entrepreneurs; visit epa.gov/greenchemistry.

PureBond meets the standards of the U.S. Green Building Council's Leadership in Energy and Environmental Design (LEED) certification system. Other winners from the corporate world and academia have found nontoxic solvents to use in specialized printing methods, and new ways of using the glycerol produced during biodiesel production. Projects started in academia often transition into commercialization, with the inventor becoming entrepreneur. Professor Richard Wool received the award in 2006 for a variety of bio-based green materials he invented and is now the president of Cara Plastics, Inc.

Living things (including your own body) are the ultimate green chemists, constantly performing myriad chemical reactions with little heat or waste—feats that human chemists often have envied. Chemistry usually requires speeding up processes, and that's where living things use special proteins called enzymes. Where human chemists often use heat, pressure, or metals for speed, nature uses enzymes found in every living cell. Molded by billions of years of evolution, some enzymes can be used to propel chemistry on an industrial scale, replacing more toxic methods.

Another strategy is to use living microbes for chemistry, giving human chemists a break. Microbes are tiny but powerful chemical factories. The right microbes with the right enzymes can be coaxed into performing a whole string of reactions inside the microbial cell, spitting out the finished product. DuPont and Genencor (a division of Danisco, based in Denmark) collaborated to produce microbes that eat sugar and produce the chemical 1,3-propanediol. This compound is used to make the bio-based Sorona brand of polymers woven into carpet and fabrics, replacing older methods and polymers that involve petrochemicals and traditional chemistry.

INDUSTRY INFO

The ACS Green Chemistry Institute, part of the American Chemical Society, also promotes green chemistry (acs.org/greenchemistry).

Not all green chemistry involves microbes. Another contribution of green chemistry is in the hunt for replacements for chemicals containing bromine used in fire retardants. These compounds are highly effective fire retardants used in a huge array of products, including electronics. But the compounds also have contaminated ecosystems and humans. For the biomimicry solution for fire retardants, the Biomimicry Guild and Benyus looked for nature's solutions for resisting combustion, working with the Warner Babcock Institute for Green Chemistry, an organization focused on green-chemistry solutions. Another biomimicry example of green chemistry in fire retardants is Molecular Heat Eater (MHE), a Swedish group that found chemical reactions that resemble molecular cycles in cells, cooling a fire and absorbing its energy to keep it from spreading.

Many players are moving green chemistry forward, including the government (the EPA, for example), industry, academic researchers, and non-profits. You don't have to be a chemist to get involved. Innovation can start small and can come from anywhere. If you are an eco-entrepreneur interested in green chemistry, check out what is going on in university labs, and see how this relates to older ways of doing things. Talk to people in the field and tech transfer offices. Start with the basic research that people are doing and trace it to a product or process you can sell, or start with a problem you want to solve and trace it back to a researcher who might hold a solution. A few good ideas and who knows? You might be the next green DuPont.

Chemists have a big advantage in developing and understanding green chemistry, and biologists can identify and commercialize the use of enzymes to replace older processes. Those with business savvy but less technical training can connect the dots from great technology to new products and new business applications. Individual researchers make key contributions in green chemistry, but commercialization often takes teams of people from many backgrounds, not just individuals working alone. Helping to bring these disciplines together and molding them into a company is as important as the science behind it.

RELATED TREND

Microbes are being used as chemists in the production of biofuels such as bio-butanol, which has physical properties that are better than ethanol for fuel use.

GREEN LEADER

John Warner is the chief technology officer at the Warner Babcock Institute for Green Chemistry. He has found that most chemists are not trained in toxicology. Warner is out to change that, to build environmental concerns into the development process for new chemical products for the companies with which he works.

Opportunities for green chemistry include:

- Reducing toxic-waste production
- Using enzymes or microbes in place of more polluting methods
- Using biomimicry to develop less polluting, greener products and processes

Chemistry will not go away as the green revolution unfolds; it will just get smarter and greener. Whether this change stems from a sense of moral duty, business savvy, or necessity, if the chemistry works, the result will be good for all involved.

OPPORTUNITY 32

Bio-Plastic Products

The Market Need	Most plastics are produced from petroleum, are non-biodegradable, and are not recycled enough
The Mission	Create eco-friendly plastics from renewable resources
Knowledge to Start	Design, plastics
Capital Required	$$ (Using existing bio-plastics to make new products)
Timing to Start	Months to years
Special Challenges	Finding markets for products

Plastics changed how we live in the 20th century. Many of the products filling our homes would not be here were it not for plastics. Plastics have been crafted to have almost any property desired; they can stretch or bend, they're lightweight, cheap to manufacture, and durable. Unfortunately, some of plastic's biggest assets are now obvious problems. Plastics are so cheap to make that there is a proliferation of cheap consumer goods and packaging. Plastics are so durable that they can reside in landfills for hundreds or even thousands of years. The opportunities to replace petroleum-based plastics with more planet-friendly products are as big as the impact plastic has had on our lives and our economy.

One problem is that plastics are petroleum based. Most of our oil is used for transportation, but about 80 million tons a year in the United States (in 2000) is used to make plastics (Michigan State University, Office of Biobased Technologies, bioeconomy.msu.edu). As the price of oil goes up, the price of everything derived from oil, including petrochemical-based plastics, also goes up. Bio-plastics also aim to be more biodegradable than their petrochemical brethren, breaking down more rapidly in landfills.

To replace plastics, we need polymers that are based in biology rather than petrochemicals. Major corporations such as DuPont, Cargill, and Archer Daniels Midland (ADM) are making plastics from corn, potatoes, and soy as part of the next plastics revolution. These bioplastics are derived from material such as starch, cellulose, and lactic acid produced by plants and microbes. This is not a token effort, but a major industrial shift. As part of its drive to green its supply chain, Wal-Mart is replacing plastic packaging with a corn-derived plastic called polylactic acid (PLA). A 2006 report from SRI Consulting found that the market for biologically-based polymers was about 85,000 tons in 2005 (in North America, Western Europe, and Asia) and expected to grow 22 percent a year. Curiously, one of the biggest producers of bio-plastics is Toyota, which is introducing bio-plastic parts in its cars and aims to expand beyond cars to be a big player in this market.

What can be done with bio-plastics? Food packaging is increasingly made from starch or PLA-based products. Businesses are already making car parts, computer cases, and cell phones from bio-plastics. Food-services companies are starting to use plasticware made from corn products, and some eco-water bottles are made from corn-based plastic (see Opportunity 51). What's next? Find something made of

INDUSTRY INFO

The U.S. plastics industry was worth more than $379 billion in 2006 (The Society of the Plastics Industry, economic statistics, plasticsindustry.org).

DEFINITION TIME

Plastics are polymers, long molecules strung together from many smaller pieces. Bio-plastics are also polymers but are produced using renewable resources (material from living organisms).

GREEN MARKETS

Eighty-five thousand tons might sound like a lot, but it's a small fraction of the total plastics market. Globally, there are 100 million tons of plastic consumed each year (waste online in the United Kingdom, wasteonline.org.uk). That leaves a lot of room for growth in bio-plastics. ❦

plastic, find a compatible bio-plastic, then see if you can replace the plastic and if there is a market for the new approach. With 99.9 percent of plastic goods still being made from petroleum, the opportunity is huge.

Another opportunity is to continue improving on the bio-plastics that are available. Just because a plastic is made from plants, is it clean, green, and renewable? Not automatically. There are a variety of bio-plastics that differ in how they are made and how biodegradable they really are. PLA production generally uses fossil fuels in the growth of the crops used and in the production of the plastic, so studies have found that the overall environmental benefit from using corn-based plastics might be smaller than thought. Products from corn described as biodegradable often require hot and controlled conditions of industrial composting, which are still not common.

EFFICIENCY ANGLE

According to a report commissioned by the largest PLA producer in the United States—Natureworks of Minnetonka, Minnesota—PLA uses 65 percent less energy to produce than oil-based plastics, as described in *Smithsonian* magazine, August 2006.

The whole supply chain could be examined for potential improvements to produce not just bio-plastics, but the greenest possible bio-plastics. Producing plastics from renewable plant resources might be an improvement over oil, but could plastics be greener still if they were made from sustainably grown crops? Does avoiding the use of genetically-modified plants improve plastic's greenness? Is the chemistry used to produce the bio-plastics environmentally sound, sticking to the principles of green chemistry? How much greenhouse-gas emissions result from the production of the material and its transportation?

The drawbacks of the first generation of bio-plastics present the opportunity to develop bio-plastics that are green from production to disposal and, hopefully, reuse. Companies such as Metabolix of Cambridge, Massachusetts, are already looking beyond corn-based bio-plastics to build the second- or third-generation materials. NatureWorks in Minnesota (owned by Cargill) is offering carbon-neutral and 100 percent renewable plastics. The physical properties of new bio-plastics may even be superior to other plastics.

These bio-plastics typically are bioutilization or bioprocessing examples. A biomimicry example of an eco-plastic as described by Janine Benyus (see the introduction to this chapter) is provided by a company called Novomer of Ithaca, New York. In photosynthesis, plants use the energy of the sun to hook together carbon-dioxide molecules and make sugar. Similarly, Novomer has found a way to take carbon dioxide and link simple molecules into polymers using specially designed catalysts. Based on the research of Dr. Geoffrey Coates, Novomer is developing a range of tailor-made, biodegradable eco-plastics with unique properties. Novomer staff can take the greenhouse-gas emissions from one industry and use the carbon dioxide as the raw material to make plastic.

Opportunities in bio-plastics include:

- Designing and producing new bio-plastic products (sporks, cell phones, etc)
- Composting bio-plastics
- Making bio-plastics from sustainably-grown crops and avoiding GMO plants
- Making bio-plastics using the principles of green chemistry

> The Sustainable Bioplastic Collaborative has issued guidelines for bioplastics with the lowest environmental impact; visit healthybuilding.net.

> **GREEN LEADER**
> Novomer is pioneering a new class of eco-plastics. These are not bioplastics, as carbon dioxide is not extracted from living organisms, but they may prove just as green.

   • Developing next generation bio-plastics with new properties

The plastics revolution continues, but is now moving from the consumer society to the sustainable society. There are a lot of players involved but it's a big field and there is always room for more. Whatever others are doing with bio-plastics, do it better, cheaper, and greener.

OPPORTUNITY 33

Natural Detox

The Market Need	The industrial world has created many sites with toxic contamination that need cleaning up
The Mission	Use nature to help clean up toxic messes
Knowledge to Start	Toxicology, microbiology
Capital Required	$$$
Timing to Start	Months to years
Special Challenges	Proper implementation and finding customers

To many, nature was so vast that leaving a mess here and there did not seem like a big problem, but the messes have a way of coming back to bite us. Mine tailings allow heavy metals to seep into lakes and rivers. Abandoned industrial waste sites become brownfields, with rusting waste drums left to fester in litigation. With the increasing need to clean up such sites comes an increasing opportunity for businesses providing cost-effective solutions where nature and entrepreneurs work together.

    Cleaning up waste sites in the past generally required tons of earth to be bulldozed and trucked to landfills, or contaminated groundwater to be pumped out. Hauling around mountains of contaminated dirt is expensive, and

GREEN MARKETS

Costs to clean up environmental hazards total between $7 and $8 billion per year, according to the Frost & Sullivan 2003 report "U.S. Bioremediation Markets."

it's not always clear that the approach works; it might just move the problem from one place to another. In response, more cost-effective and innovative ways of cleaning up toxic sites have been developed, using the power of nature. Microbes have a great capacity to digest chemicals and convert them into less toxic components. Using living systems to clean up contamination is called bioremediation.

Eco-entrepreneurs are building bioremediation companies. Potential customers include the government, nongovernment organizations, and companies on the hook for cleanups or that are working to clean up their actions and image. Rather than digging up or burning chemical spills, Spillaway International Ltd. in the United Kingdom makes bioremediation products that can speed the spill's breakdown. Focused on products for the cleanup of hydrocarbons—such as oil, lubricants, and fuels—Spillaway's products harness the power of microbes to eat a spill wherever they find it, on land or in water. JRW Bioremediation in Kansas is also making products for bioremediation, cleaning up solvents and other chemicals from wastes (including dry cleaners using perchlorate; see Opportunity 57). To clean up soil and groundwater faster, JRW is also working to speed up the work of microbes.

Renovogen in San Diego is also utilizing microbes for bioremediation. When examining a site where contaminants are found, Renovogen identifies microbes isolated from the site, tests their ability to break down the contaminants, and then grows these particular microbes to use for cleanup, avoiding foreign microbes that might disturb local ecosystems. The solution is tailored for each location and the specific pollutants encountered. Computerized modeling of the site ensures the solutions are as effective as possible. Renovogen has used this method to clean up diesel fuel, gasoline, solvents, jet propellant, and waste from asphalt.

INDUSTRY INFO

For more about Spillaway International's products, see spillaway.net. Also, providing products for bioremediation is an opportunity. The company Envirosales (envirosales.com) sells Spillaway products.

RELATED TREND

Bioremediation is related to what happens in composting or wastewater treatment. The growing number of cities employing municipal composting provides a related opportunity.

DEFINITION TIME

Using plants to clean up contaminated soil or water is called phytoremediation.

The soil at coal mines, industrial sites, and other locations often has high levels of toxic metals, such as zinc, lead, and cadmium. Left on their own, these sites will leach the metals into the groundwater and nearby watersheds, and consequently into the food chain. Researchers, such as Leon Kochlan in the U.S. Department of Agriculture Agricultural Research Services, have been investigating the ability of plants to grow in soil containing these metals and thereby remove the metals from the soil. These plants (metals and all) then can be harvested far more easily and safely than prior methods of digging up large quantities of soil and burying it elsewhere. This approach can even clean radioactive isotopes from soil around uranium mines or contaminated sites where weapons work was done. Contaminated leaves or stems can be reduced in volume and stored to keep the contaminant from being released again.

Opportunites in natural detox include:

- Developing new bioremediation solutions
- Providing bioremediation as a service
- Selling bioremediation supplies

Bioremediation is straightforward, but it still takes some know-how to use the products and monitor how well they are working. Not every team member will be an environmental toxicologist but having one close by will make a big difference. Different products are tailored for different kinds of spills, and how well they work depends on the water, oxygen, nutrient content, and temperature of the affected soil. It also takes a time commitment to get the job done right. Spraying contaminated sites with microbes and then leaving is not enough to make problems go away. This combines to create the opportunity to provide bioremediation as an ongoing service. Given how broad are the problems with contaminated soil and water, the opportunities are large.

ECO-ISSUE

There are some do's and don'ts associated with on-site bioremediation. For more information, see frtr.gov/matrix2/section3/3_1.html.

OPPORTUNITY 34

Bio-Prospecting

The Market Need	Nature contains a world of hidden treasures waiting to be discovered
The Mission	Identify commercially viable products from the natural world and preserve biological diversity
Knowledge to Start	Biology, chemistry, travel
Capital Required	$$$ (non-pharmaceutical) to $$$$ (finding and developing pharmaceutical drugs)
Timing to Start	Months to years
Special Challenges	Agreements about patents, concerns of bio-piracy, and difficulty of commercializing some products

Biology is full of surprises. Sometimes the surprise is an exotic new species, such as a bioluminescent squid from the ocean depths, but surprises can also come from the zoo of chemicals produced by living things. For billions of years, living beings have evolved to do chemistry that human chemists would never have dreamed of. By exploring the chemical diversity of nature, humans have come away with a long list of useful products. Finding and bringing natural products to market can help both the eco-entrepreneur and the endangered habitats in which these discoveries are made.

For millennia, one use of nature's diversity has been for medicines. Many of our drugs came from plants originally. This includes aspirin from willow, penicillin from mold, and Taxol (a cancer drug) from yew trees. These cures often have been discovered by native cultures and used as herbal remedies, only to be rediscovered by modern medicine. The allure of new cures continues to drive modern bio-prospectors on a quest through nature to find the next aspirin or penicillin hiding in a flower, sea slug, or a coral.

And we do need new medicines. Antibiotic-resistant strains of bacteria are more frequently producing infections that are harder to treat, steadily increasing the urgency of the quest for new antibiotics. Almost all antibiotics have been based on natural products, and many future drugs will be as well.

Biologists have cataloged less than 2 million species on the Earth (*National Geographic News*, March 5, 2002, nationalgeographic.com/news), but only a small fraction of these has been examined chemically or genetically, and the known species are only the tip of the iceberg. It's estimated there are between 10 and 100 million species on Earth that have never been documented. We have only scratched the surface of the pool of chemical surprises that nature holds.

Bio-prospecting has been pursued from many angles with varying degrees of success. One approach has been to send people into the jungle (or other biomes) to collect many different species, then test material from the species for potential use as pharmaceuticals. This approach has mixed reviews. When an active ingredient is found to be useful, the compound responsible is often notoriously complicated. Nature is such an inventive chemist that human chemists often expend considerable effort retracing nature's steps. Figuring out its structure and producing the compound can be arduous, and creating enough to use as a medicine is even harder. Finding better ways to test natural products for their usefulness and producing enough for human uses are opportunities to unlock the value of the natural world.

ECO-ISSUE

The discovery of Taxol as a cancer drug from the bark of yew trees was exciting for patients but less so for the trees. The complicated structure of Taxol was difficult for chemists to copy initially, leading some to strip bark from yew trees in search of the compound. With time, better ways of making the compound were found, and the yew trees were spared.

Another approach, called ethnobotany or ethnomedicine, looks closely at how native cultures use plants and organisms in order to find clues to the most likely starting point for a medicine. Cultures in many different parts of the world have found a variety of cures that have been confirmed in the hands of scientists and doctors. Studying the interaction between species in ecosystems can highlight the hidden molecular secrets and how we might use them.

Back in the 1990s, Shaman Pharmaceuticals of South San Francisco, California, provided an instructive example of the opportunities and challenges of bio-prospecting. Shaman was founded with the idea of studying cures from indigenous cultures and adapting the medicines to provide Western pharmaceuticals. Shaman had early success and was developing a promising diarrhea cure derived from a tropical plant but ran out of money in 1999 when the FDA required more clinical data before approval. Some have taken this story as a precautionary tale to stay away from bio-prospecting and ethnomedicine, claiming that because Shaman did not ultimately succeed, the approach is flawed. But another view is that drug discovery is risky and expensive in general, and that whatever happened with Shaman, the opportunity remains for future discoveries from bio-prospecting. Perhaps it is not bio-prospecting that failed, but the drug development and approval process that made developing the product too expensive.

In the past, bio-prospectors have not always recognized the interests of the host country, and have failed to compensate nations or their people for findings. This "finder's keepers" approach does not always go over well, leading to accusations of "bio-piracy." A new model for bio-prospecting businesses is to work in partnership with the government and people, protecting their biodiversity. By bringing governments and local people into the project as partners who will share in the profits, and by providing local people a financial incentive to make the project work, the odds of success are far better. The 1992 Convention on Biological Diversity (CBD) encourages countries to establish regulations regarding bio-prospecting, although the United States has not ratified the agreement. Regulations may include charging fees for access, requiring support for local conservation efforts, or securing a percentage of the revenue from any products discovered. Bio-prospectors such as Paul Alan Cox are working to make the industry a win-win solution. The founder of the Institute for Ethnomedicine (ethnomedicine.org), Cox helps to ensure that a portion of proceeds from discoveries goes to the people and nations where ingredients were found.

ECO-ISSUE

Bio-prospecting needs to leave intact ecosystems and the organisms it studies, sampling only enough to see what value is present. This is not the same as harvesting material from nature in large quantities to sell directly. Other methods for production are needed when material of interest is found by bio-prospectors.

A side benefit is that native people develop a financial interest in preserving the natural environment. If they profit from the biodiversity, they are much more likely to protect it. The more pressing that population and resource issues become, which they will, the more essential it is that environmental interests and business interests work hand in hand.

Biosignal of Australia (biosignal.com.au) started with an observation in nature, providing an example of biomimicry starting with chemical clues from living things, as described by Janine Benyus from the Biomimicry Guild. When bacteria grow, they sometimes can communicate with each other to grow in a tight layer called a biofilm, a key step used by many bacteria in growing and causing infection. When in a biofilm, bacteria can be much harder to kill. In thick, murky water rich in bacteria, researchers found a red algae that resisted bacterial growth. The algae was producing a compound that prevents bacteria from communicating. These compounds might be used as therapeutics to fight infections, to coat surfaces of medical devices or contact lenses, or even to prevent bacteria from degrading the integrity of oil pipelines.

RELATED TREND

Microbes have been a rich source of past bio-prospecting and are bound to hold many more surprises. Bio-prospecting for new products from microbes might require only a small sample of soil or water, and just looking at the mix of genes in a sample can provide clues about the potential of the microbes.

Looking for pharmaceuticals is only one way in which the diversity of nature can be used for commercial opportunities, and studying living things for products in other fields may be less costly and less risky. Herbal remedies and new foods often are easier to commercialize than pharmaceuticals, provided the organisms in which they are found can be farmed sustainably. Are there new bio-plastics hidden away? New pigments? The search for green chemistry solutions often looks to diverse organisms for new and novel enzymes to carry out reactions. Maintaining and exploring eco-systems and their biodiversity may hold the answers for many such challenges.

Opportunities for bio-prospecting include:

- Finding new drugs (which require long-term research and significant capital)

- Discovering herbal remedies (which require less time and money than drugs)
- Developing dyes and pigments
- Using bio-materials to replace toxic industrial materials (adhesives, plastics, solvents)
- Replicating natural patterns (Interface Inc., a floor-covering company based in Atlanta, Georgia, created one of its line of floor tiles using patterns from nature)

Even as we realize the value that natural systems hold, they are being destroyed at a breakneck pace. Tropical forests and coral reefs are some of the most diverse ecosystems, and probably hold many untapped and invaluable offerings. But they are among the most threatened ecosystems. Bioprospecting remains full of promise, but this is one opportunity that may not be around forever.

OPPORTUNITY 35

Natural Forms and Function

The Market Need	Humans often build machines that are not as efficient as possible
The Mission	Build better machines by modeling them after nature
Knowledge to Start	Physics, engineering, biology
Capital Required	$$ (adapt) to $$$$ (invent)
Timing to Start	Months (to adapt) years (to invent)
Special Challenges	Understanding natural forms and translating then into superior products

Organisms do not live in a vacuum. They move through the air and water smoothly and efficiently, and move fluids through their bodies in the same way. The shape of an owl's wing, a porpoise, or a maple seed is no accident but, rather, the result of billions of years of evolutionary pressure to move

ECO-EXAMPLE

One example of nature-inspired technology is Velcro, modeled after the small seed burrs that use tiny hooks and barbs to latch onto clothing or fur.

through their environment with the least possible effort and the greatest efficiency. The animals and plants that have survived evolutionary history display nature's best solutions. Studious entrepreneurs are improving the efficiency of human engineering to provide winning business solutions.

Human-designed systems have not always been subjected to that same pressure for efficiency. Turbulence is inefficient, but when energy is cheap, brute-force engineering can compensate by cranking up the power. For example, the shape of cars designed for market appeal may not only attract buyers but also increase wind resistance and reduce fuel economy. Taking a different approach, engineers and innovative eco-entrepreneurs are designing nature-inspired mechanical systems, learning from the finely-honed form and function of organisms.

Humans spend billions of dollars each year on industrial systems that move air and water. Air handling in buildings—moving air through ducts for air conditioning—is just one example; pipes and pumps for water are another. Then think of cooling fans; cars, computers, refrigerators, oven hoods, and many other appliances have internal fans to remove heat. These fans take electricity, and the more efficient they are, the less energy they need. The shapes of cars, trains, and planes can be designed to glide smoothly through air, and the more smoothly they move the less energy they need. This might seem obvious, but a vehicle's appearance is often a larger design concern than its efficiency—adding more horsepower often has been the solution for turbulence.

Pax Scientific of San Rafael, California, has studied the patterns of natural flow in water and air and used the information to find better engineering solutions for humans. Air and water can move in ordered, layered flow, or through the chaos of turbulence. Living systems almost always find the most elegant, efficient solution, moving fluids with the least resistance and turbulence.

The CEO of Pax Scientific, Jay Harman, studied flowing liquids and found that, in nature, they always follow the same pattern. Working in the Australian Department of Fisheries and Wildlife, Harman spent years pondering the recurring shapes he found in nature, from the spiral whorl of the conch shell to whirlpools and tornadoes. He wondered if this recurring theme might be something we could use to make engineering systems work better—if these shapes repeat over and over, there must be a reason. Harman proposed the Pax Streamlining Principle, allowing Pax to model fluid flow and find the optimal flow produced by streamlined designs like those found in nature.

Using this method, Harman and Pax Scientific have identified solutions that improve the efficiency of fans, mixing of fluids for industry, heat dispersal, and other applications. The technology discovered as a result of this has been licensed to the Pax Group, including the related companies PaxIT, PaxAuto, and PaxFan, each of which consults with clients to adopt and license their technology for the client's needs. The potential applications of this technology are huge. PaxIT is improving the fans that cool computers and other electronics, PaxAuto is designing cars to improve how they move through air; and PaxFan is working on air-handling systems, such as industrial fans and duct work.

Today the evolutionary pressure on business has changed, turning the tide in design from brute force to a more elegant and efficient approach. Air-handling systems that have been designed using the new technology already have improved efficiency between 15 and 30 percent, while producing less noise. Pax redesigned blades for the fan in a refrigerator evaporator, increasing efficiency by 33 percent (2006 data from Pax Scientific Case Study for work with partner in motor market). If you are an entrepreneur working in a related field, finding ways to integrate new technology to increase efficiency could provide a competitive edge.

There are other fields where useful biological observations are patented and then licensed to many businesses to

GREEN LEADER

For more in-depth information of the wide-ranging work of the companies in the Pax Group, visit thepaxgroup.com.

INVESTING IN GREEN

The venture capital firm Khosla Ventures is investing in a Pax Scientific spin-off company called Pax Streamline that will work on developing high-efficiency systems for heating and cooling, turbines, and other industrial uses.

apply in many products. The leaves of the lotus plant stay clean despite its muddy environment. Looking closely, Professor Wilhelm Barthlott at the University of Bonn, Germany, found that the structure of the leaves and their chemistry helped make dirt and water bead up and roll off. Barthlott patented this phenomenon and licenses it to others. Janine Benyus, founder of the Biomimicry Guild, describes the variety of companies using the lotus effect: Ferro Corporation of Cleveland, Ohio, uses it in coatings applied to glass to keep water and dirt off, and prevent fogging; paints called StoCoat Lotusan were developed by Sto-Corporation of Atlanta, Georgia; Erlus in Denmark has produced Erlus Lotus self-cleaning roofing tiles.

Opportunities in natural-form development include:

* Identifying and patenting new principles based on designs from nature
* Licensing technologies developed by others to commercialize new applications
* Working as a middleman, matching those with technologies with those who sell goods that would benefit from these nature-inspired design principles

One approach is to find useful biomimicry examples that others have pioneered and adapt these to your own work to improve performance. Another way to build a business is by finding and patenting your own observations about nature's solutions, then licensing them to others as the Pax Group and Professor Barthlott have done. What makes wood so strong yet light, for example, and how can we use these properties to design lightweight materials? Findings like these give new value to studying organisms. See how they move and live, imagine the possibilities if we could be more like them, then make it happen.

Wasting Less

It has been said that if everybody on earth were to consume and throw away material as Americans do, we would need six Earths to keep up. We don't have six Earths, we only have one, and yet we continue to consume and throw away material at a frenetic pace. According to the Environmental Protection Agency (EPA), America produced 251 million tons of waste in 2006, about 4.6 pounds per person per day. Our landfills are

running out of space and closing, with the number of landfills accepting waste constantly dwindling. If we look at this problem differently, all of the things we throw away have value if we can find the right way to capture it. One person's garbage is another person's goldmine. Sometimes literally—cell phones and other electronic waste contain a variety of valuable metals, including gold. Eco-entrepreneurs are mining this opportunity to turn the garbage into gold.

Every item that is recovered, repurposed, and reincarnated from garbage is an item that does not need to consume natural resources and energy to be born. Much of the landfill waste comes from demolition and construction—waste that can be avoided if we reuse old building materials (Opportunity 39). Artisans and designers are creating furniture from material that would otherwise be destined for the landfill (Opportunity 41). It's not smelly and dirty, it's funky and fun.

Another way to cut down on waste is to stop generating it in the first place. Plastic grocery bags are a growing waste headache, with hundreds of billions being thrown away yearly. They are such a big problem that more and more governments are banning them, driving rapid growth in the adoption of alternatives, such as reusable grocery bags (Opportunity 40). The computer revolution has long promised the switch to a paperless office, allowing documents to be moved on computers rather than paper. This has not happened. In fact, we are using more paper and generating more paper waste than ever before. A lot of paper is recycled, but the best eco-option is not to use the paper in the first place. The tools for the paperless office do exist, they just need to be integrated and adopted, making this a real eco-option (Opportunity 36). Reducing the amount of packaging we use through better and more careful design also will help slow the growth of landfills (Opportunity 38).

The plan for the long term is not just to cut down on our waste, but to eliminate the idea of waste, argue William McDonough and Michael Braungart in their influential book *Cradle to Cradle*. In nature there is no waste, no depletion of natural resources; everything is reused. *Cradle to Cradle* describes how to transform how we build products, how we re-use them, and how we cycle materials endlessly—just as happens in nature. Eco-entrepreneurs are pioneering product design to embody the cradle-to-cradle concept. Computer take-back programs are causing some computer producers to rethink how they build PCs—to allow them to be easily dismantled and their parts reused. Printed products—greeting cards, car brochures, annual reports—can be made on high quality, durable plastic and then sent to a carpet manufacturer to be melted into carpet (Opportunity 37), a model that can be applied to many other products.

We don't have to live poorly to live greenly. Quite the opposite. By selling and using products that reduce waste, we can save money and live well while ensuring a healthy economy and environment for generations to come.

OPPORTUNITY 36

The Paperless Office

The Market Need	Our offices generate mountains of paper waste, and waste time and money
The Mission	Help businesses reduce waste through effective document management
Knowledge to Start	Business consulting, information technology, electronic signature technology
Capital Required	$ to $$
Timing to Start	Weeks to months
Special Challenges	Reluctance to change business practices and stop using paper

The vision of the paperless office appeared early in the computer revolution. The logic seems impeccable: The productivity of working with electronic documents would release office workers from mindless and unproductive paper shuffling, eliminating the need for file cabinets and the cost of space for paper storage. After all, what could be more old-fashioned than printed documents in the age of e-mail and pdf files, when documents can be zapped around the world to collaborators, rather than printing, mailing, etc.? This dream has not yet been realized, but it's not too late. Helping companies change how documents are handled can revive the dream, reducing paper waste and increasing business productivity. In the vision of the paperless office, the computer revolution and the green revolution would join forces to stop the leveling of forests to make paper.

Yet, we are printing more than ever. The amount of office paper consumed rose dramatically throughout the 1980s and 1990s so that the average American worker now prints more than 10,000 sheets of paper a year (Environmental Energy Technologies Division, Lawerence Berkeley National Lab, eetd.lbl.gov/paper), most of which ends up quickly in the trash along with more than 100 million toner cartridges each year. Computers and information technology have improved business productivity, but what happened to the paperless office? Where did the dream go wrong? If the logic makes so much sense, why hasn't it happened? The answer may be that the problem lies not in the technology businesses use but is entrenched in the processes around documents.

To build a green paperless-office business, work as a consultant helping businesses to increase worker efficiency and decrease costs, and save paper along the way. Having some knowledge of computers and information technology will help to realize this opportunity, but it's not just a technology problem. Reducing paper use is as much about changing how people work as it is about changing the technology and how it works. First, talk to people in an office and watch them at work. See how much they print and trace the trail of paper and documents. After getting a feel for what is going on, create a plan for how these activities could be accomplished without paper and show people how they can get more done with less effort. Arguing for changing routines to save

INFORMATION RESOURCE
The National Resources Defense Council, a nonprofit website has a paper-reduction kit for businesses. Visit nrdc.org.

trees may get some people to change, but showing how it improves their work life will get almost everyone to buy in. Creating green teams of employees gets them engaged in the process, speeding its progress.

There are a variety of tools consultants can employ to reduce paper use and improve document handling, including some inexpensive and easy-to-implement software systems for document management. To reduce paper usage by 50 percent, use double-sided printing. To avoid printing blank pages at the ends of web pages and other documents, use software such as Greenprint that looks at pages before they are printed. Rather than print documents for review, read them online and use the editing features of word-processing packages. These steps don't eliminate paper use, but they do cut back on waste.

The steady increase in paper use is not simply due to limitations in technology. It's a matter of habit and business routine. By examining their processes large corporations have managed to make significant cuts in paper use and increase productivity. The 2002 study "Business Guide to Paper Reduction" from the nonprofit ForestEthics (forestethics.org) describes the progress made at Bank of America, AT&T, and other organizations to use paper more effectively, and outlines strategies for others to do the same. It also provides a valuable resource if starting a business in the field. The document reports that General Electric, for example, is working to save $10 billion by digitizing processes. Some of the steps other companies have taken to reduce paper use include using electronic forms, not printing internal reports, using pdf files to send documents electronically, electronic billing for customers, and electronic faxing.

Another business habit is how we think about and use signatures. When it comes time to putting our name on the dotted line, this usually still requires printing out piles of paper and pulling out an old-fashioned ink pen. Secure systems for producing electronic signatures—eSignatures—can

ECO-TIP

Removing printers from the office or making them more difficult to access removes the easy temptation to print documents for a quick review. Not having a printer forces people to get over the initial reluctance to the change. After adjusting, workers report that a fairly paperless office can be a reality, and not a bad one.

increase security compared with paper signatures, providing for an audit trail. DocuSign, the leading web-based electronic signature company, is helping people reduce paper consumption with their product to increase acceptance of e-signatures in documents. DocuSign launched a "Go Green With DocuSign Challenge" in 2007 to challenge corporations to join in saving at least 10 million pieces of paper by Earth Day 2008. "We agree it is all about changing business process habits," said Matthew Schiltz, CEO and president of DocuSign. "Our eSignature technology is proven, and it is not truly the barrier to massive change. The only potential barrier might be an organization's reluctance to change their business processes. But we know that the most successful companies embrace change and new technologies to improve their business processes to accelerate their success."

Our paper use may just be another sign of other needed changes in business practices. Rethinking how we use paper can mean rethinking how we work and increasing productivity. Creating a system to avoid printing documents is not enough. Electronic document-management systems are great, but if they are not used, they will achieve nothing. Keeping documents electronically requires creating a way to keep track of information, and requires that people throughout the organization buy into the system and use it.

Opportunities in reducing office waste include:

- Consulting to help offices use paper more effectively
- Selling tools to reduce waste and increase productivity
- Specializing in the use of electronic documents for medical records or legal records

Getting people to change can be hard, but that does not mean it cannot happen. Many offices are already doing it. Helping people move to a paperless office can make a lasting impact on businesses, helping them get more done. The payoff is not just for the environment, but for employees as well. It won't happen all at once, and businesses might never get to zero paper use, but helping them use paper wisely is good for business and the environment.

Giving Products a Second Life

The Market Need	Even with recycling, a lot of paper and other products end up in landfills
The Mission	Make products that are re-used and re-purposed
Knowledge to Start	Material science, manufacturing
Capital Required	$$$ to $$$$
Timing to Start	Years
Special Challenges	Changing habits and developing new lives for products

Most urban areas now have recycling programs, so the problem of paper waste is solved, right? Well, not exactly. According to the Paper Industry Association Council, the rate of recycling has steadily risen, and out of the 100 million tons of paper and cardboard used in the United States in 2006, 53 percent was recycled, but this still left about 35 million tons to go into landfills (the remainder was burned in incinerators, used to make energy, or met other fates). Once it goes in it never comes out, sitting in the airless depths of landfill limbo. Even the paper that goes in the recycling bin is not necessarily recycled. A better solution is to create products that don't get thrown away but are reborn as other products.

In contrast to our lifestyle, there is no landfill in nature. When a tree dies in a forest, it does not get hauled off to the dump to be buried. Nature's recyclers take over, with fungi, termites, and microbes ensuring that the tree decomposes, returning to the soil to be recycled in future plants,

INFORMATION RESOURCE

For more about paper recycling, see paperrecycles.org. Even better than recycling paper is not using it in the first place (see Opportunity 36).

microbes, and animals. We can create an economy that avoids waste in the same way. Ideally, paper and other materials in our economy would cycle again and again, so new resources are not needed to produce them, and no waste or pollution is produced when they are used. The book *Cradle to Cradle* by Bill McDonough and Michael Braungart was a landmark in the green-business movement, describing a new way to manufacture and use products so that they are reused rather than thrown away. Eco-entrepreneurs who create businesses re-purposing material, following the cradle-to-cradle model, are building innovative businesses and a new way of doing business modeled after nature.

The ReProduct product line of C2C Holdings Inc. exemplifies how cradle to cradle works. ReProduct is designing and producing printed products on special plastic sheets to re-enter the industrial ecosystem in a new form after their initial use. One of the first products was holiday greeting cards that are sent in a two-way envelope. When the receiver of the card no longer wants it, they forward it to Shaw Carpets, where the plastic in the card and envelope is melted and used to create carpeting.

The plastic used is a thin, sleek sheet of oriented polypropylene (OPP) that is printed with nontoxic soy-based dyes. The material does not pose a health risk and has less of an environmental impact than paper. To be recycled, the material needs only to be melted, and it's ready to go. The idea need not be limited to holiday cards. ReProduct is working on other products, such as brochures or annual reports. If OPP printing or a similar process can be used internally for printing at large companies in the future, it might replace paper and allow in-house recycling for printing. Perhaps the actual print on products could be erased in an eco-friendly way, and then the material used again for more printing. OPP is better than recycled paper, too. Recycled paper is better than virgin pulp, but still goes through de-inking and bleaching processes.

Cradle to cradle is not limited to greeting cards; other manufacturers are moving toward the same model. Paper is not alone in our landfills, and it is not our worst problem. Electronic waste has become a major environmental problem. Computers and other electronics rapidly become obsolete, with few good options for what to do with them after their short lifespan. If dumped in a landfill they can leak lead, mercury, and other toxic components. Even when recycled, electronics often are shipped overseas to China or other locations where workers are exposed to high levels of toxic components.

To avoid this, forward-thinking computer companies are starting to design computers that can be returned at the end of their useful lifespan, disassembled, and have their parts reused in new products. This move is influenced by the purchasing power of informed customers, and by regulators who are requiring producers to take responsibility for the products. When producers are required to consider the lifecycle of their product companies become financially motivated to redesign products to reduce their environmental impact.

Several states in the United States have already passed laws requiring the producers of electronics to take responsibility for their products at the end of their useful lives, termed "extended producer responsibility." The federal government and other states are also considering legislation. (These processes already have been implemented in Europe, Canada, and Japan.) As these programs spread in the United States, there will be opportunities for entrepreneurs to help smaller manufacturers implement take-back programs.

Opportunities for giving products a second life include:

- ⊛ Finding new ways to use existing products so they do not enter the landfill
- ⊛ Creating new products that are designed to be reused or recycled more easily
- ⊛ Creating take-back programs where they do not yet exist (look to Europe and bring ideas to United States)

Look at everything around us—all the products we buy, use, and throw away—and think how they can be reused or designed differently to allow reuse more easily. Maybe digging through your garbage or taking a trip to your local landfill can provide inspiration for the next great entrepreneurial venture. Next time you throw something away, think first about what else could be done with it, cradle to cradle.

OPPORTUNITY 38

Depackaging Design

The Market Need	Product packaging uses resources, has an environmental cost, and adds little or nothing to products
The Mission	Reduce waste by designing products to reduce or eliminate packaging
Knowledge to Start	Design, packaging
Capital Required	$$ (setting up a package-reduction-design studio)
Timing to Start	Months
Special Challenges	Finding ways to package products just as well but with less material

Take a walk down any grocery store, and what do you see? Thousands of feet of shelving filled with bottles, plastic, cardboard, paper, and cellophane. Beverage bottles are recycled in part, but most of the rest is not, regardless of what the label says. Hopefully, the contents of the package will have some use before ending up in the landfill. The package itself? It is often waste from the moment it is made. One opportunity for entrepreneurs is to reduce this waste by designing products with less packaging.

ECO-EXAMPLE

One example of reduced packaging is the shift away from the plastic "jewel box" design for CDs.

Given the amount of packaging we use, the reduction possibilities seem vast. Some toys come with more packaging than product. If packages contain a lot of empty space, can they be smaller? More efficient packaging means using less packaging material, the packages can be shipped more efficiently, and less space is needed on store shelves. Wal-Mart has started measuring the packaging used by its 60,000 suppliers worldwide and plans to work with suppliers to reduce packaging. The company expects to prevent 667,000 tons of carbon dioxide from being released and keep millions of pounds of packaging out of landfills. Suppliers that fail to reduce packaging can lose shelf space and might not be able to compete effectively in the future, according to Amy Zettlemoyer, who is leading the sustainable packaging drive at Wal-Mart.

There are many strategies to reduce packaging waste. Smaller products need less packaging. If multiple layers of packaging are used, see if one layer will do. If double-wall cardboard was the norm, see if one wall will suffice. In addition to reduced packaging, some (including Wal-Mart) want to know where the package was made. Reducing the packaging might lose its environmental benefit if the package must travel thousands of miles before meeting its contents. All in all, the way to start is by removing packaging that you don't really need. And then maybe remove a little more?

Less packaging means greater efficiency, and that means there is money to be made in finding ways to reduce the amount of packaging we use. With Wal-Mart asking its suppliers to change, the suppliers, in turn, will be looking for people who can help them, and other producers will follow suit. There is an opportunity here to build a business around consulting and designing more efficient, less wasteful packaging.

Where to look for packaging inspiration and innovation? Many European nations and companies have initiatives already in place to reduce packaging waste. The practice of "sustainable packaging" is being taught in design schools such as The Art Institute of California, Los Angeles. Ecopackaging.net and *Package Design* magazine also provide information about ways to reduce packaging.

WINNING STRATEGY
Concentrated laundry detergent may not sound green, but it takes less energy to ship the detergent, less packaging, less space on store shelves, less energy for you to carry it home, less space in the recycling bin and truck, and so on.

RELATED TREND
In addition to reducing packaging, the environmental impact of packaging can be reduced by using bio-plastics. To make bio-plastics like those made from polylactic acid (PLA) truly biodegradable, we need more municipal and industrial composting. There is an opportunity to build composting facilities, perhaps with the support of government or companies such as Wal-Mart.

One ingenious solution is for packaging to be a product itself, so there isn't any waste. For example, Tom Ballhatchet designed a TV package that becomes a TV stand (check it out at Treehugger.com). Knoend in San Francisco, California, has designed the clever lite2go lamp with a wrapper that becomes the lampshade (see knoend.com). Bird Electron of Japan converts iPod plastic cases into speakers for the iPod. There probably isn't an end to the opportunities to eliminate packaging waste altogether with innovative designs such as these.

Opportunities in packaging include:

- Building take-back programs for packaging
- Working as a packaging designer
- Producing eco-friendly packaging closer to manufacturing sites
- Running composting facilities for bio-plastic packaging
- Selling bulk material without packaging

The less we spend on packaging, the more we can invest elsewhere, such as to build a better, cleaner, more sustainable world for our kids. Building a business around reduced packaging is a good example of where less really is better.

OPPORTUNITY 39

Reusing Building Material

The Market Need	Building materials become more expensive while we continue to throw mountains of demolition waste into landfills
The Mission	Reduce demolition waste by reusing salvaged building material
Knowledge to Start	Construction, salvage
Capital Required	$$ (small-scale salvage or to work on deconstruction)
Timing to Start	Months to years
Special Challenges	Salvage is not broadly accepted yet, but it is growing

Even while we consume precious resources producing new construction materials such as wood and cement, Americans throw away more than 100 million tons of building materials and demolition debris each year—as much as 33 percent of the material goes into landfills (US EPA, 2007). Much of the wood that is thrown away could be reused, as well as an amazing variety of other potentially useful materials such as plumbing fixtures, hot tubs, solid-wood doors, double-pane windows, stone countertops, carpets, and, yes, even the kitchen sink. Cashing in on salvageable construction material, entrepreneurs are building businesses that deconstruct homes and redirect the salvage material back into homes rather than the landfill.

The landfill is not the best place to get salvaged building material, which often is damaged by the time it gets there, reducing its value. In demolition, wood and other material is often smashed and thrown into a dumpster, preventing the material from being used again. Salvaged building material is best captured at homes during remodeling by carefully dismantling or deconstructing rather than demolishing components of a home. Although some have the preconception that salvaged material is always of lower quality, old wood can be of higher quality and a fraction of the cost.

Theory is one thing, practice is another. The scale of deconstruction and reuse of building material remains small today, but The ReUse People of America based in Oakland, California, are working to change that. The ReUse People have warehouses of reusable building materials available for purchase and have salvaged more than half a billion pounds of material that would have gone into landfills. About 80 percent of The ReUse People's deconstruction comes from residential homes, with the rest from commercial and industrial work. Getting their start with construction material donated after floods in Tijuana, Mexico, in the winter of 1992–1993, and

TOOLS OF THE TRADE

Deconstruction requires specialized tools, compared with demolition. For example, see the Extractor from Hartville Tool of Hartville, Ohio (hartvilletool.com).

ECO-TIP

With the right methods and enough care, granite countertops can be removed intact, complete with fixtures and sinks. A salvaged countertop is far less costly than the material for a new one.

they have grown and gone on to do high-profile projects, including the three major sets for the *Matrix Reloaded* and *Revolutions* movies as well as the "greening" of numerous Southern California estates for Hollywood notables.

Homeowners pay deconstruction contractors to take apart building materials that can be salvaged. The contractors are often trained in the proper salvage methods. The salvaged materials are then donated to The ReUse People, which sells the materials to the public. Because the materials are donated and The ReUse People is a 501(c)3 corporation, homeowners receive a tax deduction for the fair market value of the materials, which helps defray the cost of deconstruction and remodeling. The fair market value for deconstructed material is much higher than that of material from a demolished home.

According to Ted Reiff, founder of The ReUse People, the use of salvaged construction material has grown greatly. "Yes, there's no question about it," Reiff says, "and there are a lot of things driving it. Two factors are the rising cost of landfill fees and the rapid rise of the green building movement," Reiff says. By using care and taking material apart rather than smashing it up, as much as 80 percent of the material from a home can be salvaged in good, usable condition, according to Reiff. Boulder, Colorado, is requiring 65 percent of material from demolition jobs to be diverted from landfills, and other cities are pursuing a similar strategy, further encouraging the market for reuse of building materials.

With some education, The ReUse People hope to get the word out and increase the use of salvaged material. "It's a pioneering effort but getting easier," Reiff observes. "It's hard to pick up a paper without seeing something about green building," increasing awareness and acceptance of reuse. With continued change in how people view salvaged material, there is a big opportunity for it to develop in several different business models, such as for-profit retail outlets for salvaged materials, for deconstruction contractors, and for contractors specializing in construction with salvaged materials.

Wood and other materials also can be salvaged in other ways. Terramai of McCloud, California, is scouring the globe for salvageable tropical hardwood, often from old barns or South American railroad ties, to use for hardwood floors. Liberty Valley Doors of Cotati, California, is producing "rediscovered wood doors" entirely from high-quality wood that is better and richer than virgin wood in appearance and performance. Gorgeous countertops by companies such as Vetrazzo of Richmond, California, are made from recycled glass replacing natural but less sustainable stone countertops. Concrete made using fly-ash can replace Portland cement—a key ingredient in concrete—reducing greenhouse-gas emissions, saving energy, and resources.

Opportunities for material salvage include:

- Working as a deconstruction contractor
- Selling tools for deconstruction
- Selling salvaged construction material, including specializing in niches (hardware, windows, doors, lighting)
- Manufacturing construction products from recycled material

NONPROFIT ACTION

Organizations such as Habitat for Humanity ReStore take donated building material for resale, and there are more organizations doing resale all the time.

RELATED TRENDS

Some entrepreneurs have specialized in specific materials. For example, Omega Too in the San Fransico Bay Area focuses on reusing lighting fixtures.

ECO-ISSUE

One of the factors in material salvage is that the deconstruction team usually is paid upon completion of their work, while the financial benefit for homeowners comes later, at tax time. This drives the business toward homeowners who can afford the initial outlay for deconstruction and to wait to get their money back. Including the cost of deconstruction in construction loans, or financing the deconstruction cost, will open the market to more homeowners. ❧

So far, the percentage of construction material being salvaged remains small, so the opportunity for salvage to grow is huge. The more expensive new construction materials become, the greater the demand for cheaper alternatives, such as salvaged materials. As the demand for green homes grows, so does the market for green materials going into them; salvaged materials have a big head start to be a solid green option. Changing our throwaway mentality will help to fully realize business opportunities like these.

OPPORTUNITY 40

Green Shopping Bags

The Market Need	Billions of plastic shopping bags are thrown away each year
The Mission	Replace disposable plastic shopping bags with renewable, reusable bags
Knowledge to Start	Materials, manufacturing
Capital Required	$ (for homemade bags)
Timing to Start	Weeks to months
Special Challenges	Finding a niche among competition

Between 500 billion and 1 trillion plastic grocery bags are thrown away each year, and Americans alone dump 100 billion of these (reusablebags.com). Plastic grocery bags are cheap, convenient, and a real pain in the ecosystem. Bags made from petroleum-based plastics pollute when they are made, and keep polluting after they are used and discarded. Although they can be recycled, only between 1 and 3 percent of bags actually go that route with most of the rest ending up loose in the environment or in landfills. Consumers and governments are driving a rapidly growing movement away from disposable plastic bags to more eco-friendly alternatives.

The worldwide movement to get rid of plastic shopping bags includes countries such as Ireland (which is taxing bags) and Bangladesh (which is moving to ban them). Many stores in Europe are discouraging the use of plastic bags by charging for them or paying customers who bring their own, and in 2007, San Francisco, California, became the first city in the United States to do so in grocery stores and pharmacies. As towns and countries around the globe follow suit, they are driving businesses and consumers to look for alternatives, ensuring the continued growth of the market.

One solution is bags produced from a renewable resource, such as corn. The sugars in corn can be chemically modified and polymerized to form a bioplastic (see Opportunity 32). BioBags made from a corn-based material called Mater-Bi already are sold by BIO Group USA of Palm Harbor, Florida (biobagusa.com). Their bags are biodegradable (compostable), use corn from plants that are not genetically modified, and don't use any petroleum-based products.

Is this the solution for shopping bags? The answer depends on whom you talk to. Critics say these bags are not truly biodegradable and will fill up landfills just like the old bags. This is true of just about anything in a landfill, though. Landfills, filled with airless compacted material, make decomposition of most materials very slow. To truly break down, BioBags and other similar materials need to be composted in a large-scale composting system, something that still is fairly unusual but growing more common. For cities establishing municipal composting, such as San Francisco, bags like these are probably a good solution.

Reusable bags that don't get thrown away probably are the greenest option for shopping bags. If you already own a store, selling bags with your logo on the side might be a savvy green business move, and giving them away might even pay off. With that bag, you buy increased brand recognition for your company, you associate your brand with being green,

GREEN MARKETS

Selling bags at a farmers' market is one way to reach receptive customers. Bag-sellers also should work with stores to place bags at the checkout counter. You may generate impluse sales by having the bag right there for well-intentioned folks who forgot to bring their own.

INFORMATION RESOURCE

For more information about reusable shopping bags and alternatives to disposable plastic bags, see reusablebags.com.

and you may create increased loyalty. A great variety of bags are being produced, and the nice thing about the market is that there always seems to be room for more. Bags vary in what they are made of (canvas, cotton, reused plastic, hemp, biodegradable plastic like Biobags), their shape, their appearance, as well as the market they are targeting.

One problem I have with reusable bags is that I forget them. In the rush to go to the store, I often leave the bag at home or in the car, despite my best intentions. Andy Keller founded ChicoBags of Chico, California, to solve this problem. ChicoBags are disposable bags that fold into a small easy-to-carry package. If you stick one in your pocket or purse, you can't forget it. They score points for addressing one of the big problems with reusable bags.

At first, people might worry about how they look carrying their own bags. Cool designer bags will help overcome this concern. One of the neat things about bags is that they are so simple and yet people are endlessly creative with them. The opportunity is to create not just bags, but green fashion statements. Some bags even are made from recycled material, for an extra boost of greenness. Maybe that's another use for old T-shirts. What if, from the start, green grocery bags were made to be returned in some other form, a cradle-to-cradle shopping bag?

Opportunities for green shopping bags include:

- Producing low-cost compostable shopping bags
- Creating reusable logo bags for stores to give away
- Designing novel bags for shopping
- Developing fold-up bags that are easy to take with you
- Producing homemade bags from recycled material

Like many fields, the limitation might not be the products but our habits. However, good products can help to change our habits, and the growing number of people giving these bags a try is creating a rich and diverse market for reusable bags.

OPPORTUNITY 41

Recycled Furniture

The Market Need	Most furniture today is disposable, used and then tossed
The Mission	Build furniture that wastes less
Knowledge to Start	Design, furniture, retail
Capital Required	$$
Timing to Start	Months
Special Challenges	Building sales can take time

In the drive to go green, some aspects of our lives have received more attention than others. The buildings we live and work in, and renewable energy
are getting a lot of press, but the chair you are sitting on has received less.
The furniture in our homes, businesses, and offices is an important part of
the developing green economy, and building and selling furniture that
wastes less is the right thing for the planet and a good green business.

Furniture once was an investment, finely crafted to be used by future
generations. That is not the case for much of our furniture these days. Furniture is often purchased as yet another disposable commodity, offered for
a quick buy at a low price. What happens to these items at the end of their
lifespan? When the fabric is worn, the upholstery torn, or
the table develops a wobble, the next stop is the garage sale
or the landfill. Important ways to green our furniture are to
build pieces that last, and when they show some wear, to
repair and refurbish them.

Designers are making eco-friendly furniture with sustainably produced and recycled material, often including
materials that would otherwise end up in landfills. The
materials used are not those you necessarily may think of
for furniture and can be surprising. The Peter Danko design

VARIATION ON A BIZ-THEME
Maybe the old-fashioned skill of
reupholstering old sofas is a green
trade? Better, of course, if sofas are
reupholstered with green material.
Being a green upholsterer is one
variation on this entrepreneurial
theme.

studio in Virginia works with ply-bent wood, which uses only about 15 percent as much wood as solid-wood furniture. In addition, the studio uses recycled padding and seating, such as durable and easy-to-clean seat-belt material originally produced for cars. His mission is not just to build greener furniture, but "to transform the public's concept of what furniture can be"—a high calling.

If you are artistic, designing green furniture holds great potential. Materials to work with are all around us: recycled glass can be fashioned into tabletops, old plastics into new chairs. When you work with recycled material, everything is turned on its head. Where one person sees garbage, you see a chair or table. Reclaimed wood can have a new life in furniture. Acronym Designs in Kansas City, Missouri (acronymdesigns.com), uses recycled or reclaimed wood in much of its furniture, including twice-reclaimed wood cutoff from reclaimed flooring, which otherwise would go into the landfill. Other wood used is from sustainably grown sources. Using green materials that reduce the environmental impact of furniture is an important part of how Acronym works, but the company is thinking much more broadly than just materials. Also considered are how laborers are treated, the health effects of any volatile organics, and the lifetime of products. Making well-built products that last a long time and don't end up in landfills goes a long way toward minimizing the environmental impact of what we buy.

Another opportunity is for furniture that is designed to be recycled. Designs that last a long time are preferable, but if they don't last, they at least should be recycled easily. Cardboard is a flexible design material that Cardboarddesigns of New York, is using to build furniture, toys, and other objects from recycled material. It may not last forever, but when it's done, it can be recycled again, creating a closed loop.

Mixed materials are harder to recycle, so chairs made of pure aluminum, such as Mirandolina from Pietro Arosio in

Italy, are more easily recycled than chairs made with aluminium and other materials mixed.

In addition to designing and producing green furniture, selling it is another option. Josh Dorfman is the founder and CEO of Vivavi of Brooklyn, New York, including its website and eco-friendly furniture store in Manhattan. Like the work by Peter Danko and Acronym Designs, Dorfman doesn't feature rough-hewn and raw products, but cool and modern furniture that just happens to be made from eco-friendly and recycled materials. With his radio show *The Lazy Environmentalist* and a book by the same name, Dorfman works to teach about the green shift in our furniture and other aspects of our lives. "These innovators make it easy for us to integrate environmental awareness into our lives," he writes in his book. "They understand that while so many of us are concerned about the environment, we don't always have the time, energy, or inclination to do something about it."

Opportunities for green furniture include:

- Selling used furniture online
- Running a green furniture store
- Designing green furniture
- Refurbishing/reupholstering green furniture

It seems a good bet that the green homes of the future will still contain furniture, and the greener homes get, the greener their furniture will be. Filling this need helps us all live on our planet lightly and well.

ECO-TIP

Look out: Everything that is recycled is not necessarily green. Know what you are working with and avoid toxic material that might affect the health of workers or customers. Using unhealthy or toxic material in furniture is not at all green, recycled or not.

INDUSTRY INFO

For more about cardboard furniture, visit cardboarddesign.com.

Providing Green Food

In the developed world, our food has become increasingly processed and removed from its origins, and cut loose from its cultural moorings. This is not a good thing. The United States continues setting records for obesity and diabetes, and as the American lifestyle spreads, so do American dietary patterns, and the resultant health problems. As awareness of this epidemic increases, so does the opportunity for change. We are

what we eat in many ways, and many opportunities for entrepreneurs are related to the need for better food for improved health.

Our food almost always affects the environment as well as our health. How we produce food has changed radically in the last 100 years, with farms becoming progressively larger, more industrialized, more reliant on chemical pesticides and fertilizer, and ever-more removed from natural systems. Farm chemicals filter through ecosystems, water supplies, and our food, causing problems at many levels. Conventional agriculture and the food distribution system are heavily dependent on fossil fuels, and contribute to pollution and climate change. Farmers and entrepreneurs working at every stage of the supply chain now are working to change how food is grown and delivered to reduce its environmental impact.

The greening of our food supply is confirmed by the rapid growth in sales of organic foods. According to the U.S. Department of Agriculture (USDA), the acreage in the United States growing organic food increased 40 percent from 2000 to 2005, and sales of organic food have grown between 15 and 21 percent a year (much of the organic food is imported). The growth in organics, and the willingness of people to pay more for organic foods, indicates that consumers are concerned about how their food is affecting their bodies and our planet. These consumers are showing their concern with their money.

Some conventionally grown produce has been demonstrated to contain significant residues of chemical pesticides and other chemicals that consumers wouldn't know about on their own, leaving them to mistrust inspectors and regulators to ensure the food is safe. Meanwhile, the FDA has funds to inspect only a tiny portion of food and is hard-pressed to find hazards before they reach the market. The only way to be sure about what you are eating is to test your own food. With the anxiety many consumers feel about food, there is a market for test kits, allowing people to take more control over what they eat (Opportunity 43).

The increasingly common use of genetically modified organisms (GMOs) in agriculture has been another major controversy. Researchers are finding new ways to identify strains of plants with traits such as improved productivity, pest resistance, drought tolerance, and taste. A method called marker assisted selection (MAS) can produce new strains of plants without using recombinant techniques for genetic modification (Opportunity 46). Using modern means to sort through plants and select traits makes the process more efficient than traditional selective-breeding programs. Such plants still could qualify as organic, while allowing for more efficient introduction of crops and foods with new traits and varieties.

Another issue with modern agriculture is the ever-decreasing variety of crops being produced. Once a strain of a crop with the desired characteristics is identified, it spreads across more acreage, crowding out other varieties. As sterile plants that are reproduced vegetatively, bananas are one of the prime examples. Virtually all the bananas eaten in Europe and North America come from a single strain of banana plant. The danger in this lack of diversity is that when something goes wrong such as the emergence of a fungus that attacks that strain—then the world is at risk of losing bananas—*all* bananas. The lack of diversity also reduces the variety of the food we eat. More and more people are seeking out and maintaining heritage crops as a genetic resource for the future and a rich addition to our food today (Opportunity 48).

As one of the largest of human endeavors, agriculture also contributes to climate change. Food travels around the world—grapes, for example, are shipped from Chile to New York in winter. While having year-round fruit is great in many ways, shipping food such a long distance requires petroleum and contributes to climate change. Locally grown produce, in season, almost always will be of higher quality than produce picked halfway around the world (Opportunity 44). But how do you know where your food comes from? Businesses are doing more to label the source of food as well as how it is treated, and tracking the carbon footprint of groceries is a developing trend (Opportunity 47).

Eating a vegetarian diet was once thought unusual in the United States, but is now increasingly common. Vegetarian food may have a reputation as a pale imitation of meat with limited variety, but today's vegetarians can enjoy a rich palate of flavors. Finding ways to integrate vegetarian fare into our modern lifestyle through veggie fast food provides a healthy and climate-friendly solution (Opportunity 49).

Finally, there is the inside perspective on our health. We are more than individuals; we each host a rich and diverse community of microbes in our gastrointestinal tract that is an integral part of digestion and health. How these microbes affect us is poorly understood, but studies have shown that having the right kind of microbes in the gut can support good health. Probiotics are foods that contain good microbes, helping them set up shop in the body and keep out the bad ones (Opportunity 45). Increasingly popular, there is an opportunity to provide probiotic foods in a variety of formats.

Food may be part of our problems, but it also is part of the solution. We can eat our way out of our problems just as we have eaten our way into them.

OPPORTUNITY 42

Eco-Friendly and Healthy Fast Food

The Market Need	Meat-free, fast-food alternatives to burgers and chicken
The Mission	Provide healthy, tasty, vegetarian fast food
Knowledge to Start	Entrepreneurial drive (i.e., a new concept) or willingness to follow franchise systems
Capital Required	$$$
Timing to Start	Years for creating a new concept and months for franchising
Special Challenges	Franchising takes money (estimated at between $250,000 and $500,000), and developing your own products takes even more time and money

Vegetarians were exotic creatures in the United States a few decades ago, but they're a lot more common today. There are an estimated 4.7 million vegetarians in the United States who avoid all animal products, and millions more who eat eggs and dairy but still avoid meat (Vegetarian Research Group of Baltimore, Maryland, vrg.org). A 2000 survey found that 25 percent of Americans try to avoid eating meat at least some of the time. Periodic meat recalls due to potential contamination will increase the market for meat-free alternatives. As the number of people eating a vegetarian diet has grown, so have sales of vegetarian foods, consistently outpacing growth of other food categories. People eat vegetarian food as a matter of religion, ethical concern for the treatment of animals, for health reasons, or even to fight climate change. Whatever the motivation, the rising sales of vegetarian food spell opportunity for those who can provide healthy and appealing meat-free food that fits the American lifestyle.

Meat-free food is far friendlier to our planet than the normal American meat-rich diet, and requires much less land to sustain people. Raising meat contributes more to climate change than does raising vegetable crops, particularly if the meat is raised on corn rather than pasture. According to one U.N. study, "Livestock's Long Shadow: Environmental Issues and Options," (FAO, 2006), raising meat generates 18 percent of global greenhouse gases, greater than the contribution of cars, trucks, and airplanes combined (14 percent). With a little marketing and food that tastes good, the climate benefits will be the icing on the cake.

A growing number of restaurants have gone vegetarian or feature at least some vegetarian offerings, particularly in urban centers such as New York City, Los Angeles, or San Francisco. One example is the Zen Palate in New York, owned by James Tu's company, HOV Group Inc. This and other restaurants show that vegetarian food can be prepared with great variety and wonderful taste.

Don't expect most Americans to drop their fast food ways to go vegetarian, though. For a broader market, sales of vegetarian food are most likely to be successful if people can build this choice into their existing lifestyle. In the land

ECO-ISSUE

In early 2008, 143 million pounds of meat were recalled, the largest meat recall in U.S. history, due to concerns about how cattle were handled at a meat-packing facility (*Washington Post*, February 18, 2008). That's no small potatoes.

GREEN LEADER

For more info about Zen Burger, see
zenburger.com.

of fast-food burgers and chicken, the choices for a meat-free, fast-food bite are often slim to none. Close examination of the ingredients suggests that even fries and salad may contain animal-based products. (These often are not too healthy anyway; look out for the calories and fat in that salad dressing.)

There is nothing to stop vegetarian food from being prepared and served in a to-go setting in an appealing and healthy manner. Indeed, the lower fat content of vegetarian fare may provide an answer for those in search of easy, healthy diet options. Tu is expanding from Zen Palate to create meat-free, fast food with Zen Burger, betting that the time is right for healthier fast food that is also good for the planet. The first Zen Burger opened in Manhattan in late 2007, with a design modeled after McDonald's, using upbeat, bright colors. The food is all Tu's own and all plant-based, featuring items such as vegeburgers, a meat-free ZenChicken sandwich, and a kid's meal with a toy. Foods are free of antibiotics, hormones, and artificial flavors, low in fats, and high in anti-oxidants. Even the coffee is organic and fair trade. That is green fast food.

"Business has been very good since the day we opened our doors," says Chad Carpenter, director of corporate communications for the HOV Group Inc. (which manages Zen Palate and Zen Burger). "We've had lines going out the door. I think it's a good indicator that people are ready to make healthier choices in their lives as long as they don't have to sacrifice taste, convenience, or price." By imitating the food and surroundings of other chains, but with healthier, meat-free food, Zen Burger provides a sense of familiarity for customers. "We're not reinventing the wheel" when it comes to fast food, Carpenter says. Others have perfected how to run a fast-food restaurant. Zen Burger is just taking what they have learned and using it to provide a healthier alternative.

One key to success is that the market for Zen Burger is not just vegetarians. With "ZenMeats," the company is targeting a

ECO-TIP

Zen Burger is also greening its locations by using biodegradable or compostable containers, recycled building materials, and energy-efficient lighting.

broader audience likes the taste and texture of meat, but doesn't want the associated health and environmental problems. So far the strategy seems to be paying off. With the overwhelming reception of their first restaurant in Manhattan, Zen Burger is working on its next location in Hollywood, California. From there, the company envisions at least 1,500 outlets in a decade and is working on a franchise program that aims to start in 2008.

Food can be eco-friendly in other formats as well. Vaughan Lazar and Michael Gordon have developed Pizza Fusion of Fort Lauderdale, Florida, as an organic, green, pizza restaurant. In addition to pizzas, the menu features sandwiches, salads, and other food from organic components. Lozar and Gordon are making the whole operation as green as possible to build a solid green brand from the start, according to their motto "Saving the Earth, One Pizza at a Time." It's not just the food either. Their buildings are certified by Leadership in Energy and Environmental Design (LEED), their delivery vehicles are hybrids, their power is wind, their utensils are bio-plastic, and their countertops are made from recycled materials. Things are going so well that Lazar and Gordon are selling franchises.

GREEN LEADER
For more about the food, practices, and franchise opportunities with Pizza Fusion, visit pizzafusion.com.

Opportunities in green fast food include:

- Buying a franchise of a restaurant like Pizza Fusion or Zen Burger
- Developing your own concept and food for an organic, vegetarian, or otherwise green restaurant
- Selling recyclable, or compostable plates, spoons, and cups to green fast-food restaurants

If the global-warming diet catches on, it's one fad that might not be half bad. Look for a "Global Warming Restaurant" coming soon near you, and no doubt someone has a global-warming diet book in the works (publishers, call me).

OPPORTUNITY 43

Home Food-Safety Testing Kits

The Market Need	People often are nervous about what is in their food
The Mission	Provide simple, low-cost kits for at-home use to test for bacteria and chemical residues
Knowledge to Start	Chemistry, toxicology
Capital Required	$$$ (develop new kits)
Timing to Start	Years
Special Challenges	Research costs money, but kits must be cheap

Food is one of the great pleasures in life, but with our food traveling farther to reach us and its origin often unclear, it is also a source of anxiety. A 2007 survey by the Food Marketing Institute found that American trust in food had fallen sharply, dropping from 82 to 66 percent from the year before. Consumers are worried about potential contaminants, such as bacteria or pesticides, and their fears have been stoked by highly publicized incidents such as contamination of spinach by *E. coli* in 2006, which hospitalized at least 102 people. This anxiety creates the opportunity to dispel fear with knowledge, arming consumers with the power to see for themselves what is in the food they are eating.

ECO-ISSUE

Don't assume because food is local that it's also organic or pesticide-free. Fruits and vegetables at that little roadside stand may have as much pesticide as produce found anywhere else.

While we may not all feel we are in imminent danger from our food, those who are concerned should have the ability to determine what is in the food they are eating. Food knowledge is food power. The level of concern about pesticides and other agents may be represented by the growth of organic foods. Food-safety testing generally has been performed by large, centralized government facilities, but with declining food testing and declining consumer trust, there is a market for kits allowing people to test food themselves.

Processed food can seem like a real mystery. Even though the components are listed on the label, they often mean little or nothing to most of us. (Hydrogenated oils? What does hydrogenated mean?) But the concern is not limited to processed food. Even if you stick with fruits, vegetables, and meats, it's hard to be sure what other components might be hiding in our food. Modern conventional agriculture exposes plants to a variety of chemicals—including pesticides, herbicides, fungicides, fumigants, preservatives, and fertilizers—and animal husbandry often uses antibiotics and hormones. It's often not clear how these chemicals affect us, but many scientists suspect that even minute quantities might produce unexpected health problems, particularly when the chemicals are combined, accumulate for a long time, or are ingested by pregnant mothers, nursing mothers, or young children. Toxicology testing of compounds found in food can reveal the chemicals with serious short-term risks, but it is more difficult to identify any subtler health issues that compounds might cause.

In theory, contamination of food by pathogenic bacteria or dangerous pesticides would be prevented by our food-safety-testing system, but in practice this system does not always work. The FDA has seen its resources for food inspections decline, with an 81 percent drop in inspections from 1972 to 2006 (according to Representative Henry Waxman's 2006 fact sheet on the FDA, "Weaknesses in FDAs Food Safety System"), and reports have repeatedly warned that the FDA does not test enough food to provide sufficient protection (*New York Times*, November 26, 2007). Food from overseas is tested by non-FDA labs for entry into the United States, and it has been reported that if test results are not favorable importers will have their produce checked elsewhere to get the desired results. Produce with higher-than-allowed levels of pesticides, or with residues of banned pesticides, has moved on to markets anyway. Even organic produce is not necessarily totally devoid of chemicals. While organic produce should not be exposed to synthetic compounds while it is grown, tests reported by Consumers

ECO-ISSUE

In one broadly publicized incident, pesticides were detected in sodas sold in India. Well water in many areas of India is contaminated with agricultural residues and is used in the preparation of bottled drinks.

RELATED TREND

In addition to looking for chemical contaminants and bacteria, home food-safety testing kits are made to examine food for substances such as caffeine or food allergens.

Union in 2002 found low levels of pesticides in some organic produce suggesting that the chemicals entered by drift from other fields, through residues in soil or water, or perhaps even through error or fraud. Organic foods also may contain other agents, such as bacteria.

The technology for detecting many substances in food and water already exists. The ideal kit would be relatively foolproof, simple to use, and would not require experience to operate. A model is home pregnancy tests, where the strip only needs to touch a substance and its rapid color change provides the answer. One contaminant that existing test kits look for is lead: When a material is swabbed, the test kit produces a quick pink color change if lead is detected. In 2007, *Consumer Reports* examined five different lead-testing kits and found that three worked well while two others either lacked sensitivity or produced false positives (producing a positive response when no lead was present). Kits should also be able to reliably and sensitively test for salmonella, E. coli, mercury, arsenic, antibiotics, or hormones.

One type of kit for pesticide detection is the Agri-Screen Ticket sold by Neogen of Lansing, Michigan (neogen.com). Designed to detect insecticides like Malathion, the kit can detect residues in a wide variety of backgrounds, including water, food, drinks, or soil. Hybrivet Systems in Massachusetts provides test kits with swabs that quickly change color in the presence of metals such as lead, mercury, arsenic, and chromate. Simple kits for other pesticides, metals, and residues already are available, if not widely used for a variety of reasons, leaving room for other entrepreneurs.

INFORMATION RESOURCE

For technologies that might be available to license for kit development, start cruising the U.S. Patent Office website, Google Scholar, and tech-transfer offices at universities.

One factor limiting use of these kits is their cost. Some cost in the range of $2 per test, making it expensive to test every food item. Testing water or other environmental issues is more common, especially where people rely on well water. Reusable or cheaper test kits would help them be more broadly adopted.

GREEN MARKETS

Another market for kits might be grocery stores, farmers' markets, and other food suppliers. Food retailers could alleviate consumer anxiety by doing their own testing for food contaminants and making the results available. If markets don't want to do the test, a business could sell the testing to markets as a service. ❦

In addition to selling kits, eco-entrepreneurs need to help people interpret the results. If they get a positive result, how much of a risk is involved? While providing some guidance, be careful not to run afoul of any legal issues and be sure to include the necessary disclaimers.

Testing for bacterial contamination in food generally has been more difficult than testing for lead or pesticides. Tests often have taken hours or days, and required shipping samples to a large, centralized processing facility. In response, kits for faster detection of harmful bacteria, such as dangerous strains of *E. coli*, have been developed and are being commercialized. New Horizons Diagnostics of Columbia, Maryland, has developed an *E. coli* test kit that works in 20 seconds. Invitrogen Corp. of San Diego, California, is supplying rapid E. coli test kits to ensure food safety at the Beijing 2008 Olympics. These testing systems are rapid, but still not designed for easy use at home, leaving room for further development.

Opportunities in food-testing include:

- Developing new food and water-test kits
- Developing cheaper and faster ways to detect food-born bacteria
- Finding ways to produce kits with lower costs
- Providing food testing as a service

VARIATIONS ON A BIZ-THEME

Some people are concerned about the presence of genetically modified organisms (GMOs) in their food supply. There isn't any evidence of a health risk from these generally, and the United States doesn't require labeling when GMOs are present. Providing test kits for GMOs would help people feel more secure about their food.

In the end, we live with chemicals in our lives and sometimes in our food. A small level of exposure to some chemicals probably is not going to hurt us greatly, but having a lot of chemicals in our food seems best to avoid. It's not always clear what the risks are, but many people feel that they are better off safe than sorry. Giving people the power to see for themselves what is in the food they eat might help keep those in the supply chain a little more on their toes and ease consumer anxiety.

OPPORTUNITY 44

Local Food

The Market Need	It is often cheaper and healthier to consume local, in-season produce
The Mission	Grow, distribute, market and sell local produce
Knowledge to Start	Farming, distribution
Capital Required	$$
Timing to Start	Months to years
Special Challenges	Competing with industrialized organic food

The food in your local grocery store often has traveled a long way to get there. Produce is transported across the country and around the globe, traveling between 1,500 and 2,500 miles on average in the United States to your dinner table (*Worldwatch Paper 163*, Worldwatch Institute, 2002)—sometimes much farther. The types of food grown are often selected as much for their durability in transportation as for their nutritional value or taste. To withstand the journey, produce is often picked before it is ripe and then ripened at its destination using artificial means, such as gassing with the plant hormone ethylene. The result can be food that's not the best tasting or the most nutritious and transporting of foods such long distances burns fossil fuels that contribute to climate change. Providing local-food solutions is a green business answer that hits home.

Buying local produce has rapidly developed into a major trend. There is even a word for it—"locavore," selected by the staff at the *New Oxford American Dictionary* as the 2007 word of the year. Now it's not enough to consider *how* food is grown, you also need to think about *where* it is grown. For some, this means drawing a 100-mile circle around their home on a map and buying only produce that has traveled within that region.

The growth in farmers' markets is one sign of this trend. According to the FDA, the number of farmers' markets has grown from 1,755 in 1994 to 4,385 in 2006. The food at farmers' markets reflects the changing seasons, is quite varied compared with larger grocery stores, and provides a social opportunity—consumers interact with each other and with the vendors. The food is not processed and is picked ripe. For the vendors, farmers' markets present an opportunity to collect a premium for their produce, cutting out the middlemen.

The local-food trend is spreading to schools, corporate cafeterias, and restaurants specializing in local food. School lunches have degraded in past decades into reheated, processed, plastic-wrapped food, but with a wave of obesity and diabetes threatening our kids, some schools are responding. In some parts of the country, providing local food may be a challenge, but it's also an opportunity for institutions to creatively use what is available in

INFORMATION RESOURCE

Chef Ann Cooper has written a book about bringing healthy, fresh, and local food into school lunches: *Lunch Lessons: Changing the Way We Feed Our Kids.* Given the importance of good nutrition for kids, and how bad some school lunches are, this trend is likely to grow. Other green books about local food include *Plenty* by Aliza Smith and J.B. Mackinnon and *Animal, Vegetable, Miracle* by Barbara Kingsolver.

their local economy. The increased focus on nutrition in schools and other institutions also supports the use of fresh produce and less processed food. Some groups even are requiring the increased use of fresh produce in meals. Involving larger users and suppliers of local food will help it to progress further.

Distribution is another entrepreneurial opportunity for local food. The traditional distribution system is not designed to handle local produce, even where it is readily available. Large, centralized facilities receive and deliver food all over the country, leaving locale out of the equation. Even if you have apples growing next door, you will find apples from thousands of miles away in your grocery store because that is how the system is designed. For the industrial food system local food is a nuisance, leaving smaller-scale entrepreneurs to pick up food from local growers and deliver it to restaurants, markets, and other institutions. With small-scale, local food distribution, the trip from farm to market can be measured in hours rather than days, resulting in higher quality. When necessary, farmers in some areas are forming co-ops to manage distribution together.

Organic produce was at one time synonymous with local food, grown by small farmers, but as such food has grown in popularity, it has scaled up, has become industrialized, and resembles in some ways the non-organic food system the original movement had sought to break away from. In his book *The Omnivore's Dilemma*, Michael Pollan writes of the tension between the growth of organic food and its transition away from local food into big

---

RELATED GREEN TREND

In what is called community-supported agriculture (CSA), local growers sell a share of their harvest to supporters in the region. Farmers get a guaranteed good price for their produce, and consumers get local, fresh, in-season produce to pick up or get delivered to their door. In 2005, there were more than 1,500 share farms in the United States and Canada. ❧

business. Pollan and the founder of Whole Foods Market of Austin, Texas, John Mackey, have engaged in a public dialogue about the value of organic and local food. The bigger the organic-food industry gets and the more it industrializes, the more it creates opportunities for local-food suppliers, distributors, and retailers to branch off and differentiate themselves.

> **INFORMATION RESOURCE**
> To find local food resources where you live, check out Local Harvest at localharvest.org, or localfood companies.com.

Opportunities for local-food businesses include:

- Growing local food
- Distributing local food
- Marketing local food
- Specializing in local food at a restaurant
- Providing a local-food cafeteria service

The motivations of the local-food movement are varied. If customers are seeking local food because they are concerned about food quality and unsure if industrially produced organic food is what they are really looking for, the key to success is differentiation from industrialized organic food. If people turn to local food to connect with others at the farmers' market, then the key might be providing a social atmosphere and not worrying too much about the carbon footprint. If people are seeking local food to recover a unique sense of place, then markets should emphasize their local and unique qualities. If people turn to local food to fight climate change, then providers of local food might want to verify that their efforts reduce environmental impact, for example, driving a hybrid rather than a rusty pickup truck. If all these are true for you, then do all the above.

OPPORTUNITY 45

Probiotics

The Market Need	Our health is linked to microbes in our bodies, and some-times our microbes are out of whack
The Mission	Promote health by selling products with healthy microbes
Knowledge to Start	Food science, supplements, microbiology, medicine
Capital Required	$$$ to $$$$
Timing to Start	Years
Special Challenges	Verifying quality and health benefits for high-value products

We are not alone. As we go about our daily business we carry in our gut a whole community of microscopic living organisms. While some might view this with distaste, our microbial companions generally are our friends. Too often we view ourselves as being at war with the world of microbes and have to be reminded that not all microbes are bad. While you can't trust every microbe you meet, and some deliver downright unpleasant surprises, many make essential contributions to health. The more friends you have living in your gut, the less room there is for the unfriendly microbes to move in. Probiotic products help people live healthier lives by working with the good microbes and not just warring against the bad ones.

Probiotics are foods or other preparations containing beneficial microbes, such as specific types of bacteria or yeast. Lactic acid bacteria (LABs), such as those in yogurt, are common in probiotics. Probiotics have encountered skepticism from some, but an accumulating body of medical evidence, including efficacy in carefully designed clinical trials, shows probiotics can produce real health benefits (for a summary of research results with probiotics, see information at the website of The National Center for Complimentary and Alternative Medicine, part of NIH, nccam.nih.gov). Not every health product can say as much. Researchers also are looking at the potential of specific microbes to address a wide range of conditions including:

- Inflammatory bowel disease
- Irritable bowel syndrome (IBS)
- Skin conditions, such as acne or eczema
- Vaginal or urinary tract infections
- Diarrhea, particularly when associated with antibiotic treatment
- Respiratory infections

The most commonly recommended use of probiotics is to undo the damage done to friendly microbes by antibiotics. Antibiotics can be life-saving at the right time and place, but they also clear away friendly microbes and make way for bad ones, leading to other problems, such as diarrhea. Sometimes the cure is worse than the problem. One way or another, something is going to live in your gut, and you had better make sure you know what it is.

The probiotic trend is growing rapidly, as people try to use the food they eat to improve their health. Where there used to be a handful of probiotic products, now there are hundreds. Products containing probiotics include yogurts, kefir, nutrition bars, and even cheese and chocolate. U.S. sales of Activia yogurt from Group Danone (already on the market in Europe for some time) were expected to exceed $300 million in 2007 (*BusinessWeek*, November 26, 2007). A 2008 report by Global Industry Analysts Inc. estimated the European market at $5.7 billion in 2007, and sales of probiotics are rapidly growing in the United States as well.

Creating products that contain potentially beneficial bacteria is not enough to produce probiotic products that work. The strain of bacteria is important, and the number of viable bacteria present after transportation and storage are also important factors affecting how well a probiotic product works. If the bacteria do not survive until consumption, they cannot produce any health benefits. Experts

THE BIG PICTURE

Probiotics are part of a larger trend called "functional foods," which include foods that we eat and drink hoping for health benefits, such as drinks containing ginseng or other herbal components.

RELATED TREND

Another way of influencing your intestinal microbes may be through the food you eat. One culprit in digestive diseases might be a diet that encourages the growth of unhealthy microbes. Foods that encourage the growth of good microbes are considered "prebiotics."

have counseled producers to create better labeling for probiotic products, allowing consumers to know the specific strain of microbes in the food and how many of them are present in order to use probiotics effectively.

In the rush to get probiotic products onto the market, there is a need and an opportunity for new products that really work and can prove their results. Failure of probiotics to do this may come to haunt the whole field. According to Bob Goldin, an executive vice president with food-industry consulting firm Technomic, probiotics sell only if they taste good and consumers believe they are credible (*New York Times*, January 22, 2007). Although eager to sell probiotic foods, producers need to avoid unsubstantiated health claims and continue working with researchers to verify the product's benefits. European Union regulations requiring specific wording about health claims may help to differentiate and provide higher value for European products that can meet this standard.

Regulations vary, but if microbes are taken as a nutritional supplement in the United States, they will be regulated differently than drugs and be subject to less stringent testing. Be careful of making specific drug-like health claims. Dr. Gary Elmer, one of the authors of *The Power of Probiotics: Improving Your Health With Beneficial Microbes,* says "Probiotics are regulated in the United States as dietary supplements so that all of the issues of quality control and unsubstantiated claims facing the supplement industry hold true for probiotics. There are good manufacturers and not so good. There are a few that have supported clinical trials while most imply that their probiotic works based on trials using other products." The best long-term approach for probiotic producers is to develop high-quality products, to substantiate their health benefits, and to communicate good information to consumers.

Opportunities in probiotics include:

⊛ Producing high-value probiotic products with demonstrated health benefits

- Helping others substantiate health claims for probiotic products
- Developing and selling probiotic products that encourage healthy microbes

ECO-ISSUE

Dannon was sued in early 2008, accused of changing a premium for their probiotics based on unsubstantiated health claims. How this plays out remains to be seen.

Dr. Gary Huffnagle at the University of Michigan is a probiotics expert, and in his book *The Probiotics Revolution*, he points out that probiotics are not some Johnny-come-lately fad. People around the world have produced cultured food for thousands of years, perhaps producing health benefits with everything from kimchi to sauerkraut. It's possible today's probiotics are just a return to an understanding of information we have known all along.

OPPORTUNITY 46

New, Improved Plant Breeding

The Market Need	Agriculture needs diverse crops with a variety of properties, but genetically modified organisms (GMOs) are not always welcome
The Mission	Produce non-GMO plants with the desired traits using advanced plant-breeding methods.
Knowledge to Start	Molecular biology, genetics, plant science
Capital Required	$$$$
Timing to Start	Years
Special Challenges	Developing new crop plants takes research, even though marker-assisted selection (MAS) is faster than regular breeding

Genetically-modified organisms (GMOs) have been one of the biggest controversies in biotech and agriculture. The presence of even a trace of genetically modified corn or rice in food has been enough to spark an international incident. But let's face it, the plants we eat are not "natural."

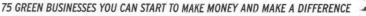

Most modern foods, organic or otherwise, are far from their origins in wild plants. Over many generations, the plants we eat have been bred for desirable traits, such as large fruit or grain, to the point that they often don't look much like they did in the wild. The wild ancestors of corn in the New World had tiny ears that were barely edible by today's standards. This development started at the dawn of agriculture and continues today. Farmers, breeders, and consumers continue avidly seeking traits such as drought tolerance, higher nutrient content, resistance to pests, and even taste. Companies large and small are bringing these characteristics to plants through a new form of selective breeding called marker assisted selection (MAS), avoiding recombinant methods (moving genes from one organism to another) and the controversy that goes with them.

Selective breeding is based on very simple principles. Desirable traits such as large kernels of grain vary greatly from one plant to the next, based on the different genes each plant holds. If you are looking for wheat with large kernels, find two parent plants that have larger than average kernels, and breed them with each other. Take the seeds resulting from breeding these two plants together, plant them, and see which of the young plants produce larger than average kernels of wheat. Keep this up long enough, season after season, and you get "artificial selection," enriching plants for the desired traits and the genes responsible for them. If you are looking for taller plants, the height of the next generation of plants would be measured to pick the tallest plants for the next round of breeding. If you are looking for larger wheat kernels, the size and weight of the kernels in mature plants would be measured and used to decide which plants to use in further breeding.

WHAT'S THE DIFFERENCE?
Artificial selection is a lot like natural selection, but humans pick the types of plants that reproduce—not nature.

This tried-and-true method of plant breeding was around long before recombinant DNA technology, and went a long way toward producing the larger and more appealing fruits, vegetables, grains, and animals we eat today. Selective breeding does not manipulate DNA artificially; instead artificial selection replaces the forces of natural selection. As long as the rules of genetics still work, the method still works.

Marker-assisted selection (MAS) adds the power of DNA technology to enhance selective breeding while avoiding recombinant methods. MAS is unique in how plants are screened to see if they have the desired trait. Previously, the young plants from two parents would be raised to maturity and then the plants would be examined to see if they had the desired trait. This method can be slow and unreliable. With MAS, breeders look at the DNA of young plants to see which plants have the desired genes. Using MAS dramatically speeds plant breeding without the commotion of gene splicing. MAS could prove particularly useful with relatively slow-growing plants, such as apple trees that take years to reach maturity.

MAS is being applied to many plants, including major crops such as wheat, tomatoes, and millet. In a collaboration between United Kingdom and Indian university scientists, drought and mildew resistance were successfully bred in millet, an important grain in much of the developing world. Researchers in the US (supported by the FDA) are applying MAS to wheat, producing strains with new traits that are not GMO and can be

RELATED TREND

Other techniques for creating new plant strains also have been widely accepted. Techniques include the integration of parts of the rice genome into wheat to create the hardy hybrid grain called triticale. Hybrid plants are common in agriculture.

RIFKIN'S OPINION

In a 2006 article in *The Washington Post*, author and biotech critic Jeremy Rifkin described MAS as "the right technology at the right time in history," and said it is likely to overcome the limitations of recombinant technology. According to Rifkin, MAS can reduce the time required for breeding by 50 percent or more. Not everybody agrees with his views about genetic engineering, but it's telling that this biotech critic has embraced MAS. ❧

grown in many countries where GMO crops are restricted. In New Zealand, fruit science company Hort Research (hortresearch.co.nz) is developing a variety of fruits and other crops using MAS. Among early successes are new strains of apples such as Jazz. These strains were produced in five or six years rather than decades required for traditional fruit-breeding programs. Hort also is working on kiwi fruit, berries, and hops, to round out the MAS-influenced meal.

One use of MAS is to make use of the great biological diversity that other researchers and farmers are preserving. Modern agricultural crops are much easier to grow and eat than their wild ancestors but also are far less diverse, with millions of acres devoted to growing a handful of varieties. In the process of selecting bigger and faster-growing plants, other traits may have been lost, traits still residing in the reservoir of genetic diversity in wild strains. If these strains disappear, their genes also are gone. Crossing wild tomatoes with their more civilized friends and using MAS to pick through their offspring for drought tolerance, or for resistance to new viruses or pests, can provide the best of both worlds.

Plant breeders who want to use MAS to kick-start their own work need some genomic information with which to work. Developing the required genetic information could take years and cost a fortune. Working on crops where academic or government-sponsored research already has made this information available probably is wisest for small organizations. Even so, working with MAS to produce new strains of plants is not a get-rich-quick scheme; it takes time and money.

Opportunities involving MAS include:

◉ Developing and marketing new strains of crop plants produced through MAS
◉ Analyzing plant genetic information to identify genes associated with desirable and novel traits

❀ Establishing collaborations and consortiums between those using plant genetic information to perform MAS and those producing the genetic information

One of the concerns about MAS is that once strains are produced, they might be subject to common agricultural concerns: produced in monocultures sprayed with chemicals, lacking diversity, and depleting soil. But MAS is not about the method of agriculture. If MAS produces plants grown in the same agricultural system that creates other problems, this reflects a broader issue with our agricultural system and cannot be blamed on MAS. If MAS increases the productivity of plant-breeding methods that have been around since the dawn of time, it's hard to see the objection.

OPPORTUNITY 47

Low-Carbon Groceries

The Market Need	Consumers are starting to think about the impact of their food and groceries on the environment, but have scant information to guide their shopping
The Mission	Build and provide systems for tracking food's journey and its carbon footprint
Knowledge to Start	Carbon auditing, supply chains, marketing
Capital Required	$$
Timing to Start	Years
Special Challenges	Carbon labeling is not yet broadly adopted

When it comes to being green, food is so simple and yet so complicated. How green is your food? The answer depends on what green means to you. Does green food have to be grown using organic methods? What about the impact of our food on climate change? Even when food is organic, it often reaches our plate after liberal dollops of fossil fuels were burned in the field, road, ships, and airplanes. The greenest food includes consideration of how it is grown, and the environmental impact of its journey to the local market and your plate. A survey of United Kingdom shoppers found that 67 percent would base shopping decisions in part on the carbon footprint of the product (Carbon Trust, 2006). Providing climate-friendly food with a reduced carbon footprint is an innovative opportunity on its way to stores near you.

The fabulous growth of organic food is good, green news for our planet and our health. But the story does not end there. What happens when the organic produce is produced on large industrialized farms and harvested with diesel combines or is shipped halfway around the world in a plastic package? What if the organic produce is picked by laborers who were not paid fairly or treated according to acceptable labor standards? The full story of food extends beyond the end product to include where the food came from and how it came to your plate.

To answer these questions, companies are looking at their supply chains and improving the traceability of products from beginning to end. With Wal-Mart's drive to reduce its environmental impact, the company is driving its suppliers to provide this information. As the world's largest retailer, where Wal-Mart goes, others will follow. Startups are developing solutions to address this need, such as Zigbeef of Tulsa, Oklahoma, which is helping to track cattle with RFID (radio frequency identification) tags. Wal-Mart is incorporating these tracking devices broadly in its supply chain, driving down the price for the tags and helping to bring others to RFID.

This story relates closely to the local-food movement. In some cases, stores such as Whole Foods Market Headquarters in Austin, Texas, are doing more to label the source of the food. But it still can be difficult to judge what is the greenest choice. The problem is not just a matter of miles. We assume that traveling farther means more fossil fuels are consumed, but sometimes that might not be true. Critics say that distance alone may not tell the whole story. If tomatoes are grown in the United Kingdom in energy-intensive greenhouses, are they still greener for the London customer than a Spanish tomato grown in a field? If lamb from New Zealand involves much less energy and chemical use than lamb grown closer to home, even after transport is factored in, is the New Zealand lamb a better buy for your plate and the planet?

As the CE-Yo and long-time leader of Stonyfield Farm, Gary Hirshberg has examined the carbon footprint of the organic yogurt they produce and found surprising results. "We have bought this mistaken idea that food miles are the Holy Grail," Hirshberg says. Rapid growth has increased the volume of organic milk they need, and caused them to look into options for how best to supply that milk. Hirshberg found that there was a surplus of organic dried milk powder from New Zealand, and that almost every farm was organic. Because of the way the dairy cows in New Zealand are raised, the carbon footprint of using this milk powder was 60 percent of the carbon footprint of fluid milk from the United States, even with the transportation factored in. While some may object to the transportation of food across such distances, having data about the overall impact on climate helps businesses and consumers make the best choice, even if it isn't perfect. "We can't make the 'perfect' the enemy of the "good,'" Hirshberg says.

To make smart, green shopping decisions, consumers need information right on the label. Already in the United Kingdom, products are starting to have transportation labeling, with a picture of a plane or a boat. The trend is likely

PREDICTING THE NEXT TREND

Some green trends move from California to the rest of the United States, but they don't all start in California. Some trends have been in other parts of the world, such as Europe and Japan, long before being imported to the United States. In looking for green trends and opportunities in the United States, look overseas and see what others are doing. ❦

to spread to the United States and improve by labeling products with their actual carbon footprint. Groups such as the Carbon Trust in the United Kingdom are developing methods of tracking and calculating the carbon emissions associated with products as well as stamping the information on the label. A few test products are appearing on shelves in the United Kingdom starting with a popular line of potato chips. The UK-based grocery chain Tesco also has joined the effort, announcing that it will track the carbon footprint of 30 products on its shelves.

To participate in the Carbon Trust plan in the United Kingdom, firms must undergo a carbon audit and any carbon-footprint product labels need to be substantiated by carbon auditors. The growth of this field creates the need for independent carbon-audit services. For produce that is coming from different sources and transportation routes, this may prove challenging. Another opportunity for those providing information-technology (IT) solutions is to trace the route of products and validate the label.

Opportunities for low-carbon groceries include:

- Creating low-carbon products and brands
- Providing tracking and auditing of carbon footprint for products
- Importing products with a smaller carbon footprint, even after accounting for transportation
- Looking for low-carbon products being developed in Europe or elsewhere to see what ideas can be imported into the United States

This is an opportunity for manufacturers who can distinguish themselves in the new, emerging low-carbon market. In concert with the new labeling, another United Kingdom company, Boots plc, is working on a low-carbon shampoo. When companies have information to validate such claims and the means to communicate this information to consumers, there will be a range of new product opportunities in every category—low-carbon bran flakes, here we come. It's not clear yet to what extent consumers will seek out low-carbon brands, but hopefully people won't make too many trips to the market in a sport-utility vehicle to buy them.

OPPORTUNITY 48

Heritage Crops

The Market Need	Biological and genetic diversity is lacking in most crops
The Mission	Grow and market traditional and often forgotten crops with unique and unusual properties
Knowledge to Start	Growing and cultivating unusual and perhaps finicky plants
Capital Required	$$
Timing to Start	Years
Special Challenges	Marketing unusual foods

While most grocery stores have a great variety of products on the shelves, diversity often is lacking in the produce section and in the fields of farmers. More and more of our food comes from a limited variety of plants. There are between 80 and 90 million of acres of corn grown in the United States—almost all of it from the same genetic background. Soybeans, rice, and other crops tell a similar story. Where once there were thousands of plant varieties grown for food, much of the ancient heritage has been lost. Stephan Fayon runs a seed bank in India and estimates that 95 percent of cabbage varieties, 91 percent of maize varieties, and 81 percent of tomato varieties already have been lost. Growing and selling heritage crops is a strong opportunity to regain the rich variety of foods once enjoyed and to protect our future food supply.

The current lack of biological diversity is a problem for consumers and farmers alike. The crops farmers grow are selected to be hardy and productive in a specific set of conditions, but when large tracts of land are all growing the same plant at the same time, the risk increases of a catastrophic crop loss. If an insect pest, virus, or mold manages to take hold in this ocean of monoculture, there is little in the genetic makeup of the plants to stop it, allowing the

ECO-ISSUE

Michael Pollan notes in his best-seller *The Omnivore's Dilemma* that much of the apparent diversity in markets is false. Many products can be traced back to corn that is simply processed and packaged different ways.

pest to spread like wildfire. Nature builds diversity in groups of plants and animals because it helps the species to survive. That's why sex is everywhere in the natural world, not because plants or animals enjoy it, but because evolution has favored the genetic diversity it creates.

For the consumer, the homogenization of our agriculture limits our food options and may affect our nutrition. The few species that we still do grow and eat are selected more for their ability to function in the mechanized and industrialized version of agriculture. The nutritional qualities of these foods are seldom examined or considered, and the great variety of foods that was once enjoyed has been pared down to a small list of produce in one section of the store, with more square footage devoted to processed food.

For the entrepreneur, this is an opportunity. People are seeking more from their food; they want food they can savor and enjoy. The growing gourmet-food and organic-food markets are indications of this. The higher end of the food market constantly looks for something new in culinary delights. One answer is heritage foods, in which the new thing is actually old strains of crop plants that have been forgotten and rediscovered.

Heirloom tomatoes are a good example of one type of heritage crop. At one time, there were hundreds of different types of tomatoes grown and appreciated in different regions with a rich palate of flavors, textures, smells, and colors. With the advent of the modern food distribution system and grocery stores, tomatoes dwindled to a handful of varieties, primarily those that are tough enough to be picked green, shipped across the country, and gassed at their destination to turn red. Their flavor is not spectacular. Heirloom tomatoes increasingly are common in farmers' markets and even grocery stores, with consumers seeking better variety and taste in their food.

Gary Ibsen is an ardent supporter of sustainable agriculture, founder of the Carmel, California, TomatoFest, author of *The Great Tomato Book*, and grower of more than 600 varieties of heirloom tomatoes. It's no surprise that he's called the "Tomato Man." This is not a newfound interest; Ibsen was introduced to heirloom tomatoes more than 20 years ago and his work has continued to grow ever since. He supplies seeds, plants, tomatoes, and other products, and he works to support the growth and preservation of these plants and their diversity. You can find more information about Ibsen and his heirloom tomatoes at tomatofest.com.

Opportunities in heritage crops include:

⦿ Becoming known for raising heirloom varieties for one type of plant (like the "Tomato Man")
⦿ Raising and selling heirloom varieties of plants at farmers' markets, cooperatives, and organic-food stores
⦿ Crossing heirloom varieties with modern strains to increase the variety of plants used in large-scale agriculture

Much of the work in heritage plants will be local, depending on the plants that grow well in each region. For each of the fruits and vegetables we see in the grocery store, there probably are hundreds of nearly lost and forgotten varieties. This work can begin as a backyard hobby and grow organically into a business. You can become the Cabbage King. Our food is more than just sugars, proteins, and fats. We have lost much of the rich variety our diet once had, but entrepreneurs providing heritage crops can help us reclaim this variety.

> **ECO-ISSUE**
>
> One of the problems with food produced from GMO plants is that when they are broadly adopted, they further reduce the variety of crops being grown.

Using Water Wisely

Water is a precious resource, perhaps more precious than oil. At some point, we will no longer use oil for energy (it's only a question of when), but we will always need water. The world's population is expected to hit between 9 and 10 billion by midcentury, but the supply of fresh, clean, usable water is decreasing and climate change may worsen the situation. Parts of Australia are currently in the grips of a prolonged and severe drought, and parts of the U.S. Southwest and South have been in a drought for years, tightening water supplies to major U.S. cities. Other parts of the world, such as China, also face major water issues. More efficient ways to use water are badly needed, and entrepreneurs are rising to the challenge with a variety of innovative water solutions.

The oceans contain 97 percent of the Earth's water, but the salt content of ocean water rules out most uses. One potential solution is desalination but this is not an easy answer. Desalination technology has improved but still requires a great deal of energy. The environmental impact of desalination must be considered in siting desalination plants and the salt produced has caused some objections. Commercial desalination is already routine in some regions, particularly those without other options for fresh water and with enough money to spend, but desalination is unlikely to solve all of our water problems.

One underutilized water resource is the water we already have. The cheapest and greenest water is that which we conserve by being more efficient. In today's water system, clean drinking water is stored in reservoirs, pumped vast distances, filtered, chlorinated, and tested just to arrive at your home and run off of the over-watered lawns into the gutter, or get flushed into oblivion. We need to use our water more carefully. One way to do this is with better toilets. The toilet commonly found in North America has not changed much over the years, and the main innovations have focused on design not function. The toilet is ripe for revolution, with more efficient toilets saving water (Opportunity 53). We also need to make better use of how we use water outside. The suburban lawn was once a symbol of 1950s affluence, and failure to have a lush and manicured lawn was taken as a sign of sloth, poverty, or poor citizenry. Where water is a valuable commodity, with cities surrounded by desert, lawns are out of place and giving way to more appropriate landscaping options. More and more homeowners are turning to gardens that are still appealing but use water more wisely (Opportunity 54).

Where we get our water from also is changing. When it rains, where does the water go? Even in dry regions, we take the rain from our roofs and direct it down drain spouts to the street, where the water runs to local waterways. Meanwhile, we import water from distant mountains to use in our garden. More and more homeowners in dry regions are saving the water that falls on their home in rain barrels and other catchment systems (Opportunity 50). Wastewater from sinks, showers, and clothes washers can be used for irrigation in greywater systems, saving drinking water for drinking (Opportunity 49). Even the air we breathe contains water, the water you see condensed on your car in the morning or as dew on the grass. This water can be collected and used for irrigation or emergency water supplies (Opportunity 52).

Dissatisfaction with the water coming out of the water tap has led to soaring sales of bottled water in recent years, but this trend is turning. The bottled water craze has created mountains of polyethylene bottles, billions of them, and a backlash against bottled water. The revelation that many bottled-water products contain nothing more than local tap water has further curbed enthusiasm. People want water that is safe, eco-friendly, and tastes good, and that means water that comes from something other than disposable polyethylene bottles. The solution is to sell reusable eco-bottles that filter water and do not add unwanted ingredients (see Opportunity 51).

The world's people have endless variation in their foods, languages, beliefs, religions, and traditions. For all of our differences, we have similarities that we often forget, including basic needs, such as that of water. It's not always clear what the future holds, but no matter what else happens, we all are going to need water. As the world's population continues to grow, getting clean water will be more of a challenge than ever. Helping people meet this challenge with water-related businesses is an opportunity sure to be around for a while.

OPPORTUNITY 49

Recycled Water

The Market Need	Water that could be used again for other purposes is lost daily
The Mission	Reuse water in homes, businesses, and communities
Knowledge to Start	Plumbing, greywater
Capital Required	$$
Timing to Start	Months to years
Special Challenges	Gaining consumer acceptance

Our supply of freshwater is decreasing, with less and less available for many uses. In our quest for new water supplies, one underutilized source of water is what we already have in our homes. Water from the shower, sink, or washing machine often can be used for other purposes, such as irrigation of lawns and gardens. Often called greywater, these sources account for 50 to 80 percent of the water that homes use (greywater.net). The more precious water becomes, the more people are finding ways to stretch our water supply as far as possible, including businesses increasing use of greywater.

Water comes in different varieties, some of which are better suited to reuse than others. Water from the toilet and the kitchen sink is called black water. This water requires sewage treatment and is not appropriate for reuse in the home because of health concerns related to contamination with fecal material or food particles that may breed bacteria. Water that is used in the bathroom sink, shower, or washing machine is another story. This water presents little or no health hazard if handled correctly.

For the do-it-yourselfers, one method of utilizing greywater is collecting water in a bucket in the shower while the water warms up and then dumping it in the toilet to flush.

GREEN LEADERS

The Greywater Guerillas (greywater-guerillas.com) are a group supporting greywater solutions, taking matters into their own hands. Describing themselves as "the water underground," they provide information in classes, on their website, and in publications on how to save water and save the world.

This works well enough, but most people will keep it up for only so long. To work more broadly, a greywater system should work on its own, without any bucket carrying. Similarly, many have hooked a garden hose up to their washing machine and run it out the window to the garden. For aesthetic reasons, and concern about putting detergents on plants, this may not work for everyone.

To provide more lasting solutions that work for almost anyone, entrepreneurs are developing and marketing products such as the Aqus from Water-Saver Technologies of Louisville, Kentucky (watersavertech.com). The Aqus fits under the bathroom sink, saving water from the sink to flush the toilet. The water from the sink may not be fit to drink, but it is fine for flushing, helping consumers save thousands of gallons a year without using a bucket. Although hidden away under the sink, the Aqus is attracting attention and winning awards such as the What's the Big Idea? contest from the Sundance Channel.

Another use of greywater is in the garden. However, the presence of soaps and other materials can make greywater a concern in the garden, greatly restricting the types of systems that many municipalities are willing to approve. The chemicals, soap, and pH of untreated greywater can accumulate in soil and hurt plants over time. Perpetual Water (perpetualwater.com) with Ralph Petroff is bringing water-reusing technology from perpetually parched Australia with systems that remove detergents from greywater before release. The Perpetual Water Home System can recycle/reuse 67 percent of the typical home's water and is already installed in many Australian homes.

As time goes on, municipalities will not only tolerate greywater, they will demand it. Some U.S. cities such as San Diego, California, and Las Vegas, Nevada, are recycling water on a large scale, taking sewage and treating it, and pumping it back out for irrigation. The more this trend spreads, the greater the market for those providing greywater solutions.

> **ECO-TIP**
>
> Many water-saving technologies are being developed in Australia, where pressure from years of drought forces every drop of water to be used wisely. If you are looking for technology in greywater, Australia is a fertile ground for new inventions that might be exported elsewhere.

Opportunities for recycled water include:

- Designing greywater systems
- Installing greywater systems (green plumbing)
- Customizing systems to fit in a variety of homes and buildings
- Consulting on home design to incorporate greywater systems

There is an opportunity for green plumbers to move away from unclogging drains and get into water conservation with systems such as those from WaterSaver Technologies and Perpetual Water. It's a lot less messy, with a great deal of room to grow, and a larger purpose in which to get involved. I would suggest that any greywater entrepreneur call the process something else, though. Greywater just is not an appealing name for marketing. How about "green water"?

OPPORTUNITY 50

Harvesting Rainwater

The Market Need	Although we don't have enough water, we throw away rainwater
The Mission	Catch and store rainwater to use
Knowledge to Start	Plumbing
Capital Required	$ (installing existing products)
Timing to Start	Weeks to months
Special Challenges	Consumer acceptance

People love to live in the sun, but the sunniest areas also are often the driest. The U.S. population is growing fastest in the west and the so-called Sunbelt. This trend is expected to continue, with some of the driest cities, such as Las Vegas, Nevada, having the fastest growth (U.S. Census Bureau, 2007). Las Vegas grew by 50 percent from 1999 to 2007, and is spending billions of dollars to pump water hundreds of miles across Nevada (Reuters News Service,

August 21, 2007). Entrepreneurs are building businesses that help consumers find water closer to home. Maybe even right on top of their homes.

The urban environment is an ocean of concrete. When it rains, water is funneled away in channels, gutters, and storm drains, lost to any use. Even in the dry Southwest, the occasional rainfall is channeled out and away from rooftops, driveways, and streets, even while freshwater is pumped from across the country. In this situation, the rain may clean cars, and allow consumers to turn off their sprinklers for a few days, but that's about it. Storm runoff can be a pollution problem when the water carries oil and other pollutants from streets into rivers or the ocean.

People are getting smarter about using water where it falls, starting at home. There was a time when it was not uncommon for rainwater to be collected and stored, and as water gets more precious, more builders and home-owners are rediscovering rainwater capture, installing home cistern systems to save rainwater for a less-rainy day. Even in a desert climate with only 10 inches of rain a year, a 2000-square-foot roof can provide 12,000 gallons of water a year. That may not sound like a lot, but it is enough for thousands of flushes. The increased use of home rainwater-collection systems also creates the opportunity to design and install them. The type of system depends on how the water will be used, how much water is collected, and the site where the system is installed.

For some, home rainwater tanks are as small and simple as a rain barrel. Adding rain barrels to a drain spout does not require a large investment or a large amount of space, but the water-storage capacity only will be about 50 to 60 gallons. Although homemade systems are one option, keeping the water clean and pest-free, handling overflow, and preventing leaks may require a more specialized system that eco-entrepreneurs can provide. Rain barrels can be built from a variety of materials, including recycled plastics or wood. One benefit of rainwater is that it is naturally soft water, free of the salt that municipal water supplies contain in many areas, and easier

THE BIG PICTURE

Of course, everything must be done in context, as part of the whole. Investing in cisterns does not make much sense without also conserving water in the home and the garden.

on plants. To get a feeling for the kinds of rain barrels people are making, search the internet, including sites such as
rainsaverusa.com/index.htm.

In the United States, harvesting rainwater at home may
just be getting started, but some European nations provide
incentives for it and it is mandatory in new homes in most
parts of Australia. Sometimes rain barrels are just barrels
collecting rain, and sometimes they are a little more.
Designed by Sally Dominquez in water-conscious Australia,
the Rainwater HOG storage system has a slender, modular
design that can blend in with its surroundings or be con-
cealed, and be installed either vertically or horizontally. Modular in nature, units can be linked to increase total water-storage capacity in
increments of 50 gallons. The unique design allows HOG units to fit in areas
where other water-storage systems would not work, for example, in tight
spaces in urban dwellings and apartments. In addition to doing a job, the
Rainwater HOG looks good and can be readily incorporated in a green home
without altering the home's appearance. According to Simon Dominguez of
Rainwater HOG, initial response to the HOG in the United States has been
so strong that the first shipment sold out in a matter of weeks. HOG units
also can be used to provide passive heating and cooling as thermal mass in
green homes. For more about the HOG units, see rainwaterhog.com. The
company currently is establishing production and distribution in the United
States to meet the great interest.

Larger systems can store more water but also require more of a commitment from the homeowner. Cisterns in the form of large tanks above-
ground or underground can store thousands of gallons of water, which if
water is used carefully, that's enough to offset a big part of the water use
in the summer garden. Such a system can involve digging a large hole
though, so it would best be done with new construction or new landscaping. Designed well, a cistern might even add a nice twist to the overall garden design.

One option for entrepreneurs is to build a better rain barrel. This will take time and money, and must address a need better than other designs. There already are a great many forms of catchment systems, but there always seems to be room for good ideas. Another option in the United States is to import and sell one of the catchment systems from Australia, or other countries that are leading the way in water conservation. Installing rainwater-storage systems is another business option, working directly with homeowners who are unsure how to do this on their own.

Opportunities in rainwater storage include:

- Designing a better rain barrel
- Importing rain-storage systems
- Selling and installing rain barrels and other catchment systems

At the end of the day, home cisterns may not provide all of a home's water needs, but they can make a contribution, and eco-entrepreneurs designing and installing these systems are making an important contribution as well.

OPPORTUNITY 51
Un-Bottled Water

The Market Need	People don't like tap water and want water to carry with them
The Mission	Get consumers out of their disposable water-bottle habit and into alternatives
Knowledge to Start	Design
Capital Required	$$
Timing to Start	Months
Special Challenges	Designing a novel product and finding a niche

Sales of bottled water have exploded, and a great variety of products have been introduced. There is high-end water and low-end water. There is flavored water, caffeinated water, and vitamin water. Bubbly or not. Even socially aware water. What's next for bottled water? The next generation is a reusable eco-bottle.

Along with the blooming bottled-water market has come an explosion in the number of water bottles going into landfills. Americans consume over 70 million water bottles a day (*National Geographic Green Guide*, July/August, 2007), and throw 38 billion bottles a year into landfills (*Fast Company*, July, 2007). Many bottles are recycled, and in states requiring a deposit on bottles, the recycling rates are much higher. But even recycling takes energy. It seems likely that the greenest water you can buy does not come in a disposable bottle. Growing recognition of this is helping to make greener drinking-water solutions a growing eco-opportunity.

THE BOTTOM LINE

In addition to creating eco-issues, bottled water is expensive, costing about 10,000 times more than tap water (Earth Policy Institute, February 2, 2006).

To find the best solution, we need to understand the problem. The first problem is that the bottles are disposable. If people want to carry water with them, they need a vessel that lasts for many uses and does not end up in a landfill. The second problem with disposable water bottles is what is inside. While the labels with pictures of mountain streams seem to promise pristine alpine sources, the reality is that the water often comes from the same municipal water supply as your tap. The greenest water solution should provide water that people like and can trust. The third problem is what the bottle adds to the water. The plastics used to make disposable bottles often leach chemicals into the water. These compounds usually are not seen or tasted, but are still a concern. The health effects of these compounds are not always clear, but they are enough of a concern to drive some eco-entrepreneurs and consumers to look for alternatives.

What type of material is best for bottles? Some plastics contain chemicals of one sort or another that leach into water over time, and these have been linked to potential health issues. The polycarbonate material Lexan can leach bisphenol-A, which some believe is dangerous, although others dispute it. Nonetheless, if you are getting into non-disposable water bottles, it's best to steer clear of these problems. Other plastics—such as high-density polyethylene (HDPE)—might be safer. Bottles from Corntainer Corporation are made from cornstarch and are biodegradable if composted properly.

Metal bottles might be the greenest solution, particularly if they are made of stainless steel. Check out the bottles from Klean Kanteen of Chico, California, for example (kleankanteen.com). Aluminum is a possibility, although aluminum containers usually are lined with an epoxy coating that still may cause concern. Metal bottles may get some dings, but stainless steel does not leach chemicals into the water and the bottles will last practically forever. Metal bottles may cost more, between $15 and $18 in the case of the Klean Kanteen bottles, but since the bottle will last for hundreds or even thousands of uses, the long-term cost to the consumer is less than that of disposable bottles.

And what about what goes into the bottle? More and more people have their own home water-filtration system, like Brita, but what about when they are on the go? People like water bottles because of their mobility, so depending only on your home-filtration system limits the use of your green water bottle. An even better eco-bottle might incorporate not just a bottle but filtration to purify water wherever the consumer goes. Straws used with

GREEN LEADERS

Brita (U.S. Headquarters in Oakland, California) and Nalgene water bottles (sold through the Nalgene International Outdoor Products Division, Rochester, New York) have partnered in the Filter for Good campaign to reduce disposable water use, as well as a Refill Not Landfill campaign that Nalgene is sponsoring. Brita is the leader in its home water-filtration market and Nalgene is a leading brand of nondisposable plastic water bottles. By working together they hope to encourage the use of reusable with bottles and decrease plastic waste. 🌱

survival gear are typically designed to remove microbes from water, avoiding infections. In addition to removing microbes, the eco-bottle straw for the developed world should remove lead, arsenic, other metals, pesticides, organic compounds, chlorine, and a variety of salts. A filter straw such as the Cleansip (Cleansip.com) might do the trick, particularly if it can be built into the bottle design.

Water is an important issue for the social eco-entrepreneur. More than a billion people lack access to clean drinking water, and millions die each year from preventable diseases caused by drinking dirty water. A number of eco-entrepreneurs are working to increase clean-water supplies in developing countries, where providing clean water has been shown to be one of the most cost-effective ways to help people. The LifeStraw of Vestergaard Frandsen, Switzerland, is a personal water filter that costs only $2 and provides protection from water-borne diseases. Hopefully, the water solution for the developing world will not be the plastic water bottle, which brings with it new problems. As an alternative to bottled water, Dean Kamen (inventor of the Segway and founder and president of the DEKA Research and Development Corporation) has developed a device to produce clean water for the developing world. The Slingshot is a low-power water-purification device that is coupled to an electrical generator powered by cow dung. The two together can provide both power and clean water for a village. Kamen is working to partner with others to bring his device to the developing world through a microfinance model in which micro-entrepreneurs would sell the water and power to pay for the Slingshot.

Opportunities to replace bottled water include:

- Designing reusable water bottles
- Designing filters to fit on existing water bottles
- Designing water bottles that incorporate filtration
- Marketing reusable water bottles
- Providing water purification in the developing world

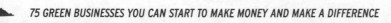

In the end, whatever the bottles are made of and whatever they have in them, they must work, and they should look good, too. These water bottles are about more than carrying water; they are sending a message about the person carrying them. Let your greenness shine with your eco-bottle business.

OPPORTUNITY 52

Condensation Collection: Water from the Air

The Market Need	We need new sources of water
The Mission	Find cost-effective ways to use the water carried in the air
Knowledge to Start	Understanding condensation
Capital Required	$$ (distribute existing product or adapt existing one) to $$$$ (develop new products)
Timing to Start	Years
Special Challenges	Competition from tap water

Most of the world's water is in oceans and ice caps. A relatively tiny fraction is swirling around unseen in the air. Although the Earth's atmosphere consists of only 1 percent water vapor, it adds up to 4,000 cubic miles of water around and over you (lenntech.com). You can see this water in the clouds and in the dew that collects overnight on your grass and car. Entrepreneurs who can extract this water from the air might find a valuable business niche in a thirsty world.

One way to get water out of the sky is to wait for it to fall in the form of rain. It works better in some areas than others. Encouraging the process by seeding clouds has been tried often with occasional reports of success, but overall seeding seems unreliable.

The plants that live in deserts might provide inspiration for another way to get at this precious resource. Dew forms on plants when their surface cools below the dew point of the surrounding air, causing water droplets to form. Some plants living in desert regions have evolved to collect the dew that forms on their leaves during the night and funnel it downward to use as their own water supply. Humans living in dry areas can use a similar proactive water approach to supplement other sources, mimicking nature's ingenuity.

Low-tech approaches use a variety of physical objects to cause condensation and collect the water. One example is a fog fence. In foggy areas, a fine-mesh fence facing the prevailing wind can collect water vapor, like dew on a spider web, and then drain the water down toward the ground. The fog fence requires favorable local conditions, but as an inexpensive and simple passive system, it has many advantages.

Low-tech solutions like the fog fence might have their place in suburban gardens and remote rural areas. Water from these systems might not always be suitable for human consumption but is suitable for watering the landscape. There's no pumping required, just drain water down to nearby plants. As such, low-tech systems might be marketed through home and garden stores.

Another way to collect water from the air is to cool a surface below the dew point. Luckily, the Earth provides a ready heat sink, maintaining a constant cool temperature. Heat-conducting materials such as metal rods inserted in the ground will encourage condensation to form. That water can then drip down the rod to the soil at its base.

Others are using more active approaches that need energy to work. The Air Water Corporation of Miami Beach, Florida, creates a range of machines that extract water from air, including the Lifesaver, capable of producing 500 liters of water per day. The AirWater System works like a dehumidifier, but keeps the water to use elsewhere. The Mirage Water Maker of Hondo, Texas, produces a smaller unit that also collects water from air, producing as much as five gallons a day. Working on a larger scale, Aqua Sciences of Miami Beach, Florida, is also producing water-from-air systems and has received awards from *The Wall Street Journal*, *Time* magazine, and the *Going Green Top 100* for its innovative design. Aqua Science units can extract water from air holding as little as 14 percent humidity, much lower than others have achieved. Targeting drinking water at a cost of $.30 per gallon, Aqua Sciences is under contract with the U.S. Army and the Federal Emergency Management Agency with Aqua Science units provide water in remote areas or in emergencies in a less expensive way than trucking or flying in supplies.

Opportunities for water from air include:

- ⊛ Using fog-fences
- ⊛ Designing low-tech condensation devices for potted plants and gardens in the developed world
- ⊛ Distributing water-condensation collection systems
- ⊛ Adapting air-conditioning systems to use the condensation water produced
- ⊛ Designing or selling larger systems for emergency water production

With water becoming increasingly precious and new sources not easy to come by, eco-entrepreneurs who are making water out of thin air are targeting a growing market in several niche areas. There are many ways to get water out of air, and the same solution is not going to work for everyone, but the opportunities are all around us—even if we don't always see them.

VARIATION ON A BIZ-THEME

Commercial or residential air-conditioning systems create condensation as they chill the air. As a byproduct, this water can be used with a little bit of tinkering. The larger the air-conditioning system, the more water that is created.

GREEN MARKETS

Water from air will have a hard time competing with the cost of water from other systems. The volume of water produced is relatively small, and tap water usually is heavily subsidized. Water from air is a niche application with the most potential in areas where tap water is not readily available, such as in developing countries, in emergency response, or to supplement other water sources.

OPPORTUNITY 53

The 21st-Century Toilet and Green Plumbers

The Market Need	Toilets take potential drinking water and flush it down the drain
The Mission	Design, promote, market, and install toilets that waste less water
Knowledge to Start	Plumbing
Capital Required	$
Timing to Start	Weeks
Special Challenges	Knowing the right toilet and other fixtures, reaching customers in crowded plumbing field

Water moves in a cycle around the earth, endlessly renewed and renewing. After being stored in reservoirs and getting pumped hundreds of miles to your house, much of this precious resource gets mixed with feces and urine, and flushed away. We needlessly flush a lot of water down the drain in inefficient toilets. Green plumbers can change this, helping us all use more efficient toilets.

Don't get me wrong. I love toilets. Sanitation is a good thing. But we need toilets that achieve sanitation without wasting water. It is estimated that the average home uses 28 percent of its water for flushing the toilet (Rocky Mountain Institute, "Water Efficiency for Your Home," third edition, 1995). A great variety of toilets already exist that can flush more efficiently. The trick is getting them installed. Low-flow toilets are being encouraged because they are such a win-win for all involved. Low-flow toilets use between one and two gallons per flush rather than the three to five gallons used by regular toilets. The first low-flow toilets did not get the job done with one flush, requiring people to flush two or three times, and giving low-flow toilets a bad reputation. However, newer models have improved greatly. (Two-button systems are a variation on the low-flow toilet, with the

user hitting either the 0.8 gallon flush button or the 1.6 gallon flush, depending on the needs of the moment.) To
encourage their installation, rebates are offered in some
areas; other areas have mandated the change. A mandate
creates a compelling business opportunity; it's an offer that
consumers can't refuse. In sunny California, big on people
and short on water, 100 percent of toilets sold must be low-
flow models by 2014. That's a lot of toilets.

INDUSTRY INFO

For more reviews of low-flow toilets,
check out Terry Love's website at
terrylove.com.

Regular models might be a little cheaper, but the more efficient com-
mode will pay for itself in water saved a few thousand flushes down the line.
And with improved design, low-flow toilets are darn pretty, relatively speak-
ing. Terry Love knows toilets well; he has tested a wide variety of low-flow
models himself, and talked to consumers and plumbers to get the straight
poop. He recommends the Ultramax by TOTO.

This is just the beginning; the toilet revolution is only getting started. To
save more water, commercial sites are installing waterless urinals. Waterless
urinals cost less to install than traditional urinals, because there isn't water
flowing in or many parts that could break. The Harold Washington Social
Security Center in Chicago, Illinois, is saving millions of gallons a year and
saving money as well. The Envirolet by Sancor Industries of Toronto,
Canada, is one example of a waterless urinal. Sites such as the San Diego Zoo
in California, have installed waterless urinals to save water, and by all
accounts, they are getting the job done just fine. In addition, there are parts
of Europe already are starting to use toilets in which urine is diverted sepa-
rately from fecal matter. When kept separate from fecal contamination,
urine can be saved and used for fertilizer.

As for the next generation of toilets beyond low-flow, the ultimate may
be no-flow, composting toilets. Maybe not everybody is ready for this, but
some LEEDs-rated green buildings incorporate composting toilets that convert human waste into usable soil. Designed and installed correctly, the composting toilet does not smell, and the owner need not ever see or deal with
the contents. A variety of vendors sell composting toilets, and they are

becoming increasingly common, particularly in cabins, parks, roadside rest stops, and other areas where access to sewage treatment is problematic. When fully composted during a period of a few years, only a small volume of mineralized material remains that's nothing like the starting point.

Homeowners and builders need the insight of green plumbers who are knowledgable about water-conserving fixtures, including toilets, showers, sinks, and appliances. Because not every toilet works the same, plumbers help consumers make the best choice. Plumbing is a competitive market. Going green is one way plumbers can re-invent themselves to stand out.

Opportunities for green plumbers include:

- Installing or selling low-flow toilets
- Installing or selling dual-button toilets
- Installing or selling waterless urinals
- Installing or selling composting toilets
- On-site waste treatment with Living Machines
- Repairing toilets to fix leaks
- Developing leakless low-flow toilets

A new world of plumbing possibilities is waiting. Imagine a future where the plumber's role goes from connecting pipes and unclogging drains to engineering ecosystems such as Living Machines with home water treatment, removing the need for a centralized treatment plant altogether. Living Machines are a form of wastewater treatment using biological systems, such as plants, microbes, mollusks, and even fish—unlike with conventional waste treatment, there is no waste left. We are a long way from making this happen, but this idea saves water, energy, and helps to restore soil. Toilets are our friends. And the less water your friends waste, the better.

OPPORTUNITY 54

Low Water-Use Landscaping

The Market Need	Clean water is precious and must be used carefully for landscaping
The Mission	Design and install landscaping that conserves water
Knowledge to Start	Landscaping, water conservation
Capital Required	$
Timing to Start	Months to years
Special Challenges	Good landscaping takes skill and knowledge

Water is increasingly precious and we should not take it for granted, yet we do. Only a tiny fraction of the world's water is drinkable, and that fraction is running dry in many places. Even in the desert climates of Los Angeles, California; Phoenix, Arizona; and Las Vegas, Nevada, municipalities move water halfway across a continent in order to water lawns. We have a 1950s water-use mentality running into a 21st-century resource issue. As more people awake to this fact, the opportunity grows to design and install water-conservation landscaping, also called xeriscaping.

Some cities, such as Las Vegas, are going so far as to pay people to rip out their lawns. What do we put in their place? Concrete is not a great option. Oceans of urban and suburban concrete already absorb heat, building urban heat islands and sapping more energy for air conditioning. In addition, concrete does not absorb carbon dioxide as plants do, but the cement it contains is responsible for releasing a great deal of carbon dioxide. Rather than paving over the land, the solution to provide wise outdoor water use is plants that use water well. Instead of planting grass and tropical plants in the desert, create landscaping with

ECO-ISSUE

Lake Mead, a massive reservoir in the U.S. Southwest, already is about half empty, and scientists at the University of California–San Diego predict the lake may run completely dry by 2021. As early as 2010, the water level may drop low enough to prevent water from being withdrawn for Las Vegas.

75 GREEN BUSINESSES YOU CAN START TO MAKE MONEY AND MAKE A DIFFERENCE

water-conserving plants that evolved through eons to flourish in a dry environment.

Native plants from dry areas around the Mediterranean, in Australia, and in North America evolved to fit their surroundings, extracting water with deep roots, hoarding water in thick stems, and coating leaves with wax to keep water in. Succulents and cacti are popular landscaping options, but they are not the only ones. A great variety of plants with many shapes, colors, and blooms can be used in xeriscaping, tailored to each home and even the position of each plant in the garden. For the customer, drought-tolerant plants can save between 25 and 50 percent of the water bill. The cost of water is likely to increase in the future, providing a financial incentive to save water. With most suburban homes still sporting lawns and water getting ever more precious, the opportunity for long-term growth in xeriscaping looks solid.

INFORMATION RESOURCE
The Las Vegas Valley Water District is motivated to get consumers to save water and posts landscaping resources online at lvvwd.com.

The tighter water gets, the greater the xeriscaping market gets. Climate modeling predicts that many dry areas of the United States will get hotter and drier still. There are opportunities at many levels, region by region. In areas where xeriscaping has been encouraged for a longer period of time, there already might be nurseries specialized in dry-weather plants. In other areas where the practice has not yet firmly taken root, there might be an opportunity to get in early and specialize in this field. There are small neighborhood nurseries, larger wholesalers, and regional providers of young plants, all of which will lean increasingly toward water conservation.

Working as a landscape designer focused on xeriscaping is another opportunity. It's good to see what others are doing before diving in, and good xeriscaping takes skill, experience, and training. Cuyamaca College in El Cajon near San Diego, California, has a program specializing in water-conservation training for professional landscape designers, with many graduates moving on to start their own businesses. Chris Wotruba of La Mesa, California, is seeing more xeriscaping all the time in her landscaping business,

Perennial Adventure Design. She moved into the field after gardening herself and became a master gardener, a process that requires "a very intense learning program about horticulture in this area," Wotruba says. To learn more about drought-tolerant plants, Wotruba volunteered and answered questions for homeowners, as well as attending classes at Cuyamaca, before opening her nursery in 1985. She also has continued learning by reading; joining clubs and associations; lecturing; writing; and returning to the school to talk to students. Turning to other experts and friends with experience is crucial, according to Wotruba.

Wotruba confirms the growing interest in water conservation among her clients. "I have had many clients looking for ways to replace lawns," she reports, with clients eager to cut down on water use as costs rise and rainfall falls short. An added benefit of xeriscaping is how easy it can be to care for. People lead busy lives, and often don't want to spend their free time mowing a lawn or paying someone else to do it. Much of Wotruba's recent work has focused on Australian plants: "Some need little or no summer water and depend on the winter rains to get through the year." Cutting back on fertilizer and pesticide use is yet another bonus; dry-landscape plants are tough and generally take care of themselves.

Opportunities in low-water landscaping include:

- Working in low-water landscape design (i.e., xeriscaping)
- Building a nursery providing low-water plants and native plants
- Opening a green garden-supply store providing seeds and equipment for water conservation

Xeriscaping may take some getting used to, but it has become a necessity and, for entrepreneurs, this change is an opportunity. As awareness of the need to use water wisely grows, more and more businesses and consumers are ready for change.

> **RELATED TREND**
>
> The use of succulents in water conservation landscaping is increasing, as described in the book *Designing with Succulents* by Debra Baldwin (see debraleebaldwin.com). One nice thing about succulents is they take neglect well, ideas for those people who like gardens but don't have time for gardening.

Delivering Green Services

Green entrepreneurs are designing, producing, and selling eco-friendly cars, buildings, energy, food, and water, but goods are only one part of the economy and not the biggest segment. According to U.S. government statistics reported by the Department of State, services represented 68 percent of the U.S. economy in 2006, and entrepreneurs are greening an array of service companies, many of them targeting the same market as less-green competitors. For any service you can imagine, there is probably a green alternative. Except that one. OK, maybe that one too.

There are many ways for businesses to be green, but in general, green services have a positive impact, or at least less of a negative impact, on the environment. Green services also are healthier for customers and workers. Each business is different, but some of the green strategies are:

- using energy more efficiently.
- wasting less water.
- producing less solid waste.
- supporting sustainable development.
- supporting fair trade.
- using renewable resources.
- avoiding resource degradation.
- respecting labor.
- avoiding polluting.
- avoiding potentially toxic chemicals.

Service-based companies are relatively accessible for entrepreneurs to start, often requiring minimal time and capital to open. However, keeping the doors open by creating and maintaining a competitive advantage can be a challenge. Providing a green alternative to an existing service is a straightforward way for entrepreneurs to distinguish themselves. As more businesses go green, the leaders in the green economy are working toward more challenging goals, such as eliminating their carbon footprints, or eliminating all

THE BIG PICTURE

To some extent, service economies inherently are greener than industrial economies. Economies moving from heavy industry to services consume fewer resources and produce less pollution for the economic value created. This can be measured as greenhouse gas emitted per unit of gross domestic product.

waste. In many markets, competition drives prices down, creating a race to the bottom to be the cheapest. In the green market, there is a race to the top to see who can build the greenest, most sustainable business.

Green service companies come in many different forms. Green bed & breakfasts differentiate themselves by providing an environmentally sustainable service (Opportunity 55). Green dry cleaners provide an alternative to unhealthy solvents and chemicals (Opportunity 57). The increasing demand for planet-friendly ecotourism is met by ecotourism travel guides (Opportunity 58). Home remodeling was a $155 billion industry in 2006 (Harvard Joint Center for Housing Studies, 2006), and the growth in green building is changing the industry, opening doors for contractors to green more existing homes (Opportunity 60). Recycling clothing can take the form of providing a service or creating products to sell, but either way it saves resources (Opportunity 63). Personal-care services often use hidden toxic chemicals in pursuit of beauty, leading a growing number of eco-salons to offer eco-friendly services for hair, nails, and skin using only natural and organic ingredients (Opportunity 65). Rating green businesses is becoming a business itself, to help green shoppers spend their money on the most sustainable products, stores, and restaurants (Opportunity 59).

The green wave is also sweeping through businesses selling services to other businesses. The U.S. Green Building Council (USGBC) is predicting there will be 100 times as many green commercial buildings by 2010, and the maintenance and cleaning of those buildings are also going green as well. Businesses are hiring green cleaning services that avoid toxic cleaning components, which can harm workers, building occupants, and the environment (Opportunity 62). Green ad agencies are working hard to get out the environmental message for businesses, nongovernment organizations (NGOs), governments, and nonprofits (Opportunity 56). As businesses go green, sometimes they need advice from others, such as green-business consultants who know the traps and pitfalls (Opportunity 61). Helping businesses avoid unnecessary travel by improving their utilization of collaboration technologies is getting easier with continued innovation, helping both business productivity and the environment (Opportunity 64).

Like businesses, customers come in all shades of green, so get ready for people to question and probe your greenness. Some of the questions—particularly the most bothersome—will be good ones. As you embark on your venture, weed out the ungreen portions by inviting criticism and taking it to heart so as to learn quickly. The quicker you learn from those questions, the greener you get, and the more competitive your business will be in the green race to the top.

OPPORTUNITY 55

Green Bed & Breakfast

The Market Need	Hotels have a largely negative impact on the environment
The Mission	Run a green bed & breakfast
Knowledge to Start	Innkeeping, sustainability
Capital Required	$$
Timing to Start	Months
Special Challenges	Investing in renovation, hard work

One of the most popular small businesses is a bed-&-breakfast inn (B&B). The attractions of innkeeping are varied, according to *Start Your Own Bed & Breakfast* (Entrepreneur Press and Cheryl Kimball, 2008). For some it's the desire to break the routine of a regular job; for others, it's the extra income; and for still others, it's the idea of living in a resort area and using their home in their business. To stand out and do the right thing, innowners are greening their business.

Hotels generally have a large impact on the environment through water use, energy use, and garbage produced, among other factors. B&B owners working to lighten their environmental impact are attracting new business while they do the right thing. One key step in creating a green B&B is creating a green home in which to base it. Most B&B owners do some renovation when getting started, spending between $35,000 and $50,000 per guest room (according to *Start Your Own Bed & Breakfast*), and green B&B owners should expect similar startup expenses in addition to renovations to ensure greenness. There are steps innkeepers can take to being green without spending any money on renovations, although bigger results are seen with green renovations. Buying green products with minimal packaging is an easy step to take; cleaning with environmentally friendly products, such as baking soda and vinegar, is easy on the budget and the environment; recycling—with bins in the guestrooms, too—and avoiding plastic containers as much as possible can be a simple green touch; and buying and serving local organic and fair-trade foods leave a favorable impression.

Kit Cassingham of Sage Blossom Consulting (sageblossom.com) in Ridgway, Colorado, is helping hotels and B&Bs reduce their environmental impact, offering advice, information, and classes. "Saving money and saving resources can go hand in hand, and [be done] without compromising the guest experience," Cassingham says. "The saving can be done as simply as stopping a leak, re-purposing items several times before recycling, and by having efficient appliances." Cassingham has a number of ideas for those B&B owners who wish to go green.

- ⊛ "If you are building from scratch, insulate beyond what building codes require."
- ⊛ "Plan a water-wise garden or landscape."
- ⊛ "Consider individual climate control in the guest-rooms"
- ⊛ "If you can't compost, find someone who will take your compostables and use them."
- ⊛ "Switch from poly-cotton sheets and towels to all-natural fiber, like organic cotton and bamboo"

ECO-TIP
Provide soaps and shampoos made from organic and natural ingredients, and consider replacing individual bottles with dispensers to reduce costs and waste.

- "Put recycling bins in your guestrooms as a way of educating your guests."

Cassingham also suggests that green B&B owners:

- Save energy by using compact fluorescent light bulbs.
- Ask guests to turn off lights and the TV when not in the room, and to be judicious with water use.
- Implement a sheet- and towel-reuse program, for example, changing sheets and towels every three days unless a guest otherwise requests sooner or later.
- Use a website to specifically tell customers what you do to be green and how it improves their guest experience.

For the breakfast part of the B&B, the food should be organic and local if possible. Guests might love an organic garden in the back that provides ultra-fresh and ultralocal produce. Coffee should be organic free trade, and owners should avoid disposable paper or plastics. Cleaning materials should be devoid of toxic chemicals. A green gift shop is a good way to earn additional money and feed the curiosity of guests about the green lifestyle.

INDUSTRY INFO

Kit Cassingham has some web resources that are a good place to get started. At EconomicallySound.com, she works to educate those in the hotel industry about their environmental impact and what can be done. For the traveler and hotel owner, Cassingham provides information about green hotels at EnvironmentallyFriendlyHotels.com. In addition to her websites, Cassingham can be contacted through theBandBlady.com.

The Maple Hill Farm Bed & Breakfast Inn of Maine has eight bedrooms and a conference center, as well as Maine's largest solar array (15 kilowatts), a wind turbine (10 kilowatts), composting, solar hot water, natural lighting, local food, and many other eco-amenities. Owner Scott Cowger is a committed environmentalist. "I believe it is incumbent on each of us, whether individuals or business owners, to take care of the environment and limit our impact," Cowger says. Guests at the inn are a wide-ranging group of individuals, including young and old. One thing they all have in common is their interest in green-certified lodging, with many choosing Maple Hill because of its greenness. "Going green was a novelty at first," says Cowger, "but it has been

GREEN LEADER

Asheville Green Cottage in North Carolina is a green B&B that has been described by Forbes Traveler as one of the 10 greenest hotels in the United States. Run by Vicki Schomer and Neeraj Kebede, this small, four-bedroom B&B showcases both their interest in the environment and in international travel. It's more than a business for them; it's a part of daily life that reflects their beliefs. 🌱

good for business" with some customers staying just to see features like the solar array and wind turbine. Going green may even keep B&Bs strong through a recession, giving them a unique quality to compete against less green competitors.

Going green can attract new business, travel agents and online resources are keeping tabs on green hotels and B&Bs to target the growing number of customers looking for environmentally friendly travel destinations. Reservation service organizations act as middlemen to match clients and B&Bs helping to bring in guests seeking a green stay.

Opportunities in green B&Bs include:

- Opening a green bed & breakfast
- Providing furnishings and supplies for green B&Bs (shampoo, coffee, tea, towels)
- Remodeling B&Bs to help them go green

"My advice to others? Go for it!" Cowger says. "Not only is being green the right thing to do, but your guests will really appreciate what you do." Cassingham agrees that running a green B&B saves you money, preserves the environment, improves the guest experience, and attracts new business. With a green B&B and great service, it's hard to go wrong. Show clients you want them to come back, and they

ECO-TIP

Maple Hill Farm has a full range of amenities for business and leisure travelers, including internet access, air conditioning, and the same TV you would find anywhere else. For many eco-travelers (probably most of them), going green is not a great sale if it means going without.

probably will. But don't forget that in addition to being green, your B&B needs to be warm, inviting, and comfortable, a green home away from home.

OPPORTUNITY 56

Green Advertising

The Market Need	To succeed, green businesses and other organizations need to reach people with their message
The Mission	Help green organizations get their message out
Knowledge to Start	Graphic design, communication, media, sustainability
Capital Required	$$
Timing to Start	Months
Special Challenges	Avoiding greenwashing, and securing business in a competitive field

There is a large and growing group of people who are realizing that our future and the future of our planet are inextricably linked, and that the road we are on is not headed in the right direction. They want to change direction, changing how they live to reduce their impact on the environment, getting things back on course. This group includes the estimated 19 percent of the U.S. adult population called LOHAS—people with Lifestyles of Health and Sustainability (lohas.com). Lohas are living their lives and spending their money in ways that reflect their concerns and beliefs. Eco-firms, nonprofits, NGOs, and governments are eager to connect their message with these people as well as reach out to those who are not yet on the green bandwagon. Green advertising agencies are helping them do just that.

The green market is growing and becomingly increasingly diverse as it goes mainstream, including people with

RELATED TREND

The number of green media outlets selling ad space has grown immensely. Maybe too much. For 2008, *Sustainable Industries* (January, 2008) predicts consolidation as well as continued growth of outlets focused on small, specific fields.

many interests, needs, and motivations. Reaching the right group with the right message can be a challenge, driving the sudden growth in green advertising. Those buying media have budgets devoted to green ads, but are media buyers spending their money well? Many members of the public increasingly are skeptical of the green buzz and tired of hearing about the problems we face. People have heard a lot about climate change and other environmental problems, and are looking for solutions. Ad businesses delivering messages that can cut through the noise will do well, as will their clients.

The New York ad agency Green Team was founded by Hugh Hough in 1993, long before the latest green surge kicked in. "Things have changed dramatically since then," Hough says, he has far more business today than when he started. Green Team has worked for ecotourism destinations, non-profits, and progressive brands making social and environmental values part of their mission. Green Team works as more than an ad company by developing communications in a variety of ways; helping clients form partnerships; and performing green audits, called Awakening Audits, of clients and products. An Awakening Audit looks at the supply chain to say "this is what you are doing right, this is what you are doing wrong, and here is what you can say about your efforts to the public," Hough says. For him, avoiding greenwashing is simple: "Just state the facts."

Take note: Success in this field means more than appearing green on the surface. Being green all the way through will show in your work and how it is received. Consumers are increasingly skeptical of green claims. Don't just say you or your clients are green—prove it.

Dwell Creative of Portland, Maine, is a small advertising and PR company that is not just promoting consumption, but communicating messages that will change how we think and live. Founder Johnny Rooks started Dwell "before I knew what LOHAS or greenwashing were."

GREEN LEADER

Hugh Hough trained with Al Gore to become one of the people helping to deliver the message on climate change. For more information about Green Team, see greenteamusa.com.

ECO-ISSUE

The Federal Trade Commission (FTC) currently is working on updating standards about what green companies can claim, fighting greenwashing.

"I expected it to be a single-person consultancy," Rooks says. "We now have an office in Los Angeles [California] and Portland, Maine, and are targeting other lifestyle-friendly cities." He has seen a growing number of other ad agencies go green as well. "When we started, I could find four other agencies doing what I wanted to do. Two years ago, we were named one of the top 25 out of 50. Now I suspect we are in the top 5 of 100."

How can green advertising agencies compete? Dwell's strategy is to go green all the way and challenge others to go there as well. "Competition is a good thing in this case. We welcome it," Rooks comments. "What we are doing to compete in this market is to get serious. To challenge our clients to move along the spectrum of 'green-ness'. Many clients are now part of our Dwell Deeper program that helps them become better corporate citizens by teaming them with other clients. Just as our competition is heating up, so is that of our clients. The greenest one wins, in a sense. My dream would be to have the reputation of 'there are many green agencies out there, but if you are serious about it and don't mind being challenged, call Dwell Creative.'" For some ad companies and their clients, going green is not an endpoint but an ongoing journey toward developing a fully sustainable business in harmony with the environment.

Opportunities for green advertising include:

- ※ Creating green advertising
- ※ Launching media outlets focused on specific developing niches in the green economy
- ※ Auditing companies to confirm green claims in ads

Developing green ads is an opportunity for creative individuals who are up to the challenge. Businesses and others needing ads often are attracted to small nimble advertising companies. Developing green ads can start as a small, at-home venture, with the internet helping to level the playing field.

Local companies might be a place to start looking for clients, knocking on their door if necessary. A little guerilla marketing might be in order, demonstrating your savvy by getting your own message out. Once you start, the path forward just gets greener and greener. By continuing to push the envelope, green ad companies will drive us all to a deeper shade of green.

OPPORTUNITY 57

Green Dry Cleaning

The Market Need	Dry cleaning that is better for our health or the planet
The Mission	Clean clothes without hurting people or the planet
Knowledge to Start	Dry-cleaning alternatives
Capital Required	$$$
Timing to Start	Months
Special Challenges	Getting customers to try new cleaning methods

There are a lot of clothes that will be destroyed if you wash them at home. I know—I've destroyed a few myself. For fabrics that cannot be cleaned any other way, we need dry cleaning. There are more than 30,000 dry cleaners in the United States, cleaning clothes by one of several methods that differ in how they treat your clothes and our planet (Dry Cleaning & Laundry Institute, 2008, ifi.org). In response to customers', and regulators', and property owners' concerns about the impact of dry cleaning there is a growing move toward greener options.

Dry cleaning uses solvents other than soap and water, and the solvent perchloroethylene (commonly called "perc") has been the most common dry-cleaning method in the United States for decades. According to the Dry Cleaning and Laundry Institute, 80 percent of the dry cleaners in the United States still use perc. This is not a good thing. Perc has been classified as a probable carcinogen and could cause other health problems, such as liver and kidney damage, in dry-cleaning workers and possibly health problems for consumers exposed to perc residue on clothes. Although perc consumption has decreased in recent years, perc remains a problem for the environment because millions of pounds have entered the air, soil, and water. Perc contamination of drinking water can force costly cleanups.

The problems with perc have motivated a search for dry-cleaning alternatives, which now include hydrocarbons, silicon-based cleaner, so-called wet cleaning, and carbon dioxide (CO_2) liquid. These are not all equally green. Hydrocarbon dry cleaning, for example, uses solvents other than perc that may call themselves green but which release compounds that might be unhealthy and can still pollute soil and water. The Environmental Protection Agency (EPA) has asked for more information about the impact of hydrocarbon dry cleaning on health and the environment. The dry-cleaning system marketed as Green Earth Cleaning, produced by General Electric and Johnson & Johnson, uses a silicone-based solvent that is reported by its producers to be safe and generally is agreed to do a good job cleaning clothes. However, questions have been raised by others about the safety of the solvent D5 used in this system, citing studies suggesting a risk of cancer.

Wet cleaning doesn't emit any volatile compounds, cleaning clothes with water and soap, using racks to prevent shrinking, and tailoring the treatment for the individual piece of clothing to prevent damage. Wet cleaning apparently is safe for workers and the environment, and does a good job getting clothes clean, but it takes more time than some methods and has been reported to shrink clothes in some cases. Most dry cleaners use wet cleaning on occasion at least for specific types of garments.

INDUSTRY INFO
To find a CO_2 dry cleaner in your area, visit findCO2.com.

Another green option is liquid CO_2, a cleaning method that doesn't produce any volatile emissions, and doesn't have any reported health or environmental issues. In addition, it does a solid cleaning job, and leaves clothes smelling and looking great. Robert Smerling of Brentwood Royal Cleaners in Los Angeles, California, has been using the CO_2

system since 2003 and reports it is the greenest dry-cleaning method for his company. In 2003, Consumer Reports found CO_2 dry cleaning to be the best, and it gained endorsements from Greenpeace and the EPA. "I'm the go-to guy for information about CO_2," Smerling says. CO_2 may not sound very climate friendly, but the process releases almost no CO_2 into the atmosphere, and uses CO_2 captured from other industries. The nontoxic and environmentally-friendly dry-cleaning process has been approved by the EPA and the California Air Resource Board. Although the number of shops using CO_2 still is small, it is growing in popularity.

Smerling has been on the CO_2 dry-cleaning scene since its inception in El Segundo, California, at a Hughes Aircraft facility. Along the way, he has worked to keep the process improving, so that "anything perc can do, CO_2 can do as well, if not better." And greening dry cleaning is not finished. "I know our industry has to change, and the government is not moving fast enough," Smerling says. Change can be hard, but the consequences of not changing can be worse.

Gordon Shaw of Hangers Cleaners (hangerssandiego.com) in San Diego, California, is another dry-cleaning business owner who has made the move into green dry cleaning with CO_2. Shaw had worked in the dry-cleaning industry for 20 years with perc when he first learned about CO_2 dry cleaning in 1999 and quickly realized that this was the future for him. Shaw got out of perc dry cleaning and opened his first CO_2 dry-cleaning location in San Diego, California, in 2001. He was the first CO_2 dry cleaner on the West Coast. Since then he has won numerous awards, received media attention, and helped spread the word for green dry cleaning around the world, getting others involved. He now has four CO_2 locations in San Diego, and has been on the San Diego *Business Journal's* list of the 100 Fastest Growing Private Companies for four years.

The Drycleaning & Laundry Institute (website at ifi.org, formerly the International Fabricare Institute) has a broad

GREEN LEADER

For more about Brentwood Royal Cleaners, visit royalcleaner.com. It's a family-run business, in the family for three generations. Customers send Brentwood Royal Cleaners clothes from across the country, not just for their cleaning method but for the great job they do.

array of services to help dry-cleaning businesses get started. They can help dry cleaners find insurance, equipment, and training at the School of Dry Cleaning Technology, and they also provide testing for dry cleaners to get certified in various aspects of dry cleaning, adding to their reputation with customers. According to the DLI, opening a dry cleaner costs about $250,000, not including improvements to the building for the business. The equipment for CO_2 dry-cleaning costs somewhat more than for other methods. The DLI also advises would-be dry cleaners to think about their target market and location carefully before opening. Are you planning to target young working professionals, families, high income, or other groups? The answer will affect the kinds of services you provide, the prices charged, advertising, and the location you choose.

Opportunities in green dry cleaning include:

- Opening a green dry-cleaning business, using an environmentally-friendly method such CO_2 dry cleaning
- Providing equipment for green dry cleaning outlets
- Selling eco-friendly hangers made from bio-plastic or recycled material

The market for green dry cleaners will be driven, in part, by customers eager to do right for the planet in every aspect of their lives. The market also is getting a boost from government action. In California, dry cleaners have to switch from perc by 2023 and other areas of the United States are likely to follow, particularly on the East and West Coasts. Because changing to a new technology is expensive, and existing dry cleaners are reluctant to switch, this leaves an opportunity for newcomers to start an eco-dry-cleaning business in their area. If you are going to get into green dry cleaning, study all the alternatives available and choose wisely.

Ecotourism Travel Guide

The Market Need	More people want to travel without hurting the planet
The Mission	Create an ecotourism travel business
Knowledge to Start	Travel, firsthand knowledge of eco-destinations
Capital Required	$
Timing to Start	Weeks to months
Special Challenges	Gaining firsthand knowledge of ecotourism destinations

The natural world is changing quickly in the face of environmental challenges. Natural areas that once seemed safely hidden in remote corners of the world are now squarely in the crosshairs of climate change, pollution, and habitat loss. With such rapid changes engulfing the natural world, many feel the need to visit and experience species and ecosystems before they change irreversibly or disappear. Ecotourism provides the opportunity to appreciate the natural world and help to preserve it at the same time. For tourists to explore the natural world without wreaking more destruction, ecotourism travel guides are needed.

According to the International Ecotourism Society, ecotourism is "responsible travel to natural areas that conserves the environment and improves the well-being of local people." Ecotourism has been growing between 20 and 34 percent per year since the 1990s, three times faster than the broader tourism market (International Ecotourism Society, ecotourism.org). In the United States, ecotourism is estimated to be a $77 billion industry, covering a broad range of activities, including:

- Eco-volunteering
- Adventure sports
- Wilderness adventure trips

- Nature travel
- Education

ECO-TIP

For local people to participate in and support preservation, they must see it as a benefit rather than another imposition from developed countries.

Ecotourism also represents an important economic opportunity for developing countries, helping them to value their natural assets, preserve them, and provide jobs and income. Clear-cutting a forest provides jobs and income only once, while with ecotourism, the intact forest can generate income month after month and year after year. If forests can generate more revenue with ecotourism than with logging, people will see the value of preservation and ensure the integrity of the ecosystems responsible for their livelihood. Costa Rica often is described as the example of what can be done with ecotourism, with more than a million visitors and a billion dollars in revenue each year, supporting conservation through lasting economic benefit.

If you want to survive in the travel business these days, you can't just sell tickets on the phone. The rapid growth in ecotourism comes amid tight times for travel agents in general. Online booking of flights and accommodations has led consumers to plan their own trips, forcing travel agents to evolve—specializing in organizing tours, for example. Ecotourism is an opportunity to do well by providing knowledge and participating directly in personally tailored trips as a travel guide.

RELATED TREND

One use of offsets (Opportunity 27) is to eliminate carbon emissions resulting from travel, whether for business or pleasure. Offset providers often have a calculator that can estimate how much is needed to make eco-trips carbon neutral. Those traveling for ecotourism may be particularly inclined to invest in travel offsets.

With ecotourism growing so rapidly and attracting so many people, there are challenges as well. While its goals are worthy, its outcomes sometimes have been less then perfect. In some cases, the popularity of ecotourism and the number of visitors results in harming locations rather than protecting them. Water resources can be strained, waste and garbage accumulated, local people displaced, habitats further stressed, and animals harmed by those who travel to see them. Ironically, poorly designed ecotourism can hurt the very thing that attracts people in the first place.

However, the answer to these problems is not to stop ecotourism. Trying to stem the tide of ecotourism seems unlikely and unwise, despite the concerns. Many of the poorest countries depend on ecotourism, and the money generated may be the best protection for the ecosystems. Parks and preserves are unlikely to remain undisturbed in areas with little money for park protection and rising pressure for resources, food, and income. For these areas, the absence of ecotourism may be worse than its presence. The solution is doing a better job.

The best opportunity for travel guides and the solution for poorly-executed ecotourism is to specialize in providing ecotourism with the most favorable impact on the environment. With firsthand knowledge from traveling to eco-destinations yourself, you can provide the best experience for your clients and have the most positive environmental impact. Don't just sell tickets or book reservations; be an ecotourism guru, investigating every facet of destinations as well as their impact on natural systems and native peoples. Are visiting tourists depleting water resources or leaving mounds of garbage? Are projects run by large hotel conglomerates, with major developments impinging on habitats and exporting cash, or are they small projects that help local people? Do large numbers of visitors create air and noise pollution? Being an ecotourist yourself to see firsthand the good, the bad, and the ugly allows you to better understand the pitfalls and build a better business.

Being a guru means informing people about the difference between greenwashed mass tourism and ecotourism that has a genuinely positive environmental impact. Most people who seek out green tourism are well-intentioned enough to make the right choice if they are informed, and many will even pay a little more to do so. It's not that easy to use the internet or a brochure to tell which travel destinations genuinely protect nature. This creates the need for a knowledgeable guide who can organize genuinely green trips.

ECO-TIP

Working as a guide and traveling to sites provides a great deal of insider knowledge, putting you in demand as a consulting resource for others. Start a website and promote this side of your business.

STRATEGY FOR SUCCESS

Giving to ecotourism-related projects is a good way to show your commitment to customers and native people, helping to ensure the long-term success of your business.

Opportunities in ecotourism include:

* Educating others about the field
* Traveling to key locations for firsthand knowledge
* Participating in industry associations
* Promoting ecotourism in the community and on the internet
* Giving back

Ecotourism can save habitats and species. As the world's population grows, there will be few, if any, areas where humans do not affect the natural world. Finding win-win solutions for local economies and nature may be essential for the long-term survival of both. There is so much to see in the world and so much that needs saving—the possibilities are immense.

OPPORTUNITY 59

Retail and Restaurant Green Rating

The Market Need	People want to buy green things, but don't always have enough information to do so
The Mission	Rank the greenness of restaurants and retail outlets to guide shopping decisions
Knowledge to Start	Retail, environment
Capital Required	$$
Timing to Start	Months to years
Special Challenges	Time to build a database of reviews

The green economy has grown to between an estimated $200 and $300 billion, and continues its skyward climb. But still it's not always easy shopping green. When people go shopping and don't buy at green stores, it's not because they are opposed to being green. Far from it—most people want to do the right thing, but don't always buy green for a variety of reasons. Some think green products are too expensive, a luxury; others are skeptical that green products work well or provide a real environmental benefit. Another limitation is a lack of good information. It's not always obvious from looking at a menu or clothing on a rack what the greenest shopping choices are. Providing information for consumers about greenness of restaurants and retail outlets as well as the products they sell is an opportunity to speed the green revolution.

It's easy for consumers to forget how much power they wield. Businesses supply what consumers buy, and if people don't buy a product, it disappears from store shelves. The way for consumers to support green business is to vote with their dollars—green economics at work the old-fashioned way. When business moves in that direction, even the crustiest business curmudgeon will become as green as grass.

How does a consumer know which restaurants are green? Certain categories are inherently greener than others, making some choices clear. Vegetarian food automatically scores greener than a steak house. But if a customer really wants a steak, which steak house is the greenest? Perhaps one provides only corn-fed beef, while another uses beef from cattle that grazed on open pasture, a much greener practice. Are there any restaurants that emphasize the use of local food in your neighborhood? Which seafood restaurants use sustainable fisheries? The answers to these questions might not always be obvious. Similarly, which retail outlets are greenest? The greenness is not just what is stocked in the store or served at the restaurant, but runs deep into the energy efficiency of buildings, how products are made, how they are shipped, the carbon footprint of supply chains, and more broadly, how workers are treated.

I don't think there is one universal definition of what is green and what isn't. For some, being green is strictly about environmental issues, but many people also consider social issues. Intuitively, this seems right; if natural capital were improved locally but at the expense of human capital in another part of the world, the end result probably wouldn't be considered green. For your green-rating business you will have to set some guidelines about how green businesses are judged, whether to include social issues, for example.

The more stores and products compete for the green label, the more consumers need an independent third party to sort out the true greens from the pale greens. When your retail dollars are based on good information, they have the greenest impact. Given the rapidly growing number of people who want to do the right thing with their money, there is a growing need for services to rank the environmental impact of stores and restaurants, and provide this information to consumers.

Greenopia of Santa Monica, California, is a green-rating service that is ranking the greenness of restaurant and retail outlets in Los Angeles, San Francisco, and New York and more cities are coming all the time. They pre-screen businesses to focus on those that are green, and then rank them with one to four leaves based on their greenness. The founder, Gay Browne, started Greenopia when she found it difficult to find green shops and restaurants. Today, Greenopia is becoming more than a book or a web resource; Greenopia is developing into a community of people trying to green their lives and their cities with the purchases they make.

If your area does not have a green guide, creating one is a way to build a business. The green economy is spreading quickly in large and small cities and towns that might not yet be served by a green guide. Another niche for a green-rating service is to target a distinct market that others have not taken on yet, such as tackling the broader retail market and not limiting yourself to ranking the greenest of the green, which still represents a small part of the market in most areas. Focusing on the top segment leaves out most stores

GREEN LEADERS

Visit greenopia.com to learn more, and see reviews for green stores and restaurants in a growing number of cities including Seattle, Washington; Portland, Oregon; and the San Francisco East Bay area. EcoMetro guides also help with green shopping in a variety of cities. Visit ecometro.com for more information. EcoMetro guides are produced by Celilo Group Media based in Portland, Oregon.

and consumers. In either case, a green rating service can start small without many financial obligations, operating from your home.

As a group of people sharing a commitment to similar causes, the green community is starting to engage in green social networking on the internet, creating green versions of MySpace. One example is dotherightthing.com, in which community members rank retail outlets by their environmental impact, with the goal of driving corporations to improve their environmental performance. One opportunity for a green rating service is to create green social networking that incorporates reviews and ranking by community members.

Opportunities in green rating services include:

- Publishing local green guides in book form
- Creating internet-based green guides ranking a broader range of retail outlets or a different market
- Creating green social networking including reviews of restaurants and retail

A green-rating service is good not just for consumers but also for the true green entrepreneurs, bringing business their way. Ratings help consumers avoid greenwashing by providing accurate assessments of vendors and their goods. And for the wannabe green businesses? Well, they are welcome to the bandwagon for now, but they need to clean up their act or risk being thrown off the back. After all, just because we're greenies does not mean we're weenies.

> **RELATED TREND**
>
> Green auditing for green guides is a service that has come with green advertising (see Opportunity 56). A green auditor helps retailers and consumers to understand and communicate the environmental impact of shopping.

OPPORTUNITY 60

Green Home Remodeling

The Market Need	New green construction gets a lot of attention, but greening millions of existing homes is equally important
The Mission	Help homeowners remodel, redecorate, and redesign in the greenest way
Knowledge to Start	Building, redecorating, interior design, sustainable materials
Capital Required	$$
Timing to Start	Months
Special Challenges	Preconceptions about green building and remodeling

Americans spent $155 billion on remodeling and home improvement in 2006 (Joint Center for Housing Studies, Harvard), seeking improvement in their homes and lives. As green building grows, more remodeling work is going green as well. Helping homeowners increase their energy efficiency is a big part of the story (see Chapter 3), but people also want their homes to look gorgeous and green, like the green homes on TV and in magazines. Homeowners have seen the look and are hungry for it, but not everybody can afford to demolish their old home and start from scratch. In addition, customers increasingly are eager to avoid the negative environmental impact of many building materials and the chemicals that some materials release into the indoor environment. Contractors who give homes green makeovers are filling a market need and a higher purpose, making homes and the planet healthier.

Appearance, cost, time, and reliability always are important remodeling factors. Green remodeling also must consider how materials are made, where they come from, and how they might affect the health of the occupants. Green remodeling avoids materials that can release a variety of unwanted and unhealthy chemicals into the air inside the home, including volatile organic compounds (VOCs), a wide range of chemicals that enter the air from building materials. The smell that fresh paint often has comes from VOCs. The EPA has found VOCs can accumulate inside homes up to ten times the levels found outside, exposing building occupants to unhealthy levels of pollution. Carpets, paints, varnishes, caulking, insulation adhesives, and plywood all emit VOCs as well as formaldehyde, a chemical known to cause cancer.

Green building materials also are evaluated for their impact on the environment during production. Organic architect Eric Corey Freed surveys building materials in his book *Green Building & Remodeling for Dummies*, identifying materials that work well for green building as well as unhealthy or environmentally damaging materials that should be avoided. Freed notes that one of the most pervasive and worst materials is vinyl. Although touted at times as a wonder plastic, Freed writes that vinyl "is the worst plastic from an environmental-health perspective and should be avoided in any form." More and more manufacturers are heeding this advice, but vinyl still can crop up in surprising places, making it essential for remodelers to have a thorough knowledge of materials.

In his book, Freed also dispels common myths about green building and remodeling. Green buildings cost more than other buildings? "With a clear budget, there is no reason why you can't build a green building for the same price or less than the cost of a traditional building," Freed writes, adding that according to recent information from the U.S. Green Building Council, green methods add 0 to 1 percent to the cost of a building. Green materials are more expensive? "Although some green materials cost more than their traditional counterparts, many more green materials cost far less than the standard." Green buildings look funny? "Most green buildings look just like their traditional non-green counterparts." Working in green remodeling, a contractor will encounter these misconceptions; as you help clients look more closely at green remodeling, the objections will melt away.

GREEN LEADER

Eric Corey Freed is a well-known green architect and much more. See Freed's website at organicarchitect.com for more information about green building, green remodeling, and green living.

Contractors can take a few easy steps to green a home significantly in appearance and efficiency. Lighting? Try daylighting, using natural light indoors rather than electric light, with Solatube of Vista, California, or lighting with compact fluorescent bulbs or LEDs. Painting? Low-VOC paint is available from several vendors, and surfaces made with colored plaster have the color embedded in the material, reducing the need for future painting. Carpeting? Green carpeting alternatives are available from sources such as Interface of Atlanta, Georgia, and Shaw Floors of Atlanta, Georgia, woven from recycled or sustainable material. Wood floors? Consider reclaimed wood, or sustainably grown and Forest Stewardship Council (FSC)-certified flooring. Countertops? Use recycled materials such as salvaged stone, or glass.

There are many resources to help existing contractors green a remodeling business. For example, the National Association of the Remodeling Industry (NARI) has a Green Remodeling educational program. Going green will help remodeling contractors to differentiate their businesses, carving out a distinct image to compete in challenging economic times. If you are an interior decorator or doing remodeling work already, becoming a green remodeler means learning the field and securing work to start building a green reputation. Prove what you can do by starting with small projects and integrating green work into jobs you already have, talking to clients about the benefits of a green approach.

RELATED TREND

Some cities, such as Los Angeles and San Francisco, are fortunate to have retail outlets such as Living Green that specialize in green building materials. The opportunities for green stores like this will grow along with green remodeling.

The clients you work with on green projects might be repeat customers, and as business progresses, you may find new clients coming your way. As in other types of remodeling work, word of mouth can draw in business.

Green remodelers doing major reconstruction work on homes should consult or work with experienced green architects and build a network of subcontractors who work well with green materials. Nobody can do it all individually; the contractor's work is only as good as that of his subcontractors, making a good network essential for success. Energy efficiency is inherently part of the green story, and doing major remodeling without including easy energy improvements is a real lost opportunity. Another opportunity with green remodeling is to find a creative use for material and fixtures that would otherwise end up at the dump (see Opportunity 39). Donating usable construction material for reuse can help the homeowner offset project costs with tax deductions.

Opportunities in green remodeling include:

- ● Working as a green interior designer
- ● Working as a green remodeling contractor
- ● Opening a green retail outlet providing eco-friendly products for the home and garden

In the end, remodeling is inherently greener than new construction. Most demolition and new construction produces tons of waste that end up in landfills. Think twice before demolishing existing homes to build new green ones. See if that old home already has a basic framework you can work with and improve on. Your work may or may not end up on TV or in a magazine, but it will certainly help us live in healthier homes and a healthy world.

OPPORTUNITY 61

Green Business Consulting

The Market Need	The greening of the economy creates risks and opportunities that businesses often are not prepared to deal with
The Mission	Help businesses go green and build value
Knowledge to Start	Experience in building business and in sustainability
Capital Required	$
Timing to Start	Years (of experience)
Special Challenges	Getting the consulting business started

Business executives face a brave new green world. The rapid growth of the green-business revolution can be exciting, but if a business is out of sync with the sudden wave of green, company leaders might feel less excited. Once a business decides to go green, what comes next? What does it take for a business to be green and what will it mean for the bottom line? What does a sustainable business look like? Environmental issues are new to many executives; they often need help from experts to deal with the risks and opportunities of the green economy. Some businesses hire a chief sustainability officer to help out (Opportunity 12), but another option is to turn to outside experts and bring in the hired greens, the green business consultants, to help make the change.

An increasing number of businesses want to go green but lack a map to get there. Green business consultants have experience dealing with the risks and opportunities of the green world, and can help companies translate the desire to do the right thing into business reality. Many of the issues businesses face in going green are core strategic issues that cut across industries. Advising about these fundamentals often depends more on the consultant's experience in building business value than on having industry-specific experience.

Jim Hartzfeld is the founder and managing director of InterfaceRAISE of Atlanta, Georgia, a consulting group that grew out of pioneering work at Interface Inc. to transform it into a more sustainable floor-covering business. Historically, carpeting has been an industry with a significant environmental impact. Ray Anderson, the founder of Interface, went through a personal revelation in 1994, "a spear in the chest" moment when reading *The Ecology of Commerce* by Paul Hawken. His change of heart moved him to adjust how Interface did business; today Interface is widely recognized as a leader in developing sustainable business practices. This journey still is under way. Hartzfeld and others at Interface looked back over their experiences to see what made the transition work, investigating "what made it stick, how it drove business

GREEN LEADER

Ray Anderson relates his story and the journey of Interface toward sustainability in his book *Mid-Course Correction*.

value," and how they could help others down the same path. They found the issues faced to develop sustainable business practices were not limited to Interface or the flooring industry. Addressing environmental issues affected core, strategic elements that every company faces: including brand and reputation, opportunities to reduce costs, access to talent, worker engagement, and productivity.

Clients are motivated by many different factors to start through the door that leads toward sustainability. "Everybody's door is a different shape," Hartzfeld says, "A unique set of circumstances that engages them on a personal level. Getting married, losing a job, having kids, [there are] dozens of different factors that come together to get people to walk through, but then there's no going back." There are three main ways companies get moving in a green direction, Hartzfeld says. The first is through a grassroots movement from the bottom up, with people motivated to come together and perhaps create a green team. The second route is spurred by a company leader (or leadership team), as was the case with Anderson at Interface. The third route is when companies are pushed by technology, customers, or energy costs to make a change in order to avoid risk or seize opportunity.

Change can be difficult, and obstacles often arise along the way, sometimes from within the organization. One of the biggest challenges Hartzfeld has found is "the mind-set that we cannot afford this." To get around this, he helps clients create a plan to start small and quickly see a return on their investment with easier changes, such as improving energy efficiency. From there, companies inevitably continue forward to tackle more ambitious projects. Once companies get started moving toward green, Hartzfeld finds they don't stop.

Daniel Esty and Andrew Winston have advised many companies on their environmental efforts, and in their insightful book *Green to Gold,* they profile the efforts of some of the largest companies working to green their businesses

ECO-ISSUE

Going green is a smart business move to increase productivity by getting workers "organized and energized around your goals," says Jim Hartzfeld of InterfaceRAISE. He found that adding "higher purpose improves productivity." Employees care more about their work when they believe in what the company is doing and can be a part of it.

and show others how to do the same. Describing businesses that succeed in their environmental initiatives as "waveriders," Esty and Winston provide actions that others can use to gain "eco-advantage." According to Esty and Winston, one of the most important success factors for waverider companies is a willingness to change their mind-set, viewing business factors through an environmental lens to find opportunities. These businesses make a commitment and stick to it, closely tracking performance on environmental factors. Along the way, companies remodel to improve performance, increase efficiency, and reduce environmental impact.

The extensive experience of green leaders is an invaluable resource to accelerate the economy's transition toward sustainability. Advisory teams also have been formed by other leaders in the green revolution, including Janine Benyus, the author of *Biomimicry* and co-founder of the Biomimicry Guild (see Chapter 5), as well as L. Hunter Lovins and Amory Lovins, co-authors of *Natural Capitalism* and founders of the Natural Capitalism Solutions and the Rocky Mountain Institute. Each of these individuals and teams has its own unique perspective about changing business practices. Just as there are many doors clients pass through to get started, once through, there are many perspectives consultants provide to move forward.

There are many ways in which green-business consultants can help businesses improve their financial and environmental performance, establishing best practices in different fields. As businesses are first forming they often need assistance in creating a business plan, and in financing, marketing, and product design. Large businesses need strategic consulting in overarching issues, helping them come to terms with how climate change and other environmental issues affect the direction of the company. Consultants can specialize in improving energy efficiency of buildings and transportation, and helping a business get access to renewable energy. Consultants can find opportunities for businesses to reduce waste and use resources more effectively, cutting costs to improve their bottom line. For some, their field of expertise will be regulatory challenges, helping businesses ensure that they comply with present and future regulation. As businesses reduce their greenhouse-gas emissions, they need help from expert consultants in how best to track, measure, and report on this and other environmental impacts. Finally, consultants can help businesses not just avoid problems but also make the most of the new opportunities that environmental issues create.

These leaders are changing how business is done, but you don't have to be the greenest or most famous green pioneer to make a contribution. You do have to be credible in selling your service as a way to build business value. Sit down and look at your experience, put your doubts aside, and show how your experience can build value for businesses while reducing their environmental impact.

Opportunities for green consultants include:

- Strategic consulting, how to get started
- Consulting for energy efficiency and renewable energy
- Encouraging waste reduction
- Ensuring compliance with regulations
- Discovering opportunities for new products
- Tracking greenhouse-gas emissions
- Writing sustainability reports

With green business growing quickly and businesses in every industry considering environmental concerns, there probably never has been a better time to be a green-business consultant. Find real business needs by talking to people, and map out how you can fill those needs with your consulting service. Businesses are increasingly receptive to doing the right thing, but they will want to know more before paying for a consultant's services. Don't be afraid to think of yourself as a product; even the greenest consultants need to sell themselves. Then, as for other businesses, the biggest hurdle in beginning a consulting business is getting started through the door. Once you start, you won't stop.

Green Cleaning Services

The Market Need	All those glistening, green homes and buildings need to be cleaned
The Mission	Clean buildings in an environmentally responsible and healthy way
Knowledge to Start	Janitorial, cleaning
Capital Required	$
Timing to Start	Weeks (to convert an existing service to green cleaning)
Special Challenges	Belief that tough cleaning requires tough chemicals

Cleaning homes and buildings can involve a multitude of chemicals—such as bleach, strong detergents, and ammonia—that can pose a risk to health and the environment. Some chemicals are added to products for looks or smell—making cleaning fluids bluer or sudsier, for example. Whether inhaled from the air or absorbed through the skin, cleaning chemicals can pose a hazard to those who clean homes and buildings, and building occupants also can be exposed to lower levels of the same chemicals. A 2000 report from the Center for Competitive Analysis at the University of Missouri estimated that the U.S. cleaning market was as large as $50 billion, with more than 68,000 businesses involved. Commercial buildings are the largest segment of business. With people and businesses working hard to green their lives and buildings, removing sources of indoor air pollution and reducing the impact of buildings on the environment, it's only natural that people want their buildings cleaned without toxic or irritating chemicals.

INDUSTRY INFO

The Janitorial Products Pollution Prevention Project, sponsored by the EPA, examined the full range of janitorial product replacements to find cleaner alternatives. It is estimated that 6 percent of cleaning workers are injured by chemical exposure each year (Culva, Alicia, et al, "Cleaning for Health: Products and Practices for a Safer Indoor Environment," INFORM Inc., 2002). To avoid this, the EPA recommends alternatives for many cleaning applications. 🦆

The number of LEED-certified buildings is growing steadily. The materials used in these buildings are hand-picked for not emitting formaldehyde, volatile organic compounds, or other chemicals. The building process also works to minimize pollution and waste from construction, and green buildings are designed to conserve water. All of this means that cleaning green buildings requires equal care. If cleaned in the usual way, the value of greening might easily be wasted. Waterless urinals can help save water, but cleaning waterless urinals with the wrong material may negate the whole investment. Green cleaning involves avoiding any chemicals that are skin irritants, toxic, or harmful to the environment. The LEED for Existing Buildings rating system looks at the cleaning methods used, further supporting entrepreneurial, green cleaning services.

One important aspect of green cleaning is the products that are used. The independent nonprofit Green Seal based in Washington, DC, certifies cleaning products as green if they pass 15 criteria, and are safe and clean for use. Green Seal certification often is used to guide purchasing decisions by government agencies, large private institutions, and universities. Companies, such as Method (based in San Francisco, California), Ecover (headquartered in Antwerp, Belgium), and Seventh Generation (Burlington, Vermont) provide green

INFORMATION RESOURCE

Government departments and offices may look for green cleaning providers. For a description of green janitorial work from the Office of the Federal Environmental Executive, see ofee.gov/gp/greenjanitorial.html.

HOMEMADE GREEN
Another alternative for green-cleaning entrepreneurs is using simple ingredients—vinegar, baking soda, and lemon juice—to make their own cleaners.

cleaning products. Clorox has even launched its own line of green cleaning products called Green Works, all the ingredients are natural and listed on the label, no hidden surprises.

Some cleaning services specialize in green cleaning, and others provide it as a premium service. Although competition is intense in the crowded market for traditional cleaning services, you can distinguish your service by going green. Another business advantage of green cleaning services is that workers are less frequently ill from chemical exposure. This may give your company a better reputation and keep business coming your way.

Currently, there isn't any special certification required to be considered an eco-cleaner. There are services that can provide voluntary certification, such as with the Green Clean Institute of Plainfield, Illinois (greencleaninstitute.com), but since eco-cleaners are not regulated, anybody can call themselves green. For now, it's up to you to prove your greenness. Going 100 percent green helps to capture the upper end of the market. Providing more services beyond basic cleaning also may help your green cleaning service to stand out. Try including small repairs. For example, in addition to green toilet cleaning, how about fixing a leaky one to waste less water? Little things—such as fixing blinds and changing light bulbs for busy clients—may help keep contracts secure.

Opportunities in green cleaning include:

⊛ Creating a green cleaning service for homes and offices
⊛ Specializing in cleaning LEED-certified buildings
⊛ Providing green cleaning products

The market for green cleaning is not limited to those sparkling green LEED-certified buildings. Many customers welcome green cleaning wherever they live and work. Starting a green cleaning service is not without competition, but with the many advantages the green approach offers, a strong green-cleaning business has many advantages and is likely to do well.

OPPORTUNITY 63

Recycled Clothing

The Market Need	Our closets are overflowing, in part with old clothes
The Mission	Reinvent clothing to reduce waste
Knowledge to Start	Creativity, sewing, fashion
Capital Required	$ (starting small, at home)
Timing to Start	Weeks to months
Special Challenges	The throw-away mentality

We spend a lot of money on clothes, often driven by the desire for something fresh, new, and trendy. We want to look young, attractive, and successful, or make other statements about who we are with what we wear. The problem with making such statements is that clothes increasingly are becoming disposable. The EPA estimated in 2003 that there was 10 million tons of clothing and other textile waste thrown away. Clothes come home in bags, get worn a few times, and then get shoved to the back of the closet and forgotten. To address this problem, some clothing entrepreneurs are rethinking the clothes they are making and looking for ways to waste less, recycling existing clothes to give them a new life.

Wearing something green is a new fashion statement, with some people proclaiming their commitment to a sustainable planet with their clothes. While organic cotton is a major improvement over conventionally grown cotton, reusing clothing we already have is even greener.

Wendy Tremaine created Swap-O-Rama-Ramas—meets that now occur in many cities, as one way to reuse clothing. At these events, people bring their old clothes, swap them, or modify them at sewing stations with help from skilled workers. When a shirt or skirt wears out or goes out of fashion, take it to the Swap-O-Rama-Rama and trim, cut, resew, mend, and refashion it. This concept has quickly spread across the country, and even across the globe, giving people something fun to do with their old clothes.

Another approach is to refashion previously worn clothing and waste textiles into something entirely new and fresh. Emmeline 4 Re (based in London, England) was founded by Emmeline Child and specializes in converting clothes from The Salvation Army and waste textiles to make original, fresh new creations with a distinct style. Using recycled clothing, each piece is unique and handmade, and diverts material that would otherwise end up in a landfill. You can see some of Emmeline Child's designs at emmeline4re.co.uk. Child built a name for herself and her brand with top retailers such as Topshop, then moved to small boutiques.

RELATED TREND

Some clothing producers like Patagonia have clothing lines that are recycled by shredding old clothes and reweaving the material into new clothes. Helping other clothing producers to create take-back and recycling programs also might be an opportunity for a new business.

With each piece produced by hand, there is no mass merchandising for Child's recycled clothing. "I made a conscious decision to move the clothing into boutiques as the product suits this environment better," Child says. The unique nature of her clothing is part of its charm; with Child's work there is no chance of two people showing up at a party wearing the same dress. This is not the cheapest or easiest approach to clothing, but customers are responding to recycled clothing positively, supporting the trend. Child says "This is definitely a growing sector of the fashion industry, in both fashion and jewelry. As it is the most ethical way to make 'new' clothes, people are exploring this while adding their own signature design . . . . [M]aking something beautiful from effectively 'waste' continues to inspire . . . . Business is growing and taking me down all different avenues so I never stop learning!" A business like this that combines creativity, business savvy, and an environmental contribution can be rewarding in more ways than one.

Lots of people have drawers and boxes full of old T-shirts that they don't wear but also don't want to throw away. Businesses are finding creative new ways to use T-shirts such as making a quilt with campusquilt.com. Handbags and purses are being made from recycled material as well, even inner-tubes. Hannah Rogge is providing ways to reuse clothing, first as a hobby, then as an author and a businesswoman. Her book *Save This Shirt* describes ways to take old clothes and revive them.

There are as many approaches that clothing re-designers can pursue as there are styles and fashions. Some customers may enjoy works that join styles from different places and times into something new for today. Others want a more subtle and conservative look, still using recycled clothing. Working as a tailor is an old but green profession to help people get more use out of clothing they already have. Recycled clothing can be either a service or a product.

Opportunities for recycled clothing include:

* Designing and producing recycled clothing
* Recycling handbags
* Recycling clothing at do-it-yourself meets
* Providing recycled clothing as a service, with people providing their clothing to be redone

A business with recycled clothing can start small, one garment at a time, and can happen at home. For creative people with skill in fashion design and sewing, all it takes to get started is some used clothing, some time and energy, and some sewing tools. There are mountains of clothes out there, waiting to be reborn. Breathing new life into clothes is one strategy to create your own green clothing business.

OPPORTUNITY 64

Virtual Business Meetings

The Market Need	Business travel takes time and energy, taking a toll on travelers and the environment
The Mission	Host virtual business meetings, reducing business travel
Knowledge to Start	Information technology, communications
Capital Required	$
Timing to Start	Weeks to months
Special Challenges	Getting clients to change engrained travel habits

The business meeting is a time-honored tradition. Doing business with someone still means shaking their hand, looking them in the eye, seeing how their eyes move, and watching their body language to get a feel for who they are. With globalization, businesspeople are traveling more and farther than ever, taking a toll on travelers, their business, and the environment. Jet travel contributes an estimated 4 to 9 percent of all human activity causing climate change (davidsuzuki.org). The time is right to provide ways to collaborate without traveling.

Constant jet travel is hard on travelers. Although we glamorize the life of the high-flying businessperson leaping from jet to jet, it's not much fun in reality. Traveling across continents for a one-hour meeting is neither a productive use of time nor healthy. In addition to the possible exposure to infectious diseases (*New York Times*, December 9, 2003), constant jet lag wears down the immune system and even shrinks the brain (*Nature Neuroscience*, 2001). Half-asleep, brain-shrunken employees might not be making the best decisions, and this might not be good for business. And if it's not important business, why have the meeting?

What are the other options? Conference calls are often more like one-way communication rather than real collaboration. People often hit the mute button and tune out, continuing to type away at their e-mail. Meanwhile, other information and communication systems for collaboration have improved. Video-conferencing draws together project teams spread across the globe, and web conferencing is another ready option. The improved technology means more people are using these tools routinely. Necessity has been the mother of invention, and with global business, constant collaboration at a distance is often a necessity for success.

Although web and video-conferencing are well-developed technologies, people often are unfamiliar with and reluctant to use these tools. Many companies have invested in video-conferencing hardware or promoted web-conferencing, only to see the tools poorly adopted or abandoned. This is bound to change, but how fast is the question. Businesses can wait for the next generation of more communication-savvy workers or companies can make change happen today.

Improved collaboration requires more than providing technology and walking away. Improved collaboration requires changing how people work. Of course, the technology must work well, but people also must be comfortable with it and see how it helps them. The tools must be as simple and natural as picking up the telephone. One way to make this change happen and increase business value is to provide classes to help employees make better use of collaboration tools. Another way is to work as a consultant,

RELATED TREND

It is estimated that 29 million Americans telecommuted eight hours or more per month in 2006 ("Telework Trendlines for 2006," *World at Work*, worldatwork.org), and telecommuting also requires collaborative tools. Telecommuting is a great resource saver—the best commute is no commute. Work is increasingly about what you do, not face time. For telecommuting to be effective, though, people need good tools to work at home. Helping telecommuting with simple tools is a growing opportunity. ❦

IN THE LONG RUN

A major disruption in travel may lead to a big boost in the use of information technology to collaborate. If a flu pandemic or similar situation arose, international travel could be curtailed for months. Ongoing security hassles at airports already might be enough to prod executives to seek an alternative approach.

coming to the organization to examine how people are communicating. Start by seeing how much employees are traveling and why, and then show the business and individuals how they can save time, be more productive, and stay home more often by using the tools of technology.

The growth in virtual worlds is another interesting business option. Virtual worlds are growing into more than just a game; they provide the means for people to interact closely even when they are far apart. If video-conferencing is not enough, meeting in a virtual world allows immersive interaction. The virtual world, Second Life, allows businesses to create secure spaces for interaction and collaboration. Crowne Plaza and other hotel chains have created virtual meeting rooms, allowing groups to book rooms for meetings just as they would a real room. IBM is moving to do business in the Second Life world, opening a business group focused on virtual worlds. With its own real estate, currency, and news service, the Second Life world allows not just meetings, but virtual conferences, classrooms, and other get-togethers. With many curious about life and business in Second Life, but uncertain how to approach it, there is an opportunity for entrepreneurs to guide others to use virtual worlds for business.

Improving travel-free collaboration requires knowledge of information systems and telecommunications, but people and business skills also are needed to sell your business. After all, collaboration is about people working together.

Opportunities in virtual conferencing include:

● Teaching people how to use video-conferencing systems they already have
● Consulting on effective web-conferencing
● Hosting virtual-world business meetings and conferences
● Providing a tool kit to support effective telecommuting

Running information systems requires energy, but it takes less than jetting around the globe. For the moment, virtual conferencing still is not quite the same as shaking hands and looking a client in the eye, but it's getting closer. We need to get more comfortable with solutions that help us cross time zones without leaving our chair. It may still seem a little "out there," and not everybody is ready to fly through the virtual landscape, but not so long ago the personal computer and the internet also were broadly viewed as lacking in practical applications. Things change, and when it comes to business meetings, the change should be welcome.

> **ECO-TIP**
>
> Part of the continued support for crazy travel schedules may be the concern of employees that the boss will think less of them if they are not traveling. Working to provide companies with data that technology saves money and helps employees produce more may have more customers jumping to board your business.

OPPORTUNITY 65

Eco-Salon

The Market Need	Hair, nails, skin, and other salon treatments often use toxic chemicals
The Mission	Provide nontoxic beauty treatments
Knowledge to Start	Hair, nails, skin treatments
Capital Required	$$
Timing to Start	Weeks to months
Special Challenges	Educating customers and workers about the health issues of the beauty industry

According to *Start Your Own Hair Salon and Day Spa* (Entrepreneur Press and Eileen Figure Sandlin) and Bizstats.com, there were 313,000 U.S. beauty salons in 2002, with steady growth expected. Ranging from high-end, luxury day spas to small strip-mall locations, salons and spas are ubiquitous. Despite their variety, one thing they often share is their use of a wide range of chemicals. Even while we worry over trace levels of chemicals and pesticides in our food, salons and spas often apply many chemicals right onto skin and hair. Green spas and salons are emerging as a growing trend, providing healthy and natural beauty treatments.

The sources of chemicals in salons are many. Permanent hair dyes can penetrate into the scalp and bloodstream and many of the chemicals used have raised health concerns. In 2006, the European Union (EU) banned 22 hair-coloring chemicals because of a potential risk of bladder cancer, and cosmetics companies in the EU must provide safety files on all hair-coloring agents. Ammonia is commonly used to help hair color set, and getting a perm can expose clients and workers to chemicals, such as the compound ammonium thioglycollate, that help change the shape of hair. Nail salons can expose workers and clients to potentially toxic compounds, including formaldehyde, dibutyl phthalate, and toluene. Cosmetics contain many ingredients—including metals known to be toxic if ingested—that make consumers cringe.

RELATED TREND

European regulation of cosmetics is more stringent than in the United States. If other environmental fields are any indication, look for the United States to move in the European direction. For more about EU regulation of cosmetics, visit ec.europa.eu/enterprise/cosmetics.

There are nontoxic substitutes available for beauty treatments, using only natural and organic ingredients. EcoColors of Atlanta, Georgia, is one company offering healthier hair coloring products as an alternative, avoiding the toxic chemicals found in some products (ecocolors.net). NaturalSolutions of Westlake Village, California, (bewell staywell.com), offers a variety of nail-care products that avoid known toxic compounds. The great variety of products becoming available helps salons go green without sacrificing the range of services they provide.

Green spas and salons that use only natural ingredients and avoid toxic compounds are opening up around the United States and the world. Sree Roy of *Nails Magazine* has reported that going green is a major trend in spas and salons (greatreporter.com, November 2, 1007). The Nova Nail Spa in San Francisco, California; the Priti Organic Spa in New York City; and the Nusta Spa in Washington, DC, are just three examples of this trend. In addition to

carefully choosing treatments, many salons are also greening their interiors, with furniture made of renewable materials, energy-efficient appliances and lighting, as well as
organic food.

Many green spas target the luxury market. One business
opportunity is to find a niche in the high-end eco-salon
market. Another market is for eco-salons that are more
affordable than their ultra-luxurious brethren. With the
broadening interest in going green, now is the time for a
lower-priced green salon that can reach more people. The
first place to focus is on the ingredients, ensuring that the
materials used are devoid of harmful chemicals and still
effective. A dramatic interior remodel might be unnecessary, but there are many small, low-cost improvements—such
as low VOC (volatile organics) paint and energy-efficient lighting (including
skylights)—that can green any location.

A green spa can start small, with one person, focused just on nails or hair,
for example. In *Nails Magazine*, Roy describes several steps that green-salon
entrepreneurs can use to build their business. Being green requires knowing
your products thoroughly, educating workers about the products, and informing customers about the difference. Networking with the local green-business
community also will help you learn more about what it takes to go green, identify suppliers for your business, and get the word out.

Opportunites in eco-salons include:

- Opening a green nail salon
- Creating a chain of lower-cost green salons
- Providing green spas and consumers with organic
  and healthy beauty products
- Selling green beauty products as a homebased business

Start Your Own Hair Salon and Day Spa (Entrepreneur
Press and Eileen Figure Sandlin) describes several ways any

ECO-ISSUE

Recognizing the health problems
associated with beauty salons, the
EPA is providing grants to help
salons reduce their use of toxic
ingredients in what has been dubbed
the "Toxic Beauty Project."
Increased ventilation of nail salons
also may help reduce health
problems in beauty workers.

GOVERNMENT ACTION

California passed the Safe Cosmetics
Act in 2005, addressing the toxic
ingredients found in many cosmetics.
Toxic ingredients must now be
disclosed on the label in
California, a step forward.

RELATED TREND

Many salons earn extra income by selling products, and the opportunity is even greater for green salons to sell green products that are not in many outlets. Some brands with organic and natural products include Care by Stella McCartney (New York and London), Aveda, and the Organics or Dr. Weil-sponsored products from Origins. Selling green beauty products as a homebased business or on the internet are also options. 🐞

salon entrepreneur can start a business, and these apply to green salons as well. One approach is to look for a franchise. Another is to take over a shop from someone else. Taking over an existing salon and turning it green will require marketing about the change, but existing customers may provide a head start toward building something larger. Lastly, you could go it alone and start from scratch. This might be the hardest but also the most rewarding way to go. If your green salon takes off, you can expand your brand into a chain—the eco-salon for the masses—selling franchises rather than buying one. Whatever the path forward is, going green provides a variety of ways for salons to head in a new direction for the health of their customers, their workers, and the planet.

Green Transportation and Cities

More of the world's people live in cities than ever before. World-wide, the number of city dwellers has surpassed the number of those living in rural areas for the first time in human history, and cities are responsible for a large proportion of humanity's environmental impact. According to the United Nations, cities consume 75 percent of global energy and produce 80 percent of the world's greenhouse-gas emissions. The coming decades will see increasing concentration of populations in mega-cities (greater than 10 million people), and transporting clean food, water, and energy to these millions will leave a significant environmental trail. In response city leaders and entrepreneurs are working together to find green business solutions.

New urban models are being developed to make cities friendlier and healthier while reducing their environmental impact. City leaders are improving transit systems, imposing congestion taxes, increasing the efficiency of buildings with new green-building requirements, and banning plastic grocery bags. China is developing the Dongtan eco-city near Shanghai as an urban model; it is expected to absorb as much carbon as it produces. The Dongtan eco-city is expected to produce all of its power from renewable energy, eliminate between 90 and 100 percent of landfill waste, and save water with a dual piping system of fresh and recycled water. In the United States, city planners are playing a leadership role in addressing environmental issues, as demonstrated by the U.S. Mayors Climate Protection Agreement that had been signed by over 500 mayors by 2007. The city of Curitiba in Brazil is often studied and copied for its green urban innovations, as described in *Natural Capitalism* by Paul Hawken, Armory Lovins, and L. Hunter Lovins.

Transportation is a crucial economic concern for cities everywhere and is responsible for a large portion of their environmental impact. As cities grow larger and denser, how will people get where they need to go? How can people and goods move efficiently, with less traffic, less greenhouse-gas emissions, and less air pollution? Even as city leaders strive to increase use of rail systems and other mass transit, there is no indication that cars will go away. The United States has more cars than ever and the number of cars worldwide is steadily increasing, with millions of new cars hitting the roads in China and India. We need more efficient and less polluting cars, or we risk being overwhelmed by their emissions.

Consumers already have started changing the cars they buy in response to the increasing price of gasoline, making the Toyota Prius one of the best-selling cars in the United States. In 2007, the U.S. government passed an energy bill requiring the major car producers to increase their fleet average fuel efficiency from 25 miles per gallon to 35 miles per gallon by 2020. Selling more efficient cars has support from all sides, and there is a great deal of room to grow in the United States (Opportunity 66). The solutions are coming from players large and small, and selling green cars does not necessarily mean setting up a traditional car dealership with the major car companies. Greener cars might not even be cars that consumers own, but those they share (Opportunity 68).

In addition to changing our cars, we are changing the fuels they use to reduce pollution and dependence on oil. New cars with new fuels need new fueling stations to keep them moving, increasing the number of ethanol and biodiesel pumps, or building the infrastructure for hydrogen (Opportunity 67).

Mass transit is also receiving renewed attention in response to the pressures of increasing urban population, with interest in alternative models rising. Buses can provide a viable, low-cost alternative to rail-based systems, and smaller flexible bus systems can complement larger fixed routes (Opportunity 70). The innovative and low-cost bus system of Curitiba served as the model for the Metro Orange Line in Los Angeles, California, and alternatives such as this can help transit systems expand and become accessible for the most possible people.

Cars and transit are a big part of the urban scene, but other factors also are contributing to greening the urban and suburban landscape. Gardening tools such as lawn mowers and leaf blowers that use gas are noisy and can cause more pollution than cars. Gardeners who convert to gas-free tools can market themselves as "eco-gardeners," perhaps gaining a competitive edge (Opportunity 69).

Another feature of the urban and suburban landscape is the ubiquitous coffee shop. Starbucks has made some green moves in its history, but there is an opportunity for the next big coffee trend, which just might be green cafés (Opportunity 71).

Natural Capitalism concludes that Curitiba's success is not only because of good design and good policy, but also because of how city leaders view the city's residents, "not as a burden, but as its most precious resource, creators of its future." The green city of the future could be a very different place to live than many cities are today, and perhaps a much better one with the help of green businesses.

Green Car Dealership

The Market Need	More efficient cars are in high demand
The Mission	Sell fuel-efficient cars that pollute less
Knowledge to Start	Autos, sales
Capital Required	$$ (for an alternative model) to $$$$ (cars on a lot)
Timing to Start	Months to years
Special Challenges	Many new, competing technologies are coming to the market

Most oil is used as gas for our cars, which are speeding climate change for%ward. However, there is no indication that Americans will give up their cars anytime soon, and developing countries such as China are adding millions of new cars to the road. We love our cars, but we don't necessarily love the gasoline they use. If there is one thing that the Toyota Prius has shown, it's that Americans are not opposed to driving a great car that also gets great mileage. The Prius is only the start. A variety of green cars are coming to the market from different manufacturers, large and small. While sales of cars overall will not grow quickly in a mature market like the United States, sales of green cars are rising as rapidly as the price of oil.

In April 2008, one out of five cars sold in the United States was a compact or sub-compact model, up from one in eight a decade ago (*New York*

STRATEGY FOR SUCCESS

Green cars don't necessarily involve new technology. According to the ACEEE (American Council for an Energy Efficient Economy) ranking of the top green cars of 2007, several of the top-rated green cars are small cars using existing technology with smaller than average engines. The Toyota Corolla or Honda Civic are examples. Cars marketed in other parts of the world routinely outperform the mileage of even the Prius. Simply selling small cars like these is one way to start selling green cars. ❦

Times, May 2, 2008). Sales of the fuel-efficient Toyota Yaris are up 46 percent, while sales of SUVs are down 25 percent overall.

Green cars have high gas mileage and low emissions; as a result, they use less gasoline (and oil), produce less air pollution, and slow climate change. Green cars also help consumers spend less money on gas. At 25 miles per gallon, Ford's 1908 Model T had better mileage than the average car in the United States today, leaving a lot of room for improvement. To address this challenge large and small companies are developing a variety of technologies to produce new cars, including gas-electric hybrids, clean-diesel cars, plug-in hybrids, all-electric cars, and fuel-cell cars. The businesses racing to build clean, green cars are producing some of the most exciting automobiles seen in ages.

Thus far, most of the production-scale green cars are being produced by the large established companies, including gas-electric hybrid offerings from Toyota, Honda, Ford, and GM. Not every hybrid is equally green, however. The Prius and the Accord Hybrid get higher mileage (between 40 and 50 miles per gallon, or higher), while some SUV hybrids get more of an improvement in horsepower than mileage. Plug-in hybrids in development by Toyota and other major auto companies should be on the market by 2010, but meanwhile small, independent groups such as CalCARs of Palo Alto, California, are creating their own conversions or offering them as kits. The expense of these after-market conversions may limit their market

GREEN LEADERS

See CalCars.org for more information about converting hybrids to plug-in hybrids.

THE RACE FOR A GREEN CAR

The X Prize of $10 million for autos will go to the team that can design, build, and race a 100-mile-per-gallon car that can be produced commercially, is safe to ride in, and produces low emissions. The winner is supposed to be decided in 2010. For more, see auto.xprize.org.

impact to ultra-enthusiasts. Other entrants in the race—such as a plug-in hybrid that Chinese automaker BYD Auto is planning for the Chinese market—may find their way to the rest of the world, giving the big players a run for their money.

Electric autos also are getting more attention as the widely publicized Tesla shows. Setting aside the question of who killed the electric car, Tesla of San Carlos, California, and others are reviving the concept. Electric cars' mileage and emissions depend on how the electrical grid that fuels the car is powered, but calculations often show more than 100 miles per gallon. The Tesla roadster is being offered for almost $100,000 in its first production run, expected in 2008, but the price has not squelched enthusiasm for the sleek, sexy auto. Faster accelerating than a Jaguar, yet all-electric and green, the expected success of the Tesla may be because it's a neat car with an eager market. Another entrant in the electric car field is Wrightspeed, which has produced the X-1 electric prototype with the equivalent of 170 miles-per-gallon and an acceleration capability of 0 to 60 miles per hour in about 3 seconds.

The Tesla is a bit pricey for most of us, leaving the door open to entrepreneurs to produce more affordable electric cars. Tesla is working on a somewhat less sporty but more accessible electric sedan that will run about $50,000. The Chevrolet Volt all-electric car is supposed to reach the market by 2010; and meanwhile Zenn Motor Company of Toronto, Canada, is producing a smaller electric car, a "neighborhood electric vehicle," for short trips. The base price of the Zenn is between $12,750 and $14,700, although its range between chargings is limited to about 35 miles. Compared with other neighborhood electric vehicles modeled after golf carts, the chassis of the Zenn car resembles other passenger cars, enclosing the passengers. The IT car from the Dynasty Electric Car Company of British

RELATED TREND

Energy storage is a big opportunity all on its own. Who will develop the batteries that finally make electric cars efficient and cheap enough to compete with gas cars, giving people the speed and range they expect from their autos?

Columbia, Canada, is another neighborhood electric vehicle. Cars such as these have limited speed and range, but can fulfill the needs for local commuting and errands. Another unique entry is the Aptera, an all-electric three-wheeled vehicle with a rounded pod shape, front wheels out to the side. The Aptera is projected to get more than 300 miles-per-gallon and production is planned in 2008.

Another interesting approach to the electric-car race is changing the business model rather than focusing just on technological improvements. Shai Agassi has founded Project Better Place (U.S. Office in Palo Alto, California), which is attempting to transform the auto industry and make gasoline obsolete. With existing technology, cars powered only by batteries can go only about 50 miles without recharging. To work with this limited range, Better Place is building stations where batteries can be quickly swapped out for freshly charged ones. To account for the high cost of electric cars and their batteries, Better Place will sell the cars for a relatively low upfront cost and charge a monthly operating fee. While still facing many challenges, Better Place is a serious entry in the race, having raised $200 million in capital already, and working on plans to roll out electric car networks with charging stations in Denmark and Israel.

What about fuel-cell cars? Hydrogen fuel-cell cars would have potentially no emissions, like electric cars, but the industry needs a way to deliver, store, and use hydrogen and affordable fuel cells. It's not clear when fuel-cell cars will reach the market. Honda has a prototype fuel-cell car, the FCX Clarity, proving that it can work, and they will lease a small number of cars as demonstrators in 2008. The question is the real cost, which still appears out of range for most of us.

Entrepreneurs are developing still more auto technologies. Guy Negre of Motor Development International (MDI) of Luxembourg, has developed the Air Car, which is

ECO-ISSUE

One neat thing about electric cars is that the cleaner the energy in the power grid, the cleaner the cars. If you charge them at home with your solar panels, your car really is emissions free.

RELATED TREND

One surefire way to save money and power is by going small and switching from a car to a motorbike or scooter. Electric scooters are catching on in Asia and might catch on in the United States as well.

powered by compressed air. MDI is licensing the technology to build facto-ries in various countries and is working with Tata Motors in India. Zero Pol-lution Motors of New Paltz, New York, is planning to release air cars in the United States by 2010.

Who is going to sell all these green cars? One option is to work with the big, established auto manufacturers, but there already are many dealerships, and as a dealer you sell a full range of cars—not just green cars. An alterna-tive is to work with the smaller, upstart, green auto producers. Zenn is look-ing for people interested in selling their cars, people such as Marc Korchin in Berkeley, California, who has established the green car dealership Green Motors. As the technology continues to improve, more and more cars will become available to fit a range of needs and markets.

Starting a traditional car dealership is a major endeavor, but another option to get started quickly is to forgo having cars sitting on a lot. Some car brokers deal in used cars one at a time, building deals between private buy-ers and sellers, as well as helping with financing, if necessary. An online green-car dealership provides access to a variety of cars, while avoiding the investment and risk of a car lot with brick, mortar, and asphalt.

Opportunities in green cars include:

- Opening a dealership for one of the emerging new producers in tech-nologies such as electric cars
- Opening a used-car dealership specializing in high-mileage cars
- Commercializing a new car technology
- Brokering sales of green cars between individual buyers and sellers

It's hard to say who will win the green-car race. People on all sides declare confidently that theirs is the only viable solution. Maybe there will be many winners, with a mix of technologies providing a variety of transportation solutions. Selling cars that stand out in the crowd in a green way is a good business, regardless of the technology used. Our cars are destined to go green. The more solutions there are to get us there, the more we all win.

OPPORTUNITY 67

Alternative Fueling Stations

The Market Need	We produce more biofuels every year, but they are not yet widely available
The Mission	Establish green-gas stations selling alternative fuels
Knowledge to Start	Cars, fuels, sustainability
Capital Required	$$$ (one station) or $$$$ (a chain)
Timing to Start	Months to years
Special Challenges	Securing fuel supplies and customers, regulatory hurdles

The transportation industry is poised for big changes. Car manufacturers large and small are racing to see who can produce the greenest car (see Opportunity 66). Biofuel producers are under pressure to continue their rapid growth to supply a large portion of our auto fuel in the decades ahead. The promise of hydrogen fuel-cell cars still is out there and also may play an important role in our future transportation. However, our gas stations still have not caught up to the change. As of early 2008, there were about 1,400 U.S. gas stations (or fueling stations) selling ethanol out of 170,000 gas stations total (Renewable Fuels Association, National Ethanol Vehicle Coalition, January 2008). Even those that do have ethanol often have only one ethanol pump. The major automakers have sold millions of flex-fuel cars that can run on E85 ethanol, but most people can't buy the fuel. As of early 2008, there were a handful of public service stations in California that offered E85 ethanol, with an estimated 300,000 cars on its roads capable of using the fuel (CalStart, 2006, calstart.org). Building alternative-fueling stations is a missing piece of the puzzle that entrepreneurs can put in place to transform our energy use for transportation.

Rick Wagoner, the CEO of General Motors Corporation, has commented that Americans need ten times more ethanol fueling stations than we have today, more like 15,000 to 20,000. GM has been trying to encourage more stations to sell ethanol but has found it "remarkably difficult." Most ethanol stations are located in the Midwest, where most of the ethanol is produced, with stations on either coast being few and far between.

For the most part, gas stations operate on low margins, earning only a few cents per gallon. A well-placed station with enough business can do well, but there is no guarantee. With 170,000 gas stations in the United States, most people have ready access to gas and there is little to differentiate one station from another. Going green could help a gas station compete.

One of the few biofueling stations in California, Pearson Fuels in San Diego, California, opened in 2003 and sells both E85 ethanol and biodiesel.

ECO-ISSUE

The regulatory requirements for opening stations vary from state to state. It's important to be aware of the local regulatory hurdles during the planning stages of opening a station. For example, certification of ethanol pumps is still a problem in California, making opening ethanol-fueling stations problematic in that particular state.

With at least nine fuels for sale, including gasoline, Pearson has been dubbed "the fuel station of the future." Mike Lewis, co-owner of Pearson Fuels, says sales of E85 ethanol fuel have increased. "All the challenges in ethanol are cost vs. gasoline, and the legislative or permit process," Lewis says. With the strong demand for ethanol, Pearson is helping other station owners install ethanol pumps with grants from the California Air Resources Board (CARB) Lewis reports that the cost of ethanol tanks adds about $100,000 to the cost of a new station and $170,000 to retrofit in an existing station. Pearson is also helping station owners with the permitting process, a challenge in California. For more about Pearson Fuels, visit PearsonFuels.com.

Biodiesel is the other major new fuel. Biodiesel is not only good for the Earth, but helps cars run better and longer by providing better engine lubrication. While the number of fueling stations selling ethanol is limited, even fewer stations sell biodiesel. Biofuel Oasis is a woman and worker owned biodiesel fueling station in Berkeley, California, run by a cooperative biodiesel producer with ASTM quality fuel made from soy oil from a potato chip factory. Customers are committed to the product, and Biofuels Oasis teaches classes helping others to set up their own biodiesel fueling station, covering all of the nuts-and-bolts details needed to get started.

Ethanol and biodiesel are the immediate opportunities, but with the passage of time, there will be others. If hydrogen fuel-cell cars reach the mass market, we will need hydrogen fueling stations. There is already a commitment at the state and federal level to start building this new fueling infrastructure. By the end of 2006, the California Fuel Cell Partnership had opened 23 hydrogen fueling stations in California and 158 hydrogen fuel-cell cars were on the road. It's a far cry from the millions of gasoline cars, but a sign of commitment to promote hydrogen as a workable alternative.

RELATED TREND
Electric cars, and possibly air cars need recharging stations. Something to think about.

Alternative fueling stations also might grow greener in other ways. Solar panels on the roof, healthy organic snacks, and distinctive green architecture can signal a green fueling station to consumers. A few prototype stations have been built, such as SeQuential Biofuels in Eugene, Oregon, with solar panels and a green roof over the convenience store. BP is experimenting with a green gas station in Los Angeles, California, called Helios House, which has solar panels, a green roof, a recyclable steel canopy, and LED lights. Ironically, perhaps, Helios House still sells only gas. The founder of Grassolean, Charris Ford, is working to provide the greenest biodiesel produced from waste vegetable oil or from environmentally sound farming methods. In addition, to encourage the greening of fueling stations, Grassolean has developed franchise plans for green fueling stations ready for entrepreneurs with the right financing and other measures in place.

Opportunities in green fueling stations include:

- Opening fueling stations providing alternative fuels such as ethanol, or biodiesel
- Opening fueling stations that green their environmental footprint by using renewable energy at the station, and building with eco-friendly materials
- Selling eco-friendly goods at gas station mini-marts

INFORMATION RESOURCE
One perspective on the developing world of fuel cells and hydrogen infrastructure can be seen at fuelcellpartnership.org.

Alternative fueling stations are a breath of fresh air from a future beyond gasoline and oil. Just as for cars, there might be multiple solutions. It is inevitable that our cars will change, and the way they are fueled will change with them. Fueling stations will evolve, but that does not mean they will all be the same. Biofuels may not provide all of our fueling needs, but they will make a difference. "Biofuels only have the ability to displace 25 percent of our dependence on oil. Let's do it," says Lewis of Pearson Fuels. This trend will continue in the coming years and decades, with twists and turns along the way. But one way or another, our fuels and fueling stations are destined to get greener.

OPPORTUNITY 68

Alternative Carsharing

The Market Need	Carsharing is offered only in the largest cities in the United States and does not fill the needs of everyone
The Mission	Develop a business around an alternative carsharing model
Knowledge to Start	Carsharing experience
Capital Required	$$
Timing to Start	Months
Special Challenges	Finding a niche, getting insurance

One of the problems with cars is that you spend a lot of money on them but the average North American car is only driven 66 minutes a day (carshare.net). Unless you drive a cab, your car is probably sitting parked for more than 90 percent of the time. It takes a great deal of energy and natural resources to produce all of those parked cars, and they take up a lot of parking spaces. Parked cars tie up a lot of money for people who only use cars occasionally, and in urban areas, it's often necessary to pay just to park your car. To address this, carsharing companies are picking up speed in North America and Europe.

There are a variety of business models for carsharing. Often, it has involved a company (for profit or nonprofit) leasing a fleet of cars, and allowing members (customers) to use the car on an hourly rather than the daily basis required by rental car agencies; gas and insurance are included in the rates. Cars are parked in strategic neighborhood locations, and reservations are made online. Availability is posted online, and access to get into the cars and drive them is provided remotely and electronically.

Each carsharing vehicle is parked in a specific spot and can be reserved by members when they need it for a period of hours, specifying when the car will be checked out and when it will be returned. The company takes care of maintenance, insurance, and arranging the parking space so the customer only deals with driving the car. When the customer is done, the car is returned to the space, and the hours billed electronically.

In the United States, the two largest contenders in this growing market have been Zipcar and Flexcar, which merged under the Zipcar banner in late 2007. Independent research indicates that every carsharing vehicle displaces between six and ten privately-owned vehicles, or more. Zipcar also reports their

ECO-ISSUE

One of the biggest hurdles for carsharing is insurance. It's difficult for small operations to get coverage because it's a specialized type of commercial fleet policy; however, there are at least two insurance companies that have provided coverage for carsharing fleets. Vehicle insurance continues to be an issue for startups. David Brook suggests working with a broker for one of the large insurance companies to obtain fleet insurance, or working with an insurer who offers personal auto insurance and then recruit your customers from the same insurance company so the insurer knows the risk of the drivers in your system. 🌱

ECO-TIP

Establishing carsharing in a community requires there be enough cars and customers to make money. Zipcar's David Brook estimates that starting a business requires at least 50 to 100 cars, about 20 members enrolled in the network per car available, and each car used at least four to six hours a day.

customers cut back on driving by using other modes of transportation, and that more than 50 percent of members said they decided not to buy a car of their own. With thousands of cars on the road, and tens of thousands of customers, Zipcar and other companies have proven that carsharing can work in the United States and provide green solutions for urban transportation.

Zipcar and other carsharing companies have grown rapidly, but they have not solved all of our transportation needs. One of the founders of Flexcar, David Brook has years of experience making carsharing work. He sees "plenty of room for competition" still, with opportunities for entrepreneurs to address market niches, such as smaller cities.

The number of large urban centers with Zipcars is growing, but the company is not everywhere yet. Brook says, "There are lots of college towns with 150,000 to 200,000 [people] for example, where a person or a small group of people can make a living from [a carsharing business]." To get started as a small operation, there are a variety of companies that help provide billing and reservation systems, and install the technology to track car use and location. "If several smaller organizations go together and do one billing system, reservation system, or a common website, they can share the expense and play to each other's strengths," Brooks suggests.

Another option is to try variants on current Zipcar practices. Brook writes in his report on carsharing, "One of the major complaints that new members have with carsharing is the requirement to specify a return time." The solution? Try providing open-ended return on certain cars in the fleet, an approach for which early pilot studies have been positive. Similarly, try allowing cars to be returned at one of many spots, not just the point where they were checked out. The technology to make this happen is out there. While it's difficult for established companies to change, Brook observes that smaller, startup carsharing

GREEN LEADER

You can find David Brook's report on carsharing business models on the web. Look for "David Brook" and "Carsharing—Start-Up Issues and New Operational Models, 2004."

companies can experiment more because they "don't have their resources committed to a particular model."

There are a variety of other models that carsharing entrepreneurs might pursue. One of the most promising Brook sees is the "cash car." One of the problems with starting a carsharing business is the cost of the cars themselves. Generally cars are leased, and each must be occupied for at least four to six hours per day to cover costs of the lease. In the cash-car model, a carsharing company doesn't lease cars it rents privately-owned cars. In this case, the car is outfitted with an onboard computer to allow entry and to track vehicle use and location. With the cash-car model, the company only pays for cars when they generate revenue and fewer hours of use are needed each day to make the business work. This approach opens doors to possibilities where other carsharing businesses could not compete, as in smaller towns and less densely populated areas. While this model is not yet being commercially used in the United States or Europe, it was demonstrated in a research project in Germany. Some owners might be reluctant to let others drive their car, but owners who make hundreds of dollars a month from their car might see their reluctance rapidly fade.

> **RELATED TREND**
> Other forms of informal ridesharing services are springing up as well. Visit goloco.com, or spaceshare.com for a social networking-based form of ridesharing. If people in your network are going to the ballgame on the weekend, the system can help you all share a ride and the cost. You may not want to give rides to strangers, but with systems built into online networks and communicated via cell phones, it's easier to find help getting where you need to go.

Opportunities in carsharing include:

- Opening a carsharing business that focuses on smaller towns like college towns
- Creating a carsharing business with open-ended return on cars and flexible return locations
- Linking carsharing with social networking systems
- Developing a "cash-car"-based carsharing business, using cars owned by others

There are many opportunities to use our cars more efficiently. By weaving a variety of uses and models, creative entrepreneurs can build businesses by helping cities and drivers get more out of their roads and cars.

OPPORTUNITY 69

Gas-Free Gardening

The Market Need	Gardening often uses chemicals and noisy, polluting engines
The Mission	Clean up gardening by helping customers go organic and gas-free
Knowledge to Start	Gardening, landscape maintenance
Capital Required	$
Timing to Start	Weeks
Special Challenges	Knowledge of best practices in organic gardening, and education of workers and customers about the benefits

Gardening used to be a nice, quiet endeavor of getting back to the earth, and mowing the lawn was a weekend workout in the days of push mowers. Not anymore. With the plethora of loud and polluting garden implements, gardening has become a noisy, noxious activity, with nothing natural about it. Lawn mowers prowl our lawns, gobbling gasoline and spewing more smog than your car. According to the EPA, gas mowers produce 5 percent of our air pollution. And leaf blowers? Don't get me started. Leaf blowers are a noisy, dust-raising nuisance. Landscape-maintenance businesses can provide a green alternative, taking care of lawns, parks, and other areas without causing air or noise pollution.

Change is coming to gardens and lawns in the form of gas-free gardening and tools powered by humans and electricity. For homeowners and professional gardeners (landscape maintainers), cleaning up gardening is motivated by

GREEN MARKETS

Two big advantages of hand tools are that they are cleaner and quieter. Many cities have required leaf blowers to be below certain volume levels, leading to some improvements, but the quietest leaf blower is still louder than a rake. If you are a professional, providing clean *and* quiet service with hand tools could be a selling point.

the desire to do the right thing and by government action. Leaf blowers may not seem like the biggest environmental threat, and they probably aren't, but there are about 20 million used in the United States (*Washington Post*, August 19, 2004). Gasoline-powered leaf blowers produce as much air pollution in an hour as driving a car 350 miles. And blowers produce infinitely more air pollution than a rake. To rein in leaf blowers, some areas are having leaf-blower exchange programs, providing cleaner versions for a reduced price in exchange for older, more polluting blowers. Cities such as Los Angeles, California, are even banning gas-powered leaf blowers.

There are alternatives to using gas-powered tools in gardening. One is hand tools. Not everybody will be excited about hand tools or think they are practical. Check out some blogs about leaf blowers to see the depth of the controversy. The story plays out with modern-day John Henrys in man-vs.-machine YouTube videos, battling rakes with leaf blowers. Another option that is greener than gas tools is electric tools, such as the Neuton (drpower.com), a battery-powered, electric lawn mower. The Neuton doesn't generate any exhaust and produces half the noise. In addition, there's isn't any gas to spill, messy oil, or frustration caused by not being able to start it.

The EcoBiz program in Portland, Oregon, is helping landscape professionals go green by providing information and a landscape-business certification process. As local government regulations increasingly motivate gardeners to change, professionals can either wait and be forced to change, or get ahead of the game. Working in organic landscape maintenance and making the change early may put a gardening business in the lead and help to create a competitive edge.

In addition, if you are staying away from gas-powered mowers and blowers, you might as well go organic: staying away from chemical pesticides and fertilizers, and using organic methods to control pests and encourage plant growth. Plantscapes in Fairfield, Connecticut, has been providing organic landscape maintenance services since it was

INDUSTRY INFO

To find out more about what is required to be an organic landscaper, see the Northeast Organic Farming Association at nofa.org. It's not just for farmers; the organization publishes a handbook for organic lawn care for professionals and standards for organic land care.

co-founded by Michael Nadeau and his brother in 1981. According to the website for Plantscapes, "The demand for organic landscaping services has never been greater." This growth is driven in part by customer concern about using chemicals (plantscapeorganics.com). The same people fueling the rapid growth of organic food in stores don't want to step off their porch and encounter pesticides in their lawn and garden. By removing synthetic chemicals and fertilizers, and changing practices to eliminate the need for their use, organic landscaping may even save customers money.

Another benefit of organic gardening is for workers. The exhaust from backpack blowers is particularly bad for the person carrying it, not to mention the dust and other particles raised into the air. Fuel spills also are a common hazard. Avoiding pesticides in your business goes a long way to removing the risk of accidental exposure.

Opportunities in green gardening include:

- Starting a landscaping business that replaces gas-powered equipment with electric or hand tools
- Creating an organic gardening business, avoiding synthetic pesticides and fertilizers, and changing gardening practices to enrich the soil
- Teaching classes about organic gardening for professional landscape contractors, their workers, and for homeowners

Organic and gas-free gardening helps the land and people who live on it, and fills a growing need. If you are interested in the landscape-maintenance business, or already have a business in the field, organic landscape maintenance using gas-free tools is worth a try.

OPPORTUNITY 70

Bus Solutions

The Market Need	More cost effective, efficient, and flexible urban-transit solutions
The Mission	Better busing
Knowledge to Start	Mass transit
Capital Required	$$ (within existing system) to $$$$ (creating a new system)
Timing to Start	Weeks to years
Special Challenges	Working with municipalities

Although cars are not going away, cities need the best possible urban-transit solutions to get as many people out of their cars as possible. Rail systems are the flagship of most large, urban-transit systems, but buses also are important. While buses are not as sexy as a rail-based system and do not always attract as much attention or funding, they get the job done. Buses do the job so well, in fact, that with innovative designs, they can give rail-based systems a run for their money.

In Curitiba, Brazil, the city government has pioneered many ideas for supporting low-cost, people- and environment-friendly solutions. When looking at potential transit solutions, city leaders found that a rail-based system was going to be much too expensive. Previously, a bus system was thought to be a cheaper, but less efficient and slow option. To deal with Curitiba's transit needs, the city redesigned how buses work.

The Curitiba bus system is called "Bus Rapid Transit," to distinguish the many innovations it encompasses. The designers of the system created special stations where customers paid fares before the bus arrived so they could board quickly. Designers also created tube-shaped platforms at each stop that eliminated the need for climbing stairs into the bus. Bus routes are color coded and organized around different functions, such as health care, shopping, express, or tourism. The payoff for the city was significant.

Natural Capitalism by Paul Hawken, Amory Lovins, and L. Hunter Lovins, found that after the Curitiba bus system was redesigned, it carried four times as many passengers at 0.5 percent of the cost as the subway in Rio de Janeiro, Brazil.

Los Angeles, California, is another city working to improve its mass transit. The city was not known for its mass transit system in the past, but it started building rail systems in the 1990s and now has more than 73 miles of urban rail service covering much of the metropolitan area, with plans for further growth still underway. The Orange Line between the Warner Center and Hollywood created a special problem for the construction of a rail line, however. LA Metro owned the right-of-way for many miles of rail line, but was prevented by law from using it for a new rail system or from using money to dig a subway. To get around these limitations, they turned to the Curitiba model and used the right-of-way for a bus line, creating the Orange Line. The Orange Line has many characteristics of a light-rail system, including that customers pay fares at the station rather than on the bus, with less frequent stops, and a dedicated right-of-way.

GREEN ISSUE

Some critics have charged that the comparison of transit systems in large North American cities with Curitiba is not fair, that such solutions cannot replace rail systems in other locations. This concern seems to be false, however. Rather than replace rail systems, perhaps bus systems like Curitiba's can complement rail-based systems where appropriate and extend the capabilities of mass transit.

Bus systems around the world have followed a variety of models. Providing low-cost bus solutions that have been tested elsewhere is an opportunity for businesses and municipalities to work together toward transportation solutions. In most American cities, buses are run by the municipal transit system and require close coordination with city governments.

One problem with buses is that they often are perceived as slow and inflexible. Ridership in many bus systems is low, particularly at certain times of the day. Ridership in New York City, one of the largest bus systems—has been declining for years, with riders turned off by long waits and buses getting stuck in congestion. A fully loaded bus can be quite efficient, but a full-sized bus with only a few people on board probably is not a great investment of resources.

Increases in ridership with rising gas prices may change the situation some what, but introducing greater flexibility in bus services and more innovative entrepreneurial models will still help to improve service and get more people out of cars.

RELATED TREND

With integration of mobile messaging and computerized coordination, minibuses can change their routes to optimize trips for both the passengers and drivers.

There are a few ways that bus systems can be made more responsive to the needs of riders. One is to move away from fixed routes. Fixed routes make buses very predictable but also limit their accessibility, keeping many people away. In some countries, the alternative solution is flexible routes, often using minibuses. Minibuses carry fewer people than a full-sized municipal bus, generally fewer than 16 people. Working like shared cabs, minibuses take passengers wherever needed, and the more flexible the route the better. Managed properly, a system of minibuses working in conjunction with a fixed route for a full-sized bus can provide the best of both worlds. In this model, joining an existing system could be as simple as buying a shared cab, getting a cab license, and starting to drive a route. Creating a new system could take much longer.

Minibuses can create problems if not managed properly. Bogota, Columbia, had a problem with private minibuses racing through the streets causing accidents. To bring order to the system, area governments took over management of the minibus systems by providing licenses to operate in specific regions or routes.

Opportunities for improving mass transit with buses include:

® Designing buses, stations, and fare machines
® Implementing private minibus systems to supplement public bus systems
® Using flexible routing
® Working as a driver of a shared cab or minibus

Providing transit solutions is not a go-it-alone opportunity, but by working together, cities and entrepreneurs can revitalize transit systems to provide flexible, efficient solutions that work for as many people as possible.

OPPORTUNITY 71

Green Cafés

The Market Need	Greenies like their coffee and tea but they want it green
The Mission	Provide an environmentally sustainable coffeehouse experience
Knowledge to Start	Restaurant businesses
Capital Required	$$ to $$$
Timing to Start	Months
Special Challenges	Building sufficient customer base

Coffeehouses are hot. Maybe you've heard of a little place called Starbucks. Doing all right, I guess. They have one every 100 yards or so. Why do people love it so much? Is it the coffee? The coffee is OK, but it's more than buying coffee; customers are buying an experience. Customers are there to sit in a coffeehouse and read a book or socialize, to soak in the slower and easier café life we dream of having. They are getting a little luxury. Now that Starbucks is so popular, though, the mystique is gone, and it's become more like the McDonald's of coffee rather than a higher-end small luxury. And with McDonald's getting into the espresso coffee market, Starbucks has little room to maneuver. The coffeehouse market is ripe for a disruption, and going green is a strategy for challenging these giants.

The very aspects that made Starbucks successful and led to the company's meteoric rise now play against it. When Starbucks was less ubiquitous, going there was an escape from the nine-to-five daily grind. Now Starbucks has become incorporated into expectations of the nine-to-five, not really an escape, but a part of the status quo. Starbucks has a standardized menu from coast to coast and beyond, but even though people like familiarity, it also can breed contempt. A 2007 memo from Howard Schultz (the man who built Starbucks) was leaked to the press, expressing doubts about the direction of the business. He has since returned to the CEO post, but the problems he outlined in his memo remain. The time is right for a green competitor to give Starbucks a run for its money.

If you are going to start a new coffeehouse, it should be different than Starbucks, and that could mean being green. To be fair, Starbucks has taken some measures to be green: The company gives a discount if you bring your own mug and is supposed to provide a mug for drinks consumed in the store. Starbuck's cups are now 10 percent post-consumer plastic, although the plastic lining for the cups makes them unrecyclable. The company saves paper by providing the cup holder instead of an entire second cup. Nonetheless, there is room for improvement. In 2004, Starbucks used an estimated 1.5 billion cups that were thrown away (*New York Times*, November 17, 2004). And for the coffee Starbucks sells, only a small fraction is organic or fair trade. Starbucks has helped protect coffee growers and the environment with Coffee and Farmer Equity Practices (CAFE) guidelines published in 2001, although the benefits to growers and the third-party certification have, in some cases, been lacking (*Sacramento Bee*, September 23, 2007). This leaves a lot of room for a creative upstart. Given a choice, green customers will choose the green coffeehouse across the street that better reflects their beliefs.

The Green Restaurant Association provides guidelines and resources for all types of restaurants to green their operations, including coffee- and teahouses. To be green, a restaurant needs to reduce its water waste, use recycled materials, energy-efficient appliances and lighting, nontoxic cleaners, and, of course, the beverages it serves should be eco-friendly. In the world of coffee, this means organic and fair-trade coffee.

Opportunities in green coffee houses include:

- Creating a chain of green coffeehouses, targeting the green market
- Helping coffeehouses to green their locations, wasting less water, energy, and materials
- Developing coffee cups with higher recycled-paper content or with other material that can be recycled

Starting a restaurant, or a coffeehouse, is not easy. It takes time, perseverance, and money. Many will try, and not all will make it. But if you do, this could be big. In addition to being green, of course, the coffee must taste great and the service needs to be efficient and friendly. But what about the experience? One option is to make the atmosphere a little slower, higher quality, and no more expensive than you-know-who. And leave out the merchandising racks.

Green Farms

Although more of the world's people live in cities than ever before, we all depend on farms for our food. The world's demand for food is expected to grow 50 percent globally by mid-century as its population continues to rise. While humans need farms, farms also have a significant impact on the environment and play a major role in the degradation of ecosystems. The productivity of 20th-century farms in the developed world has been driven by industrialization of farming. Fueled by cheap petroleum, massive farm equipment plows the land and harvests crops. Conventional farms also use large amounts of chemicals—an estimated 1.2 billion pounds of pesticides in 2001 in the United States and 5 billion pounds worldwide (EPA, "Pesticide Sales and Usage, 2000 and 2001 Market Estimates"). With one crop grown in large tracts of land, soil nutrients are rapidly depleted and soil erosion further degrades soil quality. Animal wastes pollute water and air, releasing greenhouse gases. With so much land planted with a small number of crop species, biodiversity is threatened around the world. In the long run, conventional agriculture is continually diminishing the ability of the land to produce food and of ecosystems everywhere to support life.

In response to environmental concerns, government regulation, incentives, and market pressure, more and more farmers and researchers are turning to alternative forms of farming, working to grow the food we need while preserving our farmlands and environment for the future. Organic agriculture has grown rapidly around the globe, and according to the Organic Trade Association, U.S. sales of organic food have been growing between 15 and 21 percent a year for more than a decade. To reduce soil erosion as well as the loss of carbon and nutrients from soil, farms are starting to turn toward conservation tillage, which leaves crop residues on fields and minimizes soil disruption, or even no-till agriculture, which avoids plowing the land. Looking even further down the road, researchers are developing a new way to grow crops using perennial plants in prairie-like communities for biofuels and food.

One consideration for farms is how they affect climate change. Dairy cows produce large volumes of milk, but that's not all they produce. A farm's thousands of cows produce a great amount of manure, which pollutes air and water, smells terrible, and releases significant quantities of methane, a potent greenhouse gas. Methane digesters can capture this and use it to minimize the problems. The energy gained from burning the methane can reduce costs for farms or even be sold to the local utility, producing income. Widely adapted in many parts of the world, methane digesters still are getting started in the United States, and offer an opportunity for farmers and other entrepreneurs to decrease pollution and climate change while building value (Opportunity 72).

Fish are an important food source for much of the Earth's population, but wild fisheries are largely overexploited. Aquaculture—farming fish— has expanded rapidly but can have a negative environmental impact. Growing large numbers of fish in close quarters can pollute water and harm aquatic ecosystems, and coastal areas have been degraded or cleared to make room for shrimp or fish farms. An alternative and improved form of aquaculture called the Partitioned Aquaculture System (PAS) may hold the answer, helping fish farms produce more fish than ever at a lower cost, while reducing environmental impact (Opportunity 73).

The transformation of our economy from fossil fuels to renewable energy includes biofuels as an important component, but the current environmental and social effect of raising crops for fuel might be too great. In addition to driving up the cost for food, the use of conventionally grown crops such as corn and soybeans for biofuels harms ecosystems and soil. Rather than growing corn or soy as a single crop as is currently done, a more efficient and less harmful approach may be growing fields of perennials with many species mixed together—as occurs in the native prairie ecosystem. Research suggests that returning land to mixed communities of grasses may provide a better way to produce future biofuels and preserve the land without competing for food (Opportunity 74).

The rapid growth in organic-food production leaves farmers looking for new ways to control pests without synthetic chemical pesticides. One approach is the use of beneficial insects that eat or become parasites to insect pests. Another approach is using microbes to control agricultural pests such as nematodes, or baiting traps—with insect sex attractants to monitor insect pest populations and lure them to their doom in the trap. Producers of a wide variety of innovative means to control insect pests without chemicals are seeing business grow along with the organic-food market (Opportunity 75).

Farms are essential to our survival, providing food and many other products. We must work to build strong businesses that improve farms for today, for future generations, and for the planet. Future generations will thank us.

OPPORTUNITY 72

Methane from Manure

The Market Need	Raising cows can be a messy business, producing large volumes of manure
The Mission	Convert manure into methane to save energy, and reduce the smell and air pollution
Knowledge to Start	Engineering, anaerobic methane digesters
Capital Required	$$$
Timing to Start	Months to Years
Special Challenges	Regulations

There are about 100 million cattle in the United States (National Cattlemen's Beef Association, beefusa.org) and more than a billion worldwide. Dairy farms can have hundreds or thousands of cows producing manure that pollutes air and water, and produces a smell commensurate with the number of cows. A single dairy cow can produce 40,000 pounds of manure a year (*San Francisco Chronicle*, May 14, 2004), which can enter run-off from the farm and contaminate groundwater with bacteria. The manure also can release methane into the atmosphere, acting as a potent greenhouse gas and contributor to climate change. Pig farms are another major manure source. However, there is a solution for the manure problem: methane digesters. In methane digesters, the manure is digested by bacteria that break down the organic components and release methane, which is captured to prevent it from reaching the atmosphere.

DEFINITION TIME

Methane produced biologically, as in methane digesters, is sometimes called "biogas," a renewable energy resource.

Capturing the methane from manure prevents a variety of environmental problems and can provide a useful form of renewable energy.

Anaerobic methane digesters not only prevent methane from being released into the atmosphere but also allow farms to capture the methane and burn it for energy. A variety of designs are used, ranging from covered ponds to enclosed tanks where the bacterial fermentation takes place. The type of bacteria used can vary as well, ranging from bacteria that grow at moderate heat levels to bacteria called thermophiles that thrive when their environment is hotter. Compared to leaving manure in the open to release greenhouse gas into the air, methane digesters both prevent climate change and provide a source of energy.

The energy from methane can be significant. Nonprofit group Sustainable Conservation estimates that "if all 65 billion pounds of manure that are created yearly in California underwent methane digestion, the fertility and productivity of farm soils would be greatly enhanced, while supplying an estimated 200-plus megawatts of power." The National Dairy Environmental Stewardship Council estimates that a dairy farm with 550 cows can produce $30,000 worth of electricity each year, yielding a payback period of three to six years on the investment in the digester. Others who have installed digesters estimate an even quicker payback in some cases.

A variety of grants at the local, state, and national levels provide support for installation of methane digesters, speeding their introduction into the market. The California Energy Commission has set aside $15 million to support digester installations in that state, and other states also are providing incentives. The U.S. Department of Agriculture (USDA) and the Environmental Protection Agency (EPA) have provided grants, and even nonprofits such as the Natural Resources Defense Council (NRDC) have provided support. Still, the market in the United States is just getting started compared with Europe, where there are thousands of sites generating methane energy.

GREEN LEADER

Sustainable Conservation (suscon.org) is a nonprofit in California encouraging environmental solutions that make good business sense in farming and other industries.

Microgy, a subsidiary of Environmental Power in New Hampshire, licensed thermophilic digesters from Danish Biogas Technologies. Thermophilic digesters can produce more methane and keep producing even in cold weather. At an installation cost of $11.5 million, one plant installed at Huckabay Ridge in Texas is expected to produce $4.6 million a year in revenues. To allay farmer concerns about the initial cost outlay for systems like this, Microgy and others are, in some cases, installing the systems themselves and selling the gas as their product, rather than selling digesters.

Methane digesters also can generate coproducts in addition to methane and electricity. One is the solid or slurry material that remains after digestion, which can be used as fertilizer or as bedding for animals. Methane collection can provide an opportunity for carbon offsets, in some cases, with groups or individuals investing in methane-capture projects to help fight climate change (see Opportunity 27).

For individuals whose business is installing anaerobic methane digesters or for those working to improve these designs, an engineering background is important. Also, those with a business background can help farmers with financing, including finding grant money to alleviate one of the main obstacles methane digesters face. If you are fairly savvy with both business and engineering, a methane consulting business might be the way to go.

Opportunities in methane digestion include:

VARIATIONS ON A BIZ-THEME

Manure is not the only source of methane generated by livestock. Livestock also produce methane by belching. The volume of methane produced can be reduced by changing conditions in which animals are raised. Changing animal husbandry practices is one way of generating carbon offsets. For details, see the AgStar program at the EPA, (epa.gov/agstar). ❧

- Designing digesters
- Consulting about biogas
- Installing and maintaining digesters
- Capturing and selling methane gas
- Selling offsets
- Financial consulting for methane-digester operations

Methane digesters make a great deal of sense for farmers and the environment. The main obstacles generally are the initial investment, regulatory hurdles, and attitudes toward acceptance. With more money available, regulatory hurdles disappearing, and attitudes changing, methane digesters will continue their steady increase in the United States.

OPPORTUNITY 73

Better Fish Farms

The Market Need	More eco-friendly aquaculture
The Mission	Convert fish farms to be more efficient and produce less pollution
Knowledge to Start	Aquaculture
Capital Required	$$ to $$$
Timing to Start	Months
Special Challenges	Farming fish without harming the environment

Fish always have been a key source of food, there for all to enjoy. The seas are less bountiful today, however, with many fisheries depleted from years of overfishing. While traditional fisheries have been flat or declining in their yield since 1990, production from aquaculture has steadily increased. Wild fisheries are not likely to meet demand for fish by the increasing world population, leaving aquaculture to make up the difference. Aquaculture can quite successfully produce fish, such as catfish, or shellfish such as shrimp.

Aquaculture is moving to produce new species over time like abalone, but this approach often has come with negative environmental consequences. Growing large numbers of fish in confined areas can lead to an accumulation of waste that pollutes the water, and coastal fish farms can damage or destroy area ecosystems. Large areas of coastline in Southeast Asia have been converted to aquaculture farms, particularly shrimp farms, removing mangrove swamps in the process. Finding less harmful ways to raise fish would help the environment and the business of aquaculture.

Biosystems engineer Dave Brune at Clemson University has spent years developing and testing a practical system to avoid some of the problems of aquaculture. Brune has created and helped the university patent the Partitioned Aquaculture System (PAS), in which catfish are farmed and their waste removed to grow algae, which is then used to feed tilapia. By connecting these components, overall fish production is increased while waste discharge is reduced, using resources more efficiently. In the case of catfish, PAS produces 18,000 pounds of fish per acre each year, compared with only 5,000 pounds in a conventional system: PAS also reduces the cost and pollution from the fish farm. Similar results are obtained with shrimp farming using PAS, increasing production from 5,000 pounds of shrimp per acre to 35,000 pounds per acre, and lowering costs as much as $.10 per pound (*Clemson World Online*, Fall 2006, clemson.edu/clemsonworld).

According to Brune, "tilapia coproduction can significantly reduce the need to import protein to grow fish, one of the arguments against modern aquaculture." In recent years, U.S. fish farmers have been caught in a squeeze between the high price of fish feed and the low price of imported fish. Brune also suggests that PAS might make

U.S. fish farmers more efficient, with lower costs, helping them to compete with low-cost imported fish. Fish farmers in other parts of the world also might adapt the system, or variations on it, to become more efficient and less polluting.

Brune also is involved in a project to solve another environmental problem: the nitrogen waste that runs off agricultural land. Agriculture uses millions of tons of fertilizer each year, much of which runs into rivers, lakes, and the ocean. When fertilizer reaches these bodies of water, it fuels the growth of algae, which die and cause bacteria to grow, removing oxygen from the water. The Mississippi River carries fertilizer from vast areas of farmed land in the United States down to the Gulf of Mexico where the fertilizer creates a "dead zone" with so little oxygen that large quantities of fish and shellfish perish every year. Such a process plays out in other parts of the world: the Salton Sea in California, surrounded by farmed land, is steadily shrinking, growing progressively saltier, and becoming overwhelmed by algal blooms as a result of the fertilizer.

While algae can create a problem they also could provide an opportunity if harnessed properly. If the water flowing into the lake were captured (before entering the lake) and the fertilizer nutrients used to grow algae, the algae could be harvested and used to grow fish. Brune and others have been working to remodel the lake and prevent its pollution with fertilizer, capturing these nutrients to use in other ways. The main barrier to implementing the plan is politics, not science or technology. The clock is ticking though, and with every passing year, the environmental condition of the Salton Sea continues to deteriorate. If successful there, similar plans could be implemented in other rivers and lakes, reducing pollution and supporting aquaculture at the same time by growing and using algae to reduce fertilizer runoff.

Opportunities for better fish farms include:

ECO-TIP

Setting up a catfish farm costs between $3,500 and $5,000 per acre of pond. Selling fish directly to consumers is one way to get a better price for your product and make more money.

RELATED TREND

Tilapia is a hardy fish that grows quickly in fresh or brackish water, and is becoming increasingly popular. More tilapia is sold than trout in the United States, and its ready adaptability makes tilapia a good candidate for continued aquaculture growth.

- Creating aquaculture for new, high-value species (like abalone)
- Improving aquaculture to be more efficient and less environmentally damaging
- Working in environmental remediation in conjunction with aquaculture

GOVERNMENT ACTION

For more about plans for the Salton Sea, visit saltonsea.ca.gov. One proposal is to build a massive dike all the way across the lake, splitting it in two. One half will receive the remaining freshwater flow, and the other will be left as a salt sink.

With the world's fisheries under increasing pressure, the aquaculture market is likely to continue its steady rise. While some forms of aquaculture have proven problematic, there are ways to improve. Finding clean, efficient, and environmentally sound ways to perform aquaculture can provide an important approach to providing food worldwide.

OPPORTUNITY 74

Prairie Biofuels

The Market Need	Biofuels without the environmental cost
The Mission	Produce biofuels with farming modeled after the prairie ecosystem
Knowledge to Start	Farming, ecology, biofuels
Capital Required	$$$ to $$$$
Timing to Start	Years
Special Challenges	Transforming how we farm

Biofuels are a hot topic and a hot industry, but they also are producing a lot of controversy. Most people agree that we need alternatives to oil-based transportation fuels, but the devil is in the biofuel details. Producing corn-based ethanol as it's generally practiced today takes almost as much energy from fossil fuels as it yields and has little climate benefit. In addition, long-term farming of a monoculture such as corn is hard on the soil, and pushing farmers to produce more with more chemicals takes its toll. The loss of carbon from soil caused by conventional agriculture also is an underappreciated factor contributing to climate change. Many of the problems with biofuels and the crops from which they are made can be traced to the use of annual crops in the bulk of modern agriculture.

Since the dawn of agriculture, the grain crops that occupy the bulk of agricultural acreage have been annuals. Annuals are plants that grow from seeds with each new season. With annuals in agriculture, each year the land is tilled (breaking it up), seeds are planted in the broken soil, water and fertilizer supplied (and other chemicals, today), and grain harvested. The next year, the process is repeated. One of the consequences of till agriculture is that over time, breaking up the soil depletes its nutrients and causes erosion. The invention of the plow and agriculture with annuals probably led to the birth of civilization some 10,000 years ago, and probably has led to the demise of more than one civilization as soils gave out and the food went with them.

An alternative way to grow and farm plants is offered by the model of the prairie grasslands growing in mixed communities of perennials. These grasslands once covered vast tracts of the American Midwest but have been replaced by farms with their massive annual plantings of corn, wheat, and soybeans. Although apparently simple at first glance, the prairie is a complex ecosystem with many plants and organisms living in an interconnected network. Perennial grasses in the prairie grow back each year from their deep-root system, which can extend for meters into the soil. There is no plowing, planting, or breaking of the soil. Rather than depleting the soil, the plants enrich it over time and erosion is virtually nonexistent. Biofuels can copy this model and recover some of our land in a prairie-like system that can be farmed, harvesting its energy to make biofuels.

David Tilman of the University of Minnesota has completed a 12-year study on the use of perennial prairie grasses for biofuel farming, and what he found is surprising a lot of people. A mix of prairie grasses produced 240 percent more energy than fields with one or two species. These high-energy yields could produce more energy than fields of corn or even switchgrass, which is being contemplated as the next generation of biofuels. In addition, Tilman found that plant populations and productivity were more stable from year to year with different grasses planted together. These plants take care of each other and help each other. When its time to harvest, just mow the grasses and wait for new growth in the following spring.

With a yield of 240 percent more energy, these systems might be able to outperform other sources of biofuels, restore soil quality, and even sequester carbon in the soil. Compared with soy biodiesel or corn ethanol, fuels from prairie grasses would slow climate change more. Also, these plants store carbon dioxide in their roots and soil—as much as 1.8 tons of carbon dioxide per acre of land planted—helping to further fight climate change by taking this greenhouse gas out of the air (*Scientific American*, December 7, 2006). The grasses can be grown on land that cannot support food crops, reducing competition between fuel and food production. The fuels from these grasses could be converted to ethanol, using cellulosic technology, or burned to produce electricity. This approach to biofuel production could be one of the keys to slowing and stopping climate change while continuing to grow the economy.

Beyond organic agriculture, or even the trend toward local food, the concepts discussed here for growing biofuel crops using prairie-like perennial communities also are being applied to food crops. At The Land Institute in Kansas, Wes Jackson and his colleagues have been tackling the problem for more than 20 years, working to develop what they call Natural Systems Agriculture. Around the world, Jackson's group and others are researching food crops that may grow as perennials, going back to plant breeding to find grains that grow well and are edible. The key to the work is a great deal of plant breeding.

Many of the annual grains we use have related grains that grow as perennials. Breeders at The Land Institute are hybridizing established annual crops such as wheat with the perennial cousins to develop plants that have grain like the wheat we know but the lifecycle of a perennial. To accelerate the process, plant breeders also are incorporating modern methods, such as marker-assisted selection (Opportunity 46).

Switching to perennial crops will take time, but other trends (such as no-till farming) are happening today to improve the sustainability of agriculture. No-till farming uses the crops we already have, but avoids plowing the land to minimize soil disruption and maintain soil quality. More and more farmers are using this method as it proves itself to be economically competitive. Some farms are selling offsets or carbon credits as an added support for making the switch to no-till agriculture.

Opportunities to use prairie-like ecosystems in agriculture include:

- Farming mixed cultures of perennials to produce sustainable biofuels
- Developing strains and mixtures of plants that optimize energy production while maintaining soil and biodiversity
- Developing food crops that grow as perennials
- Developing tools and equipment for no-till and conservation tillage forms of farming

The change to growing perennial crops is a big one for farms. The modern farming system, based on annual crops such as corn, has been developing for millennia. It will take time for farmers and others to get used to a new perennial-crop approach to agriculture. Perennial food crops, such as wheat or corn, are a long way off, but growing prairie-like communities for biofuels probably is closer. With ongoing changes in agriculture such as these, our farms will continue to produce food for the long run.

IN THE LONG RUN

Developing new perennial crops for food is a long process, and the research may take decades. This isn't a scheme for quick money, but for visionaries who want to invest in saving our farms for the decades and centuries ahead. The Land Institute is online at landinstitute.org.

INDUSTRY INFO

At the Agricultural Sustainability Institute at the University of California–Davis is finding new ways to produce the food we need for the long term, preserving or replenishing soil and other resources at the same time.

OPPORTUNITY 75

Eco-Friendly Pest Control

The Market Need	Organic agriculture and gardening needs alternative solutions for pest control
The Mission	Provide beneficial insects for organic farming and gardening
Knowledge to Start	Insects, organic farming
Capital Required	$$
Timing to Start	Months
Special Challenges	Knowing your bugs and how best to control them

As unwelcome visitors, insect pests can be a problem for farmers and gardeners, damaging plants and produce, and spreading disease. Keeping insect pests off crops is a major industry with millions of pounds of pesticides sold each year. The publication of *Silent Spring* by Rachel Carson in 1962 about the environmental problems with the pesticide DDT led to its ban in the United States and many other countries, and helped launch the modern environmental movement. The book also helped to propel the growth of organic agriculture, which avoids the use of synthetic chemicals for pest control. But organic farmers, home gardeners, and others still need to control insect pests. One way to do that is to use good bugs to control the bad ones.

Insects can seem to be fearsome opponents, but they are not invincible. In nature, insects are part of ecosystems; insects prey on plants but are preyed upon, in turn, by other creatures. Some insects survive by preying on other insects or by acting as parasites of specific insects. Ladybugs, praying mantises, lacewings, and other beneficial insects can keep the number of insect pests low without chemicals. One market for beneficial insects is organic

ECO-TIP

Using insect predators, or parasites, to control insect pests is often called biological pest control. Beneficial insects also are one of the tools in integrated pest management, which uses a variety of methods to reduce, although not always eliminate, pesticide use.

farmers, but greenhouse growers and home gardeners also may need help controlling pests without chemical pesticides.

The Beneficial Insect Company in North Carolina (thebeneficialinsectco.com) is one producer of biological pest control, raising and selling insect predators including ladybugs, lacewings, nematodes, and praying mantises. Company representatives recommend using biological pest control as part of a program that also includes keeping a close eye on your plants. It helps to know a little about pests so you know which ones you are dealing with. Not every predator eats every pest; some of these insects are specialists. Predators can go a long way toward controlling pests—a single adult ladybug eats 1,000 aphids a day.

In addition to using insect predators, organic farmers can use other forms of pest control. Insect traps are laced with pheromones, luring bugs to their doom rather than a mate. Microorganisms are another alternative to chemical pesticides. Scientists have identified microbes from around the world can infect and kill agricultural pests, including nematodes, fungi, and insects. Sales of these "biopesticides" based on microbes or related products are increasing steadily, with sales of $672 million in 2005 and growing 10 to 15 percent a year (Business Communications Company, Norwalk, Connecticut, 2005). The most common biopesticides (based on bacteria, called B.T. for short) produce a protein that kills insect larvae when they eat.

The biggest challenge in starting a business selling beneficial insects (and other living forms of biological control) is learning how to raise them in large enough scale to be commercially viable. Luckily there are a variety of resources available to learn how to do this, the most valuable of which being the experience of others who have worked in the field. Locate and connect with an industry veteran, and see if they might be willing to share their time and insight. University and

ECO-ISSUE

Biological control of pests has had unintended consequences in some cases. The cane toad was introduced into Australia to control cane beetles, a pest in cane sugar. The toads ate the beetles, but the toads also ate many other species and grew out of control to become a pest and environmental hazard themselves.

INDUSTRY INFO

The Association of Natural Biocontrol Producers represents producers of biological pest control (anbp.org).

government-run labs working in the biological control field are another valuable resource. Many information resources can be found at the National Sustainable Agriculture Information Service (attra.ncat.org). Another resource is the book *Beneficial Insects—How to Mass-Rear and Make a Profit* by Bob Saffell, from Mayfield Press.

Opportunities to build businesses around eco-friendly pest control include:

- Raising and selling insect predators and parasites
- Raising and selling bio-pesticides, microbes, and nematodes that protect plants and increase soil productivity
- Selling traps and pheromones to kill insects and disrupt reproduction without exposing crops to insectides
- Helping farmers create farm practices that attract beneficial insects and help them proliferate

Although doom was once predicted for agriculture without chemical pesticides by the opponents of Rachel Carson's book, organic farmers and others have found that their business can thrive without such products. Beneficial insects, biopesticides, traps, lures, and other pest-control solutions can help farmers and gardeners do their work without chemical exposure for themselves, their produce, or the land. Not bad work for the humble ladybug.

Resources

These resource lists are not comprehensive, but rather provide a few key choices to get started with.

Books for Further Reading

Benyus, Janine M. *Biomimicry* (New York: William Morrow, 1997)

Chiras, Daniel D. *The New Ecological Home, A Complete Guide to Green Building Options* (White River Junction, Vermont: Chelsea Green Publishing Company, 2004)

Esty, Daniel C., and Andrew S. Winston. *Green to Gold: How Smart Companies Use Environmental Strategy to Innovate, Create Value, and Build Competitive Advantage* (New Haven, Connecticut: Yale University Press, 2006)

Freed, Eric Corey. *Green Building & Remodeling for Dummies* (Hoboken, New Jersey: Wiley Publishing, 2008)

Gore, Al. *An Inconvenient Truth: The Planetary Emergency of Global Warming and What We Can Do About It* (Emmaus, Pennsylvania: Rodale, 2006)

Hawken, Paul, Amory Lovins, and L. Hunter Lovins. *Natural Capitalism: Creating the Next Industrial Revolution* (New York: Little, Brown and Company, 1999)

Hawken, Paul. *Blessed Interest: How the Largest Movement in the World Came into Being and Why No One Saw It Coming* (New York: Viking Press, 2007)

———. *The Ecology of Commerce* (New York: HarperCollins, 1993)

McDonough, William and Michael Braungart. *Cradle to Cradle: Remaking the Way We Make Things* (New York: Farrar, Straus and Giroux, 2002)

Pahl, Greg. *Biodiesel: Growing a New Energy Economy* (White River Junction, Vermont: Chelsea Green Publishing Company, 2007)

———. *The Citizen-Powered Energy Handbook: Community Solutions to a Global Crisis* (White River Junction, Vermont: Chelsea Green Publishing Company, 2007)

Pernick, Ron, and Clint Wilder. *The Clean Tech Revolution: The Next Big Growth and Investment Opportunity* (New York: HarperCollins, 2007)

Pollan, Michael. *The Omnivore's Dilemma: A Natural History of Four Meals* (New York: Penguin Press, 2006)

Vaitheeswaran, Vijay V. *Power to the People: How the Coming Energy Revolution Will Transform an Industry, Change Our Lives, and Maybe Even Save the Planet* (New York: Farrar, Straus, and Giroux, 2003)

Websites

75 Green Businesses You Can Start: 75GreenBusinesses.com

Starting Up Green: StartingUpGreen.com

Treehugger: treehugger.com

Grist: grist.com

Sustainable Industries: sustainableindustries.com

Ecogeek: ecogeek.com

Lazy Environmentalist: lazyenvironmentalist.com

Organic Architect: organicarchitect.com

Inhabitat: inhabitat.com

Greenbiz.com: greenbiz.com

Department of Energy/Energy Efficiency and Renewable Energy: eere.energy.gov

Environmental Protection Agency: epa.gov

Rocky Mountain Institute: rmi.org

Natural Capital Solutions: natcapsolutions.org

Biomimicry Institute: biomimicryinstitute.org

Renewable Energy Weekly: renewableenergyweekly.com

US Green Building Council: usgbc.org

NRDC: nrdc.org

Sustainable Conservation: sustainableconservation.org

National Renewable Energy Laboratory: nrel.gov

About the Author

As the author of *75 Green Businesses You Can Start to Make Money and Make a Difference*, Glenn Croston writes extensively about the wealth of opportunities for businesses providing solutions for environmental challenges. Helping others join the booming green economy, he has broad expertise spanning green businesses in renewable energy, building, water, food, services, transportation, fuel, farming, finance, and waste reduction, described more at 75Green-Businesses.com. A green entrepreneur himself, Glenn is developing Starting Up Green (StartingUpGreen.com), helping entrepreneurs

entrepreneurs to connect to resources they need to succeed, including expert partners in promotion, human capital, business plan writing, financing, legal issues, green business operations, green facilities, and certification.

With a Ph.D. in biology from University of California—San Diego, Glenn knows the importance of finding environmental solutions for the rest of the living world and for ourselves. Living green with his wife and two daughters in San Diego, Glenn continues working toward a more sustainable world, starting at home with a hybrid car, solar panels, compact fluorescent light bulbs, and compost. He is currently working on future publishing opportunities, and he looks forward to the time when all businesses are green.

Glossary

Agribusiness. Large businesses involved in industrialized agriculture, generally by conventional means. Businesses include seed suppliers, farmers, chemical providers, and food-processing companies.

Biodiesel. Biofuel produced from plant or vegetable oils and fats by reacting them chemically with alcohol.

Biomimicry. Using living systems as a model for human-designed systems in business—including natural forms, processes, and ecosystems.

Bioprospecting. Finding and analyzing samples of organisms, including their chemical components and genes, to find commercially useful material.

Carbon credit. Part of market-based emissions trading to reduce climate change. Carbon credits are provided to greenhouse-gas emitters and can be sold, giving emitters credit that can be used to meet targets for reducing greenhouse-gas emissions.

Carbon footprint. Net amount of greenhouse-gas emission for which a person or business is responsible.

Carbon neutral. Reducing a person's or business's net level of greenhouse-gas emission to zero, either directly through conservation and other measures, or indirectly through mechanisms such as offsets.

Cellulosic ethanol. Technology that breaks down the cellulose in plants into sugar that is fermented into ethanol as a biofuel.

Clean Development Mechanism. A component in the Kyoto Protocol to reduce climate change that allows those in industrialized countries to invest in carbon-reduction projects in the developing world to meet industrialized countries targeted reductions in greenhouse-gas emissions.

Cleantech. A variety of technology-based green-business solutions, including renewable energy, transportation solutions, waste reduction, and climate-change mitigation.

Climate change. Disruption of global climate patterns caused by greenhouse gases, traced to human action.

Cogeneration. Capturing heat along with electricity to make power production more efficient.

Ecotourism. Travel to natural settings intended to benefit local people and the environment.

Fuel cell. Technologies using electrochemical reactions rather than combustion to produce power.

Greenhouse-gas emissions. The production and release into the atmosphere of gases, such as carbon dioxide and methane, that trap heat in the atmosphere and contribute to climate change.

Greenwashing. An exaggerated promotion of the environmental benefits of products and services.

Greywater. Water that has been used in the home, and can be reused for some purposes such as irrigating gardens. Toilet water is not included.

Kyoto Protocol. The international climate-change treaty adopted in Kyoto, Japan, in 1997, which created the European Union Emission Trading Scheme and the Clean Development Mechanism to reduce greenhouse-gas emissions from developed countries that have signed the agreement.

Load management. Arrangements in which energy consumers volunteer to reduce power use during peak hours, usually in exchange for some form of compensation.

Locavore. People who prefer to eat local food.

LOHAS. Stands for Lifestyles of Health and Sustainability, a large group of green consumers.

LEED. Stands for Leadership in Energy and Environmental Design, the green-building standard created and implemented by the U.S. Green Building Council.

LED. Light-emitting diode, an efficient and durable form of lighting.

Microbe. Microscopic organism like bacteria and yeast.

Natural capital. The value of natural systems and natural resources.

Offset. Systems in which individuals or businesses make voluntary payments to projects working to reduce greenhouse-gas emissions in order to reduce the individual's or business's carbon footprint.

Organic. The form of agriculture that avoids synthetic chemicals and fertilizer use to grow crops.

Photovoltaic (PV). Solar power produced with silicone-based panels that produce electricity directly when struck by light.

Probiotics. Foods and products containing living microscopic organisms that can help sustain health and prevent disease.

REC. Renewable-energy credit, also called renewable energy certificates or green tags. RECs represent the attribute of power produced from renewable energy, apart from the actual electricity. People can buy a REC to purchase green energy indirectly and reduce their carbon footprint.

Renewable energy. Energy produced using natural resources that are constantly replenished, including solar power, wind power, biofuels, wave energy, and geothermal. Renewable energy does not include fossil fuels such as oil or coal.

Smart meter. Electrical meters that track when power is used at a home, and generally capable of remote communication between the home and the utility.

Social entrepreneur. A person using business methods to create social or environmental change.

Sustainability. Organizing green-business processes and products so that the resources they require will not be depleted and will be available for the indefinite future, and so that natural and social systems are renewed rather than depleted.

USGBC. U.S. Green Building Council, the creators of the LEED green-building certification system.

White tag. Energy efficiency certificate, tradable certificates representing one megawatt-hour of energy conserved through the course of a year, and through verified conservation measures.

Xeriscaping. Landscaping using plants that require minimal water.

Index